Craft Brew

F

FRANCES
LINCOLN

Frances Lincoln Limited
74–77 White Lion Street
London N1 9PF

Craft Brew
Copyright © Frances Lincoln Limited 2016
Text copyright © Euan Ferguson 2016
Recipe photographs copyright © Charlie McKay
Further photography copyright: p59 © Randy
Duchaine/Alamy Stock Photo; p86/p87 © Two
Birds Brewing; p131© Gustav Karlsson Frost;
p100/p101 © Gigantic Brewing Company; p108/
p109 © Mikkeller; p118/p119 © Brewdog; p143
© Beavertown; p189 © Dalini Sagadeva/Ubrew.
Design: Ashleigh Bowring
Commissioning editor: Zena Alkayat

Quarto is the authority on a wide range of topics.

Quarto educates, entertains and enriches the lives of
our readers—enthusiasts and lovers of hands-on living.

www.quartoknows.com

First Frances Lincoln edition 2016

A catalogue record for this book is available
from the British Library.

ISBN 978-0-7112-3733-9

Printed and bound in China

3 4 5 6 7 8 9

MIX
Paper from
responsible sources
FSC® C104723

FRANCES
LINCOLN

EUAN FERGUSON

Craft Brew

50 homebrew recipes from the world's best craft breweries

Contents

—

Breweries

USA

Introduction

—

Why brew your own beer? After all, pubs are full of it; the shelves of bottle shops groan under the weight of all those lovely stouts, pale ales and lagers. Can you really make it better than a professional? The answer to that is: maybe, maybe not, but it doesn't really matter. Brewing your own beer is fun, satisfying and creative.

The life-affirming qualities of fermented grain have been known to humans since at least 9000BC, and today it's the world's most popular alcoholic beverage. There's been a lot of excited talk about a 'renaissance' or 'revolution' in beer, which might seem odd, given that it never went away. But it's the way we think about beer that's changing: its versatility, taste, strength, potential, even its place in society. At the heart of this is what's come to be known as craft beer.

What is craft beer?

'Craft'. Does that word in front actually mean anything? Some people say craft brewers have a small output. Well, compared to a brand like Budweiser, perhaps they do. But Lagunitas, for instance, produced 600,000 barrels of beer in 2014 at its California site. Other people think craft brewers are all independent. For the most part, that's true: craft beer lovers will tell you that a brew free of the taint of big money tastes much sweeter. Others claim that craft beer has in-your-face flavours and cancel-tomorrow ABVs, and is full of ingredients that don't belong anywhere near beer, like foraged herbs or grapefruit or tonka beans. But try Marble's Manchester Bitter (p173), a modern interpretation of an old, old style, which sits down beside you for a gentle cuddle rather than whacking you over the head: things become less clear-cut. So let's make our own definition – craft beer is about values over volume, it's about spirit over finance, it's about soul over cynicism. If that sounds like the sort of thing you like, then craft beer is for you.

And this book will help you not only become a craft beer drinker but a craft beer brewer. Homebrewing is an integral part of the craft beer revolution – most commercial craft brewers started making it at home and there's still a close connection between them, their product and the people who drink it.

The world's best breweries

All the recipes here come direct from the world's most exciting, groundbreaking, fearless and uncompromising breweries. Take inspiration: having a go at Mikkeller's Cream Ale or Gigantic's Ginormous imperial IPA is much more enticing than making plain old generic versions. Start with something simple and move on when you feel like you're getting to grips with the techniques and you understand your equipment. And when you get more confident, use the recipes as springboards to dive off into your own creations – more/fewer/different hops at different stages, a touch of roasted malt or rye or oatmeal, complementary ingredients like fruit, herbs, spices, tea, chocolate, vanilla, coffee... You're only limited by your imagination.

Kit, extract and all-grain

Anyone can buy kits that contain
everything to make beer. (Well, a
sort-of beer.) Open a packet of mixed
malt-and-hop extract, pour it in a bucket
with some water, wait a while, drink:
more or less, that's it. But you can also
buy microwaveable meals and flatpack
furniture – it doesn't mean you should.
You may get a passable approximation
of a distant relative of beer from a kit,
but it will lack life and will provide a mere
droplet of the enjoyment that comes
from brewing from scratch. The next
progression from kit brewing is to use
dried malt extract in place of fermentable
grain: extract brewing uses a soluble
powder or syrupy substance in the
mashing stage. This can lead to decent
beer, and many homebrew journeys
begin this way. It's easier, certainly, but
will probably leave you feeling like you're
missing out on the mistakes, trials and
triumphs of real brewing. This book
recommends taking the plunge and going
all-grain from the start. You'll learn heaps
from your misses and miscalculations.
So here, all recipes are all-grain – using
real malt and real hops. It involves a bit
more work, but it's worth it.

And is 'craft' homebrewing any different from regular homebrewing? In theory, maybe not, but in principle, yes. Homebrewing as we know it today hasn't been a historically continuous practice (at least not a legal one). In Britain, for instance, homebrewing regulations insisted upon a licence until 1963; in the US, making beer at home with a higher ABV than 0.5% was illegal until 1978. Early exponents of late twentieth-century homebrewing were often attracted by financial benefits rather than creative ones, giving the practice an unenviable reputation for producing sinister buckets of undrinkable sludge (a reputation it struggled to shake off for a long time). The new generation of homebrewers find inspiration in the huge range of ingredients and beers they find within their reach.

So now, your local bottle shop or bar sells beer brewed thousands of miles away (hopefully as well as a lot brewed within walking distance). Beavertown's Smog Rocket porter, made in north London, is available in North America. Kiwis can wake up to Mikkeller's famous Beer Geek Breakfast oatmeal stout; a whole hemisphere away in Denmark, Mikkeller's online shop sells beer from New Zealand's estimable 8-Wired. Homebrew shops sell hops from all over the world, from classic English varieties like Fuggles or Bramling Cross to Australia's tropical Galaxy. You can buy malted grains of every colour – from tried-and-trusted barley to spelt, buckwheat and rye. If you're a craft beer drinker, you probably have a good idea what a saison or a witbier or a cherry sour or an imperial stout tastes like. You probably have your favourites. And now there's nothing stopping you from making your own.

Start simple, then experiment

Before you start your journey into homebrewing, remember: a recipe is just a starting point. In this book they come straight from the breweries and have been formulated and tweaked for their own processes, which are probably very different from yours. You should consider your first brew to be a test. Keep records. Also, your own equipment is just as important as ingredients; as is taking accurate measurements, hitting targets, experimenting, practising, balancing ratios and consistency.

Equipment

—

Brilliant batches of beer have been brewed for years on homemade A-Team-style collections of equipment. Don't feel like you need a full complement of steel kit before you can call yourself a homebrewer.

What you need

At its core, making beer is a simple enough process, but it's worth investing a bit of time and money getting things right.

Your kit will have a huge effect on the end product, more even than the recipe. As you become a better brewer, you'll get to know your equipment: how it behaves, what it can do, what *you* need to do to get it to achieve your targets. A fundamental understanding of the processes involved will give you a solid base to move on from. This chapter details what could be considered a minimum of what's needed to make quality craft beer at home, plus a few more bits and pieces you might consider investing in if you get serious.

Homebrewing has a history of innovating, inventing, hacking, adapting, making do, converting and ingenuity. Many bits of equipment can be adapted at home from everyday components. You can add to it as you go on. And before you splash out, consider the idea of a cooperative: open breweries, like Chaos Brew Club in Chicago, or Ubrew in London, are spaces where members can use top-grade equipment, buy ingredients and share knowledge. But it doesn't have to be so organised. A few people can pool together to install a brewing set-up in a spare room or even a shed, meaning less individual investment and more hands to join in the work (plus more mouths to drink the results). The creation of beer, much like its consumption, is better with friends.

01 Hot liquor tank

To begin a brew, you'll need to heat water to a fairly precise temperature (water when warmed becomes 'liquor' in the trade). A sizeable stovetop pan is the entry-level option. It has to be big enough to hold the total water for your brew (see 'mash' p53), to save you having to heat up twice for mash and sparge; and also if you're planning to alter the water's chemical make-up before you begin (see p28). But a purpose-built HLT with an element is more accurate and makes multi-rest infusions easier; it will also have a tap to make liquid transfer safer. Advanced models come with volume sight gauges and built-in thermometers.

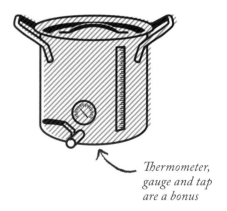

Thermometer, gauge and tap are a bonus

02 Mash tun

An insulated plastic chill box with a lid makes an inexpensive and straightforward mash tun, following the fitting of a drainage tap and some sort of filter. You can fit these yourself with basic DIY skills and basic DIY store parts – online guides abound – or you can buy them ready to use. The next step up from plastic is stainless steel. Size is important here too. The tun has to be big enough to fit your batch size; however, if it's too big the grain bed will be insufficiently deep to create effective filtering. For most of the recipes in this book, 30 litres / 6 gallons capacity will work (although for the extra-high ABVs, something bigger would be helpful). A filter to separate post-mash liquid from solids is essential. These come in various forms, and all homebrewers have their favourites:

01. False bottom: a mesh that sits proud of the floor of the mash tun, with a run-off tap below it. It holds the grain but lets liquid through. This is probably the most effective homebrew method.

02. Manifold: an arrangement of copper or plastic pipes covering the bottom of the tun, with small holes to allow hydraulic drainage of the wort. This works well too, but can be harder to clean.

03. Braid: a stainless-steel weaved hose that works in a similar way to a manifold.

04. Bazooka filter: more often used in the boil kettle, but some brewers think it works just fine in a mash tun too. It's a single steel mesh tube which attaches straight to the drainage tap. Issues have been reported with sugar extract efficiency, however.

05. Bag: some brewers fill a nylon bag with their grains, which can be lifted right out after the mash.

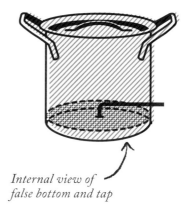

Internal view of false bottom and tap

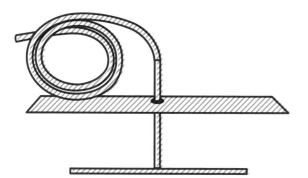

03 Rotating sparge arm

Very handy for the sparging stage, this simple bit of kit rests atop the tun and rotates when water is passed through it, showering the mash in a fine spray that won't disturb the grain bed. A cheap and easy hack is to pierce holes in a piece of aluminium foil big enough to cover the grain surface, then very slowly pour the sparging water over that with a measuring jug.

04 Boil kettle

To extract bitter flavours from hops, a vigorous boil is necessary, and household cooker hobs aren't usually powerful enough to maintain this. Boil kettles are therefore heated by an internal electric element or sit on top of a gas burner. They have to be large enough to hold the batch without boiling over – for safety's sake, for a 20 litre/5 gallon brew you'll need a 30 litre/8 gallon capacity. The shape of the kettle is important too: if the diameter is too wide, the evaporation rate will be higher than desired and too much wort will be lost. A diameter/height ratio of about 1:2 is recommended.

05 Filter

Dried hops are a beautiful thing, fragrant and flaky; boiled hops are a sludgy mess and must be kept away from the fermenter. So as with the mash tun, the boil kettle needs a filter to separate hop matter or other ingredients from the wort at the end of the boil. The options are a false bottom, a bazooka filter or a bag (although there's some suggestion that hop bags don't allow a proper extraction of oils and acids at the boil stage).

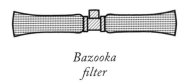

Bazooka filter

06 Wort chiller

After the boil stage, it's usually vital to cool the wort down as quickly as possible to minimise air-exposure time and chances of infection, plus it saves you hanging around. (The exception is in the case of a 'hop stand' or 'whirlpool', when hops are added to the wort after the boil and left to stand.) An immersion chiller is a coiled length of tubing which connects to cold water at one end and drains from the other; it's placed in the wort 15 minutes before the end of the boil to sanitise, and when the cold water is turned on it transfers out heat. You can make your own relatively easily from copper pipe and plastic hose.

Store-bought plate or counterflow coolers do the same thing faster and, inevitably, more expensively.

07 Airtight fermenting tub, glass jar or metal tank

A good fermentation is essential for good beer. Fermenting tubs can be made of plastic, glass (a carboy or demijohn) or steel. Plastic is cheapest, lightest and blocks out sun, but scratches relatively easily; glass allows the brewer to easily see the progress of the fermentation, but is heavy when full and can crack; steel protects the beer from sunlight and is, as ever, the most expensive.

Two such vessels allow for a secondary fermentation (see p47). They need tight-fitting lids and airlocks or blow-off tubes, and they need to be the right size to accommodate your wort plus its krausen (not a mythical sea monster, but the unappealing-looking froth that forms at this stage). A tap at the bottom makes racking easier.

08 Airlock

A bubbler airlock has water-filled chambers that keep bad stuff out of your lovely beer but let CO_2 escape: you can see fermentation taking place this way. Simple airlocks have a lid that does the same job, or a blow-off tube leads from the stopper into a small vessel of sanitised water.

09 Racking cane

Beermaking involves a lot of liquid transfer. A racking cane is attached to a siphon tube and has a sediment trap at the bottom to filter out unwanted solids when moving liquid out of the fermenter into a keg or bottling vessel. You'll need one if your fermenter doesn't have a tap at the bottom. Again, steel is pricier but more pro than plastic.

10 Bottle filler

A simple tap/tube combo that makes the final stage of brewing that bit more enjoyable. A stainless steel syphon filler allows you to fill several bottles at once.

11 Bottle capper, bottles and caps (or Grolsch-type swingcap bottles)

All that beer needs to be stored somewhere before drinking. Bottling is the usual option: you'll need caps and a capper too. Go for brown bottles to avoid the beer becoming 'lightstruck' – a term for when natural light causes a breakdown of hop acids creating a most unpleasant smell.

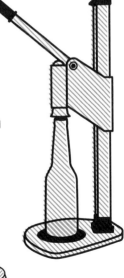

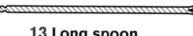

*A fridge can
be fitted with
a thermostat*

12 Heater and/
or brew fridge

Optimum fermentation occurs at fairly specific temperatures (18-20C/64-68F for ale, lower for lager), which usually have to be maintained for the duration. Too hot and the yeast will go into overdrive or die, too cold and it just won't wake up enough to do its job. Depending on environmental conditions, the wort might need to be warmed or chilled to hit these targets. Heating is easier – if you're fermenting somewhere cold, a heat pad will help maintain temperature. Chilling is harder, especially for lagering (see p113, for example). Lagering is definitely an advanced homebrew technique, but then there's not much more satisfying than a cold, crisp pilsner on a summer day. Some people use a fridge with temperature controls. A more basic option is to put the fermentation vessel in a larger tub of water, which can be iced if necessary: like the sea, it will be less susceptible to environmental temperature changes as it's a bigger body of water. Monitor temperature regularly, whichever option you choose.

13 Long spoon

Steel is best for stirring.

14 Digital scales

Grams and ounces matter in homebrewing. Digital is the way forward.

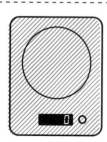

15
Thermometer

Some models clip on to the side of a pot, some float in liquid; some are digital, others use mercury. The more accurate yours is, the more closely you can follow recipes and control your process. Temperature is hugely important.

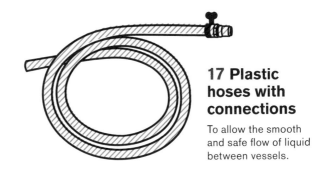

17 Plastic hoses with connections

To allow the smooth and safe flow of liquid between vessels.

16 Measuring jug

Essential for recirculation, tasting and drawing off wort.

18 pH papers or digital tester

As explained on p28, the pH of water can have an effect on the beer you make with it. Science-class strips are cheap but hard to read. A digital tester is more accurate and won't cost too much. Neither is essential for a homebrewer just starting out, but to take your brews to the next level, the chemical composition of your water has to be taken into account.

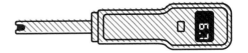

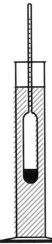

19 Hydrometer or refractometer

You probably only need one or the other, but these two bits of kit measure the specific gravity (density) of your brew at various stages (see p53). These readings help you calculate alcohol content as well as efficiency. Pure water at 20C/68F has a specific gravity of 1; wort's is higher due to suspended sugars. As a wort's sugar is converted to alcohol and CO_2 throughout the brewing process, it loses density. A hydrometer (left) is a basic instrument: it's a weighted glass thermometer-like tube with a scale, and it floats in a sample of wort in a trial jar. You can also use a refractometer, which gives readings calculated from

a few drops of liquid on a prism: it's more accurate, and doesn't require temperature to be taken into account.

To use a hydrometer (which is more properly called a saccharometer, since it's measuring sugar content), firstly take a small sample of wort using the (sanitised) trial jar. Cool it down externally to around 20C/68F by immersing in cold water or swirling it around – temperature affects density (or, use a temperature conversion graph). Slowly lower the hydrometer into the wort and give it a little spin to dislodge any air bubbles. When it rests on its own, take a reading from the bottom of the meniscus at eye level.

Brew like a pro

Advanced equipment to make your beer even better.

01 Hopback

If you seriously get into hops and want to add even more of that drink-me-now aroma to your brews, consider a hopback. It's a sealed container which fits in line between the boil kettle and the fermenter: it's filled with whole or plug hops, which impart loads of flavour without losing any of their oils to boil-off. You can make your own – it's not too hard.

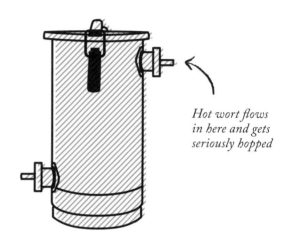

Hot wort flows in here and gets seriously hopped

02 Wooden barrels

Chances are you've tried a barrel-aged beer recently. Ageing ale on wood is becoming big news as brewers look for new and exciting roads to take their beer down. Ex-wine, whisky, sherry, bourbon and even tequila barrels are used; if you've got room for a brewing set-up, you might have room for a little barrel too. They're sold in different sizes and can be reused a few times for many styles of beer. Wood chips in secondary fermentation are sometimes employed as a substitute.

In general, beers with higher ABVs and rich, dark flavours age better than lighter, fresher ones, but who's going to stop you making that port-barrel-aged witbier if you really want to?

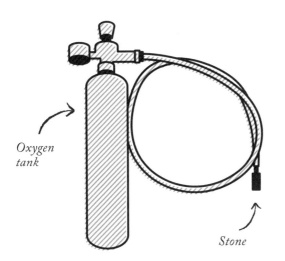

Oxygen tank

Stone

03 Aerator

At later stages of the brew, oxygen and beer are not best of pals. An exception is when racking from the kettle to the fermenter: yeast needs O^2 to live. A bit of splashing, stirring and shaking is the hands-on solution, although you can buy a tank with a ceramic or steel diffusion stone to do it more effectively. An aquarium stone with an electric pump is a thrifty hack, provided of course it hasn't spent time keeping Goldie's tank fresh.

04 Kegs, taps and CO^2

A keg-and-tap combo creates the closest legal thing to a pub in your house. Add a dartboard and you can probably start charging neighbours by the pint. Advantages of kegs: they keep beer fresh between serves, they're bigger and easier to clean and sanitise than a caseful of bottles, and they can be force carbonated (the use of a gas canister to quickly carbonate beer without having to wait for yeast to do the job in the bottle, a system employed by many craft breweries). Modern Keykegs are a plastic bag-in-barrel system that allow brewers to keg beer and dispense it using a bicycle-style handpump.

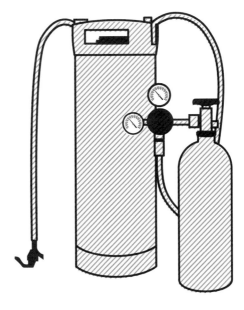

Ingredients

—

Just as you really don't need much equipment to make beer, its ingredients can be reduced to a core four: water, malt, hops and yeast. From this holy quaternity, miracles happen – every element comes in many variations, but together they form the basis of most beers.

01 Water

It might seem like the most straightforward ingredient, but even plain old H_2O needs a bit of consideration before it goes into a brew. It makes up the largest percentage of beer. Traditionally, the mineral content and pH of local water determined the types of beer that would be made in an area (London's high-carbonate water meant stouts and porters dominated, whereas the soft water in parts of Germany make an ideal base for lager). There are solutions and tablets you can add to brewing water to raise or lower the pH or hardness, but it might feel like it takes a chemistry degree to fully understand the effects of various chemicals and minerals on your ingredients. Unless your own area's water has a notably extreme chemical make-up, or you really want to recreate a particular style of beer exactly, the stuff that comes out your tap will probably be fine for your first few brews. Your water company will be able to supply a report on the compounds present in your supply if you want to get scientific, and then you can begin to tailor the water chemistry for each brew.

02 Malt

The first thing you'll probably add to brewing water is malt and other grains (collectively known as grist). Malt is a catch-all term for any type of 'malted' cereal – a grain that has gone through the process of being soaked in water to begin germination then dried in hot air to stop it. The drying is done to different degrees of intensity (heavy roasting, even). Germination allows the natural starches to be converted into sugar during the beermaking process.

Pretty much any cereal can be malted and used in beer – millet, buckwheat, spelt even – but the most-used varieties are barley, wheat, oats and rye. The intensity of the post-soak heating results in different characters – pale malt, for instance, is used as a base for many beers and doesn't add much colour; 'chocolate' malt lends deep, bitter flavours and a rich dark hue. (Roasted barley isn't malt, but is often employed in the same way, in stouts and porters.)

Malts are classified by colour in three scales – degrees Lovibond (from light 10L to 300L-plus dark malts), and the newer ERM (European Reference Method) and EBC (European Brewery Convention).

Grains need to be crushed (into about three smaller bits) before use. Brewers working towards a homemade product take on the crushing themselves using a grinder, but if you buy malt pre-crushed, try to use it straight away. It will last well in its whole form but loses potency when broken up.

Enzymes produced during germination break down long and complex grain starches into shorter lengths which can be consumed by yeast – lower temperature mashes favouring beta amylase will in general create higher alcohol but less body in the beer; mash temperatures towards the higher end of the scale favour alpha amylase, which leads to lower alcohol production and more body. A balance between both is usually favoured.

03 Hops

In a beautiful balancing act with malt, hops are the other primary flavour-creators in beer. Brewers use the (usually) dried flowers of the hop plant, which also have medicinal and antibacterial properties (before the days of scrupulous sanitation, hops had a welcome side effect of killing bacteria). They can also add a barrel-load of taste, ranging from subtle and warm to unrestrainedly floral or totally tropical, depending on the variety. Hops added at the start of the boil provide bitterness; when added throughout the process ('late hopping') they provide more powerful flavours, and at the end they create aroma in beer. Those American-style IPAs that seem to fill the room with

their ultra-fresh fruit and garden bouquet – you can guarantee a whole heap of late hops have been employed. Some hops are best for bittering, some excel at aroma, and the all-rounders do both. Hop packets list an alpha acid percentage (AA), which varies by crop and year, and to ensure consistency, brewers have to take this into account. It gives us an idea of the amount of bitterness a hop will provide. For example, the US Chinook has a relatively high AA at around 12%, whereas New Zealand's Wai-Iti brings only around 4% AA but smells like a citrus orchard in summer. Some recipes in this book list the brewers' recommended AA – if you're aiming for accuracy, you need to take this into account.

04 Yeast

Yeast is the final component in the alchemical series of reactions that end up as beer. When added to cooled wort after the hop boil, yeast sets about vigorously gobbling up the sugars in the liquid, turning them into alcohol and CO_2. Without yeast, beer would be a flat, dead and impotent liquid and the world would be a sad place. Most homebrew yeasts are of the Saccharomyces genus, although others exist, including the harder-to-handle Brettanomyces (see p57, for example). Saccharomyces comes in top-fermenting and bottom-fermenting varieties – top is more common and used for most ales; bottom needs lower temperatures to get to work and is used mainly for lagers and pilsners.

There are many varieties of commercially grown yeast, some of which add unique flavours and cope differently with the traits of the beer being brewed. Saison yeast, for instance, will introduce spicy and aromatic notes. Some yeasts are described as 'clean fermenting': they don't impart much personality but convert efficiently and quietly. Breweries often use house strains that they 'harvest' from finished brews to use in the next: this can be done at home, which is a slightly more advanced technique but ensures you have a regular supply of healthy and strong yeast.

You can buy yeast dry (to 'pitch' or add into the wort from a packet) or liquid (which may have to be fermented separately in a 'starter' along with dried malt extract and water, or wort, before pitching – see p44). Dry is convenient, easier to use and recommended for beginners, but comes in a limited range of strains. Wyeast sells 'Smack Packs', slap-activated bags of liquid yeast plus nutrients which make starters on their own; White Labs sells vials of liquid yeast that are shaken to the same aim.

Each variety of yeast has its own characteristic measurements: attenuation, which is the amount of sugar that it will convert to alcohol and carbon dioxide; flocculation, the amount it will 'clump' together into solids during the latter stages of fermentation; the optimum temperature range it prefers; and its alcohol tolerance – the level of booze it handle before it gives up. We all have that.

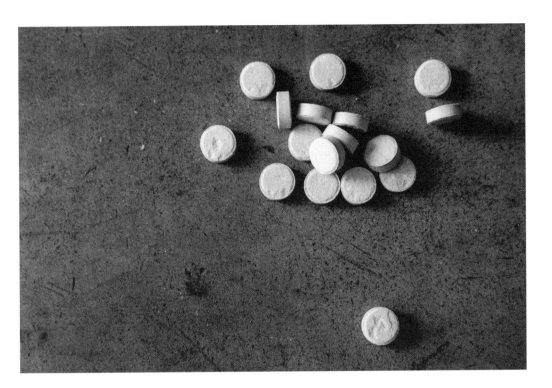

05 Other ingredients

'Adjuncts' refers mainly to unmalted grains added to a mash – corn, oats, rice – which don't take part in sugar creation but have other desirable properties: they might improve foam retention, say, or provide mouthfeel. The term can also refer to sugars – the likes of corn sugar or Belgian candi sugar – added at different stages of the brew to increase fermentation or alcohol content.

Sugar is also added to 'prime' beer just before bottling or kegging – this creates carbonation in the finished product. Light, refreshing styles – lager, amber, wheat, for instance – need more sugar than rich, comforting styles like porter or bitter.

And beer can be best pals with a huge range of other ingredients. Espresso stout, raspberry wheat beer, lemongrass saison, citrus IPA, salted porter… Those are a few uncontroversial combinations. But what about Rogue's Voodoo Doughnut, made with bacon and maple syrup? Or Two Birds' Taco Beer, a fiesta of corn, coriander and lime? Or the Popcorn Pilsner made by Indiana's Sun King brewery? There are no rules beyond what's actually drinkable – and homebrewing gives you the chance to raid the store cupboard and get creative.

Finally, many beers benefit from clarifying agents (finings). In some styles, clear beers are prized by the brewer for both visual and taste reasons, but three things can cause cloudiness: proteins (from darker grains, malted and unmalted); tannins (a grain by-product of the mash); and suspended yeast. A traditional type of clarifying agent is Irish moss (actually seaweed), added at the boil stage; it encourages the flocculation (or 'clumping') of proteins, which sink to the bottom to form sediment. Protofloc and Whirlfloc are tablet versions of finings.

Brewing your own beer

—

Brewing is a lifetime's journey, but immerse yourself in the fundamental techniques and you'll have a solid base from which to make great beer.

Sanitisation

Cleanliness, they say, is next to godliness, and in brewing it's also right beside tastiness (and safeness). Sanitisation has to come first – its importance can't be stressed enough. A whole batch of beer can be spoiled by the infiltration of unwanted bacteria or wild yeast. Warm wort is a playground for rapidly reproducing cells, and infected beer is fit only for the drain. (Unless you're Belgian – the likes of lambics are intentionally infected. But that's another story…) Every part of every piece of equipment used post-boil has to be thoroughly free of germs. Get into this habit early and you'll save yourself heartache further down the line. It's helpful to think about a 'two-steps-back' regime: sanitise anything that will touch the wort. Bottles, too, have to be thoroughly cleaned and sanitised – use a special brush or rinser.

Preparation

Most homebrewers use the power of gravity to transfer liquids between vessels in the various stages of the brew. If you have the space, a stepped podium-type arrangement will make this easier; if not, limber up for a bit of lifting and lowering. Electric inline pumps take out the struggle.

A Wyeast Smack Pack will have to be activated at least three hours before you need it. White Labs vials need to be brought to room temperature then activated 15 minutes before use. A traditional liquid yeast starter will need to be prepared 12 to 18 hours in advance. Grain should be ground as near as possible to mash-in time.

Set aside about four to five hours for a brew, longer for your first few – this is not an activity that benefits from haste. It's also not an activity that you can pause for a few hours while you go to work/sleep/the pub. And don't get too carried away with thoughts of sampling your beautiful beer any time soon. Grain to glass is about four to five weeks, when fermentation and conditioning are taken into account. It's worth the wait.

Step 1 **Mashing**

Extracting fermentable sugars from crushed grain in hot water.

01. Heat the total liquor (see 'mash' p53) in your hot liquor tank to about 10C/18F more than the recipe specifies. This could take an hour – get everything else ready, weighed and laid out while it's warming. This higher temperature allows for a bit of cooling in the tun to optimum mashing temperature, which is usually between 65C/149F and 68C/154F, although individual recipes call for variations.

02. Add the hot liquor (for volume calculation see 'mash' p53) and the well-mixed, crushed grains to the mash tun simultaneously, while carefully mixing. This can be done in half-stages, taking temperature readings to ensure it's not too hot or cold. Leave the lid off and add cold water to drop the temperature; add more hot water to raise it if necessary (record the volume of water additions, subtract from sparge).

03. Stir gently to mix everything together, distribute the water/grain and eradicate clumps. Too much vigour at this stage will drop the temperature more than desired and can lead to a 'stuck' mash, which is akin to a sloppy loaf of bread in the mash tun – just try draining wort out through that.

04. Put the lid on the mash tun. For single-rest infusions, leave for one hour (longer won't hurt). For multi-rest infusions, as a few of the recipes in this book require, it's necessary to increase the temperature during the stage to extract different malt characters. The rests are intended to develop enzymes and lead to greater efficiencies. Modern 'modified' malts, however, are designed to allow high levels of extract without multi-step infusions. This method is easier if you have a temperature-controlled mash tun; otherwise, you'll have to start off with a thicker mash (see 'mash' p53) and add hot water to hit the temperature targets. It is harder to master, certainly, and harder to keep consistent – many homebrewers deem it mostly unnecessary, some swear by it. Try it if you like to see how you get on.

05. Some brewers carry out an iodine test at the end of the mash. Take a grain-free sample of wort, put a couple of drops of common iodine in. If it turns black, there are still unfermented starches (remember that from school science?) and you should keep mashing for longer. If it stays clear/ turns slightly red, your mash is efficiently finished.

Step 2 **Lautering**

Rinsing the mashed grains of all their fermentable sugars and creating the desired pre-boil wort volume.

01. Raising the temperature of the mash to 77C/170F is known as a 'mashout'. This is done either with external heat or by adding very hot water – about 93C/200F – and serves the dual purpose of making the wort flow more freely and halting the enzyme conversion process. Some homebrewers do it; others don't bother and skip this stage without disastrous results. 'Sticky' grain bills, such as those with a lot of wheat or finely ground rye, may benefit from a mashout.

02. There are two stages of lautering – recirculation and sparging. Firstly, to recirculate (which 'sets' the grain bed), cut a piece of foil to fit the top of the grain and perforate it a few times. Draw off one or two pints of wort from the tun's tap into a jug, close the tap, and gently pour back over the foil. This is also known as 'vorlauf'. Repeat this recirculation two or three times until the runnings are free of husks and big bits of grain debris. The clearer the better.

03. There are two methods of sparging: batch and fly. This book only deals with fly sparging (see right), which is usually considered more efficient. Ensure water in the hot liquor tank is at 78C/172F, and that you have at least the volume required for the lauter (see 'mash' p53). Sparging effectively rinses the grains of all the fermentable sugars formed in the mash, creating the correct volume of rich, sweet wort.

04. A stuck mash is when grains become too thick to allow filtering of the wort and can happen with batch or fly sparging. The sign of a stuck mash is when no wort flows out the bottom, even though the tap is open and there's liquid in the tun. To fix it, close the outlet tap on the tun and give it all a little

stir; recirculate a couple of times after this as in step 2 to 'set' the bed again, and leave for 15 minutes before running off again. If this doesn't work, you might need to try other methods like a more forceful stirring or the reapplication of heat to loosen the liquid.

05. Before the wort is boiled in the kettle it can be useful to take a gravity reading at 20C/68F (see p53). This will be your pre-boil gravity.

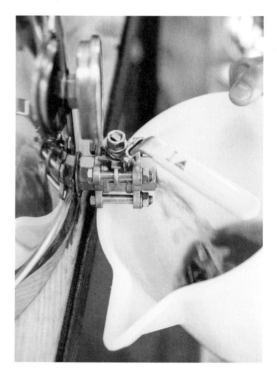

06. If you're using a sparging arm, set it up above the tun. Connect its inlet hose to the hot liquor tank, and a hose to the tap at the bottom of the tun. Lead the other end of this hose to the boil kettle.

07. Partially open the hot liquor tank tap, causing the arm to spin and water to sprinkle out; simultaneously open the tap at the bottom of the tun. The object here is to produce a continuous and steady flow of wort down through the grain bed and out. If the grains seem to 'pull away' from the walls of the tun a bit, increase the water in; if there's a layer of water above the grain bed, decrease it. Too much water weight could collapse the bed, making filtering impossible.

08. As soon as the kettle's element is fully covered in wort, you can turn it on to begin to boil – this will save time. Keep the water flowing until you've reached the desired pre-boil volume in the kettle (see 'mash' p53).

An alternative fly sparging method involves a flexible, perforated food-grade plastic hose, which sits atop the grain bed and is connected to the hot liquor tank and trickles water. Or, easier still, continue sparging with the foil method described on the previous page: refill your jug with 78C/172F water from the hot liquor tank and gently sprinkle it over the top. Repeat this several times.

Yet *another* method that homebrewers use is to spread water over the grain surface with a big metal spoon and a hose that's connected to the hot liquor tank.

Whichever way you do it, the principle and aim is the same, and it should take anything from 45 minutes for a standard grain bill up to 90 minutes for heavy mashes. Make sure you only use the right amount of sparging water as calculated at the start of your brew (see 'mash' p53).

Step 3 **Boiling**

Extracting bitterness, flavour and aroma from hops (and killing unwanted bacteria).

01. By now you should have the correct volume of wort in the kettle, and it should be on its way to boiling. Putting the lid on the kettle will get you there quicker.

02. Adding hops before the water even boils is known as 'first wort hops'.

03. When the wort hits a rolling boil, you're ready to commence the hop schedule. Break up any big lumps in the hops then drop each addition straight in as the recipe directs, giving it a stir each time. Leave the lid partially off throughout the boil. This allows for the escape of sulphur compounds (which give beer an unwanted 'cooked corn' flavour), or chlorine, should your tap water contain it; it also lets you see if the liquid is in danger of boiling over. You will lose some wort to evaporation (see 'mash' p53), but you should have allowed for this.

Your first couple of boils will give you a clear idea of exact measurements. If you're using finings of any sort, like Whirlfloc (see p33), this is the stage you'll add them (usually ten or 15 minutes from the end).

04. Keep the water bubbling merrily for the duration. If you're using a coiled immersion cooler and not performing a hop stand, insert it (without water flowing) 15 minutes before the end to sanitise.

05. At the end of the boil, remove the heat source (brewers call this flameout) and add any final hop additions (ie for a hop stand or whirlpool).

06. Take a small sample and use a hydrometer or refractometer to take a gravity reading (OG).

Step 4
Hop stand

Giving hops a long, lazy bath in warm wort for maximum aroma.

Conventional wisdom claims that the wort needs to be cooled as quickly as possible after the boil. However, as some of the recipes in this book indicate, a hop stand can add huge aromas to the final beer and many homebrewers now incorporate it. Basically, it simply involves adding a load of aroma hops and leaving them in contact with the cooling wort for anything between ten and 45 minutes. This is also known as 'whirlpool hops', due to the pro technique of spinning the wort, creating centrifugal force to form a pyramid of solids in the middle of the kettle, allowing for easier drainage. You can do this if you wish, but a hop stand can still be performed without a whirlpool. If your recipe doesn't call for a hop stand, skip to Step 5 on the following page.

Step 5 **Cooling & aerating**

Dropping the wort temperature and preparing it for the introduction of yeast.

Whether you've performed a hop stand or not, it's imperative the wort is now cooled as quickly as possible to minimise risk of infection (and for two other reasons: to get it to the yeast-friendly temperature indicated on the packet and to minimise hanging-around time. A batch of wort can take hours to cool naturally). See p20 for the different chillers you can use (or simply dunk the whole kettle in a big bath of iced water, which takes a long time and only works for non-electric stovetop pots, of course). From now on, anything that comes into contact with the wort must be considered a potential risk to the health of your beer. Sanitise. Also, at this stage it's a good idea to think about yeast – if it needs to be rehydrated, start it while your wort is cooling.

Immersion cooler

If you're using an immersion cooler, connect hoses to the ends – one for cold water in, one out. Turn on the cold water tap as high as it safely will go and ensure the output leads to a drain or sink. Stir the wort with a sterilised spoon to ensure maximum cooling efficiency.

Take regular measurements until the wort temperature is within the range specified on the yeast packet. Turn off the cold water input and remove the chiller.

Transfer into the fermenter will have to be carried out now – either with gravity or a siphon. Splashing is desirable at this stage – oxygen in the wort is essential for the yeast to start fermenting.

Plate cooler

Connect hoses to the correct inputs and outputs.
You'll be extracting the wort as it chills – so you'll
have to balance the output carefully to ensure that
the liquid flowing directly into the fermenter is at
the right temperature (around 20C/68F or less).
If it's too high, close off the tap at the bottom of the
boil kettle a little. Splashing at this stage is to be
encouraged – oxygen in the wort is essential for
the yeast to begin fermenting. Keep this going until
you've drained the boil kettle into the fermenter.

In the fermenter

01. Depending on your efficiency and evaporation,
the volume of wort at this stage may vary. If you
have more or less than the intended batch size,
the chances are that your gravity will be a bit off
target – the beer will still be eminently drinkable,
just not exactly the ABV you were aiming for.

02. Take another gravity reading. This will be
your original gravity (OG), vital in determining
final ABV. Compare it to the target OG in the
recipe (see p53).

03. Give the wort a stir to avoid any hot spots,
then take a temperature reading. If it's too hot, the
yeast you're about to pitch will not work or could
even die off, and you'll have to pitch another batch.
Which you may or may not have hanging around
somewhere. It's a good idea to have a spare.

04. Aerate the wort. Like us, yeast can't live on
beer alone – it needs oxygen. (Don't aerate wort
above 26C/80F – it can cause oxidation, which
is not the same as aeration and makes your beer
taste weird.) Homebrew shops sell aeration
equipment; the simple way of aerating is to put
the fermenter lid on tight and shake it all for a
few minutes.

Step 6 **Pitching yeast**

There's a party going on in your fermenting vessel. The sugars are sitting guarding the booze stash and the hops have got boring old water up on the dancefloor. But it's not going off just yet. Pitching the yeast is like chucking John Belushi in and locking the door: things are going to get wild.

How much yeast should you use? One packet per 20L/5 gallon batch will probably be enough for beers up to 11% ABV or so. For higher-gravity beers, it's advisable to use two packs or make a starter culture. As mentioned on p32, there are two forms of commercial yeast, dry and liquid. Liquid yeasts should be stored in the fridge until use, although it's best not to keep them for too long (anything more than a few months will render them sluggish and feeble). Dry yeast is much hardier. A third kind, wild yeast, is floating all around you right now – it would get involved with your beer if you gave it the

chance, but the outcome would be unpredictable to say the least. Stick to the store-bought stuff at first; spontaneous fermentation is for the confident only.

Some manufacturers of dry homebrew yeast recommend rehydrating dry yeast before pitching. They'll tell you that the rehydration process has the potential to damage yeast cell walls, and so should be carried out on a smaller scale at a certain temperature before pitching. Some homebrewers disregard this advice and sprinkle the yeast straight on top of the wort, which is most of the

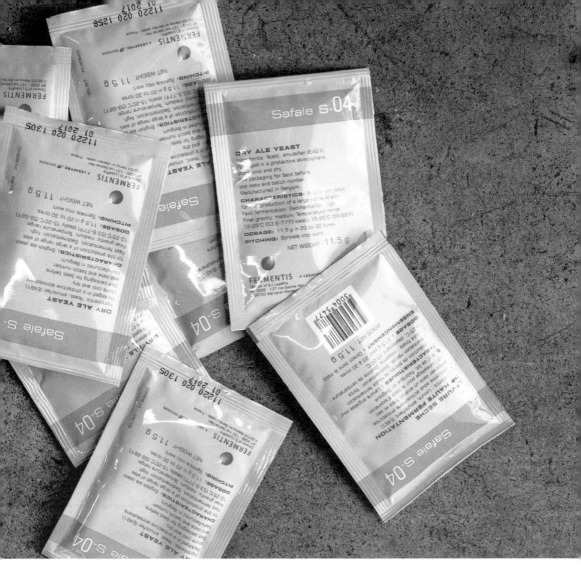

time absolutely fine, but not guaranteed to work. Best follow the instructions on the packet (and always sanitise the outside of the packet too before opening). If the packet doesn't have instructions (where did you find this stuff?), do it like this: boil four times the amount of water as you have yeast. Allow to cool to around body temperature (hopefully 37C/98F) in a sanitised jar. Sprinkle room-temperature yeast over and leave for 15 minutes. Stir it in gently, and after another 15 minutes, check

first that the yeast temperature is within 10C/18F of the wort it's going into, then send it in. Liquid yeast, provided the nutrient pouch (if there was one) was activated three hours before and it's at the correct temperature, can be poured right in too.

When you've pitched the yeast, wave goodbye to the wort and shut the lid or seal the top. Next time you open it, you'll have beer. Put the airlock in the hole (with a bit of sanitised water, if it's the bubbler type).

Step 7 **Fermenting (and dry-hopping)**

Good beer demands a good fermentation. Give the yeast what it needs and it's hard to fail.

In some ways, fermenting is the easiest step in brewing, because it involves passing over all the work to the yeast: but fermenting is also perhaps the most important. Give the yeast a hand by ensuring the fermentation vessel is stored in a dark place at the temperature indicated in the recipe. Primary fermentation should begin within 12 hours of pitching: the evidence will be activity in the airlock as lots of CO_2 is produced. (If nothing happens after 24 hours, the yeast has probably not worked. Don't despair: pitch your spare packet, making sure you follow the condition instructions carefully.) If you have a glass vessel you'll be able to see the scummy-looking krausen forming on the top of the wort, but if you're fermenting in steel or plastic, don't be tempted to open the lid to have a look. That's asking for infection.

Under normal conditions, this phase could last up to ten days for ales – it's hard to be accurate, because yeast is free and alive and doesn't follow instructions. Keep monitoring it – when the activity from the airlock has slowed right down, it's time to either rack off into a secondary fermenter (not strictly essential for a homebrewer, most of the time) or simply leave for longer to condition. The yeast is still working, albeit at a slower pace, and the beer is clearing. Three weeks is about the maximum you'd want to leave it on the yeast cake without racking off.

When you're satisfied the phase is over (and satisfaction comes with experience), it's time to take a gravity reading. This will be your target final gravity (FG), and will be used to determine ABV (see p52).

If you're making lager, it's time for the lagering phase – another fermentation stage at a lower temperature.

Some brewers then practise 'cold crashing' on lagers or beers, chilling the beer to between 1C/33F and 5C/40F for between a couple of days and a week to aid in clarifying.

If you're dry-hopping, as many of the recipes in this book suggest, after primary is the time to do it. How long should you dry-hop for? As with most aspects of homebrewing, there's no straight answer. Three to five days is a good bet, but experiment with less or more if you like. The hops need to be in contact with the wort long enough to give up their oils. Your choice of fermentation vessel will affect the method you use: some people dry hop using a muslin bag, to avoid extra matter in the wort, but that becomes hard to physically fit into a plastic or glass carboy. So hop plugs are handy at this stage because they're just more practical. If you're not racking and filtering out to a bottling vessel (see Step 8), a bag is pretty much essential to avoid hop lumps in your beer.

Step 8 **Priming, bottling & conditioning**

The last few stages before the best one (drinking) involve setting the stage for carbonation and giving the beer somewhere peaceful to rest.

You're so close to having real beer. The liquid in the fermenter is no longer wort: it's malty, hoppy and alcoholic, but flat and underdeveloped. For fizz, it needs priming with sugar, usually brewing sugar (a simple glucose which adds no flavour and is easily converted to CO_2 by the yeast). Mix up a solution according to the volumes of carbonation required: brewing software makes this a cinch. You can rack the beer out into another vessel before bottling, to minimise sediment transfer into bottles: if you do this, put the sugar solution in then rack on to it. Or just use the fermenting vessel and be careful. Pour the solution into the almost-beer, stirring very gently but ensuring it's well mixed. Attach the scrupulously sanitised bottling tap to the vessel and fill the scrupulously sanitised bottles. To suffer contamination at this stage would be like breaking your ankle on the last 100 yards of a marathon. Using a capper, fix the sanitised caps on solidly. Put the bottles somewhere dark and cool for two weeks, although you'll find that another one or two on top often helps. (Some beers, like Nøgne Ø's barleywine on p162, need longer to mature.)

And as for the next stage, you probably don't need any guidance. Get a couple cold, say cheers, and drink the best beer you'll ever taste. Until the next batch.

How to follow these recipes

—

Beer recipes come with their own code, one of gravities, yields, times, weights and percentages. Once you understand how they correspond to what you actually have to do at home, they're simple (and you can start writing your own!).

All beer recipes are created with efficiencies and equipment in mind – the same ingredients could lead to different results on different sets. So consider your first brew a test. Keep records. Equipment is just as important as ingredients, as is taking accurate measurements, hitting targets, experimenting, practising and consistency. The recipes in this book were created by pro brewers; if you can't recreate a particular mash schedule or fermentation profile, adapt, but keep the principles intact!

When laid out in steps, homebrewing seems simple enough. But delve a bit deeper into the science and it can become a bewildering mass of figures, percentages, weights and measures. Like most hobbies, you can get as geeky as you like. Don't be alarmed: dive in, figuratively speaking, and before long a beautiful calm will descend over your brewing. The relationships between ingredients and their properties will be revealed. Efficiency and consistency will move within reach. Your equipment will become an extension of you and you'll be at one with the malt, hops and yeast.

Or, at least, you'll get the hang of it. Either way, great beer is the result. There are good homebrew calculators online and in app form, but to get to grips with the science underpinning the art will lead to better beer. You only need a basic understanding of maths to brew, and if you don't have that, are you sure you're even old enough to be drinking beer?

ABV target

Alcohol by volume. This is a pretty vital figure – will you end up with a breakfast beer, or one you need to clear space in your diary to drink? ABV is a target, not a guaranteed figure, though. To calculate it, you'll need OG and FG readings (see p53), which are also targets. A simple homebrew formula is:

$$ABV = (OG-FG) \times 131.25$$

Use specific gravities with a point (ie 1.054). The relationship between gravity and ABV is not linear, so this formula is never going to be completely spot-on, especially at higher ABVs. Use software or an online calculator for increased accuracy.

Yield

All the recipes in this book are to a homebrew batch size of 20L/5 gall. That's the amount you're aiming to get into the fermenter, although even after that, some liquid may be absorbed by yeast, dry hopping, dead space etc. Water, malt, hops and yeast can be scaled up or down effectively to make more or less beer, should you want to. The yield figure is also a target – if it's higher or lower, your gravity and ABV might be awry.

OG and FG targets (original gravity and final gravity)

The two most significant targets in a homebrew recipe are original and final gravity. Not only do they allow us to calculate ABV, but they're an indication of how efficient a brew was, and also, the FG will tell us when fermentation is finished. When brewers talk of 'brewhouse efficiency', they're referring to the ability to which their system can extract potential fermentable sugars of the grains from start to finish. Due to differing ingredients, efficiency can't be considered uniform across brews. All the recipes in this book assume a 75% efficiency, which is not a bad target. As you become a better brewer you'll want to take efficiencies into account and measure your own. A good software like Beersmith is invaluable.

Grain

All recipes in this book suggest grain weights as well as percentages. Basically, if you don't want to concern yourself too much yet with efficiencies, use the weights; if you have a clear idea of how your equipment performs and what efficiency you can hit, use the ratios and the results will be more accurate.

Mash

Mashing is, simply put, grain plus water. Mash water is split into two volumes – strike water and sparge water – and you'll have to know how much to use of each. To calculate strike water we firstly calculate mash thickness, ie the ratio of water to grain. A standard ratio is 2.6L of water to 1kg of grist (1.25 quarts to 1lb). To then calculate the sparge water, we have to allow for losses to, among other things, grain absorption, trub absorption (see p183), hops absorption (boil and dry), all vessel dead space and boil evaporation. You'll only really know how much your system is likely to lose after a bit of trial and error. (Boiling water for an hour in your kettle, volume measured before and after, will reveal your evaporation rate.) You can assume that 1kg of malt holds on to 1L of water (roughly 1lb/1 pint). So to work out total liquor, add lost volume on to target yield; to get the sparging volume, simply subtract the mash volume from this total. As a guideline, you'll probably need to be putting around an extra 7L/1.5 gall above final yield into the boil kettle.

Hops

Some breweries in this book specify alpha acid percentages in their recipes. Alpha acids are compounds extracted from hops in the boil which provide bitterness in beer. Bitterness is measured in International Bitterness Units (IBUs). AA and IBU are related: more AA leads to higher IBU; a greater weight of hops or a longer boil time also leads to a higher IBU. Alpha acids in hop varieties vary from crop to crop, so to achieve exact IBUs, hop weights will need to be adjusted.

If you need to adjust a hop weight to your own packet AA%, get your calculator out. Here's a formula:

Original AA% x original hop weight / AA% of new hop = weight of new hop

And as with grain, you might not always be able to get the hop variety specified in a recipe, especially in times of agricultural shortage. Alternatives abound.

Yeast

Many breweries use a house strain: the recipes here suggest commercial strains and, again, you can find substitutes in case of unavailability. Choose something similar.

Fermentation

Stick to this temperature as closely as possible till FG is reached and fermentation has finished.

Carbonation

Introduce the correct weight of priming sugar to give the finished beer the correct amount of fizz. This varies according to temperature, volume and style of beer, so it's always easiest to use an online calculator.

Wheat, saison & sour

—

Wheat, weizen, wit: when malted it makes beer smooth and refreshing; unmalted wheat is sharper. Saison is a light and sparkling Franco-Belgian farmhouse ale that takes on added flavours perfectly, while sours use different yeasts and bacteria to result in a recognisable tart taste.

Bruery Terreux

Orange County, California, USA

BERET
RASPBERRY IMPERIAL SOUR WITBIER

20 L / 5 GAL | ABV 9%
OG 1.076 | FG 1.010

There's a group of craft beer lovers who don't just buy it and drink the stuff. They buy it, cellar it, trade it, age it and show it off (then hopefully drink it too). In the world of rare beer collecting, one brewery's name comes up again and again: The Bruery (this Terreux side brand was created for sours in 2015). There's emphatically no IPA – founder Patrick Rue's team specialise in barrel-aged, sour, experimental, rested-on-fruit styles, plus revivals and completely original creations. Many of these beers blossom after a long dark rest on wood; Beret, however, can be fermented on steel (or a neutral wine barrel, or a demijohn/carboy) and enjoyed fresh (although it too will pick up complexity over time). The base is a smooth Belgian wit with minimal hopping, but the Lacto bacteria and Brett yeast take it to a new level. The Brett will get stuck into any malt sugars left over (and sugar from the raspberries), all the while producing its trademark spicy, fruity, farmy flavours. Brewer Andrew Bell recommends using sturdy bottles capable of withstanding a lot of CO_2 (you should aim to carb to around 2.75 volumes).

GRAIN
Weyermann pilsner malt, 3.4kg/7lbs 8oz (60%)

Great Western unmalted wheat, 2.27kg/5lbs (40%)

MASH
67C/152F for 60 mins

HOPS
(60 minute boil)

German Magnum 15.2% AA, 6g/0.21oz, first wort hops

YEAST
White Labs WLP400 Belgian Wit Ale or Wyeast 3944 Belgian Witbier

Your favourite Lactobacillus brevis (12 days into fermentation)

Your favourite Brettanomyces bruxellensis, 1,000,000 cells per ml (12 days into fermentation)

FERMENT
18C/65F, then allow to free rise; full fermentation and souring will take around 2 months

OTHER INGREDIENTS
Crushed coriander, 12g/0.4oz, boil for 10 mins

Bitter orange peel, 12g/0.4oz, boil for 10 mins

Yeast nutrient and Whirlfloc, boil for 10 mins

Raspberry purée, 726g/1lb 9.6oz, or whole raspberries, 826g/13.1oz, 12 days into primary

Brooklyn Brewery

Brooklyn, New York, USA

The story of the Brooklyn Brewery is so fascinating it deserves its own book. Luckily it has one. Beer School: Bottling Success at the Brooklyn Brewery is full of anecdotes and details, facts and figures, history and legend behind the Williamsburg enterprise, which is still as cool as a freshly cracked cold one after almost 30 years on the scene. Brooklyn is truly craft beer royalty: it was founded in 1988 by an ex-Middle East correspondent and keen homebrewer (Steve Hindy) and a banker (Tom Potter), and the unquestionably iconic emblem was created by

Milton Glaser, designer of the I ♥ NY logo. Since 1994 the output has been under the stewardship of brewmaster Garrett Oliver, who's become something of an authority in the world of craft brewing. Brooklyn has built a reputation with its non-traditional advertising and its no-compromise beers, including the the harmoniously balanced East IPA, the made-for-outdoor-drinking Summer Ale and the world-famous Brooklyn Lager, which has been surprising, intriguing and converting major-label beer drinkers since 1988 with its Vienna-style malty richness.

Brooklyn Brewery

Brooklyn, New York, USA

SORACHI ACE
US-HOPPED SAISON

▬

20 L / 5 GAL | ABV **7.2%**
OG **1.062** | FG **1.008**

A relatively recent addition to the Brooklyn gang is Sorachi Ace, a classic Belgian farmhouse ale with a New York accent. Traditionally, saisons were made for hardworking agricultural workers in the countryside of the Wallonia region, with a fairly tight selection of ingredients – European malts and grains, low-alpha acid noble hops – but they're great fun to brew because they can cosy up with all sorts of other hops and flavourings. This twenty-first-century reimagining uses only one hop, the Northwestern-by-way-of-Japan Sorachi Ace, which provides a flowery, lemony character you won't get anywhere else. And the technique in this recipe is great evidence of the way that staggered deployment throughout the boil can draw out a real range of flavours, from bitterness through flavour to aroma. An essential element of saison is Belgian yeast, which makes its presence known through fruity, spicy, ester notes. The result is straw-coloured, refreshingly carbonated, food-friendly and supremely thirst quenching – ploughing fields will be a breeze after a couple of these.

GRAIN
Pilsner malt, 5kg/11lbs (92%)

MASH
50C/122F for 10 mins, 63C/145F for 60 mins, 67C/152F for 15 mins, mash out at 75C/168F. Draw off wort at 1.054 SG and add corn sugar

HOPS
Sorachi Ace 12% AA, 14g/0.5oz, 60 mins

Sorachi Ace 12% AA, 14g/0.5oz, 30 mins

Sorachi Ace, 56g/2oz, 0 mins

Sorachi Ace, 84g/3oz, dry hop 5–7 days

YEAST
Wyeast 1214 Belgian Ale or White Labs 500 Trappist Ale

FERMENT
22C/71F

OTHER INGREDIENTS
450g/1lb corn sugar (8%)

8 Wired Brewing

Warkworth, New Zealand

SAISON SAUVIN
NZ-HOPPED SAISON

---

20 L / **5** GAL | ABV **7%**
OG **1.055** | FG **1.002**

In New Zealand, they say anything can be done with a bit of No 8 wire. It was a gauge used for fencing, and came to symbolise the classic Kiwi DIY attitude: adaptability and resourcefulness and just-bloody-get-on-with-it. It seems you can even make good beer with No 8 wire – Søren Eriksen has won awards including NZ Champion Brewery in 2011. Compare this saison, which stars the one-of-a-kind Kiwi hop Nelson Sauvin, to Brooklyn's Sorachi Ace on p60, or Burning Sky's Saison à la Provision on p68, and you'll see the huge variations in malt, hops, yeast, additions and techniques that exist in the style. Some advice from Søren: "The higher finishing fermentation temperature is important for proper attenuation. You can use many kinds of yeasts, but it's important to get the extreme level of attenuation that we get from the 3711. So if you use a lower attenuator, include up to 10% dextrose in the fermentables. Plus, a small amount of dry-hopping with Nelson Sauvin doesn't hurt, but we don't do it…" There is no substitute for Nelson Sauvin either – this beer won't be the same without it.

GRAIN
Pilsner malt, 2.71kg/5lbs 15.6oz (59%)

Pale ale malt,1.06kg/2lbs 5.4oz (23%)

Wheat malt, 370g/13oz (8%)

Caramalt, 180g/6.3oz (4%)

Flaked wheat, 180g/6.3oz (4%)

Acid malt, 90g/3.2oz (2%)

MASH
Mash at very low temperature to get the required attenuation, 64C/147F (or lower if you are comfortable with it), for 60 mins

HOPS
(60 minute boil)

Nelson Sauvin, 42g/1.5oz, first wort hops

Nelson Sauvin, 84g/3oz, whirlpool

Motueka, 42g/1.5oz, whirlpool

YEAST
Wyeast 3711 French Saison

FERMENT
Start fermentation at 21C/70F, then let it rise to 27C/81F or so over the course of 4–5 days

Three Boys Brewery

Christchurch, New Zealand

THREE BOYS WHEAT
BELGIAN-STYLE WIT

20 L / 5 GAL | ABV **5%**
OG **1.050** | FG **1.012**

New Zealand is a small country with a widescreen outlook. This is especially true in the country's craft brewing industry, which punches well above its weight in both hemispheres. Three Boys' Ralph Bungard is president of the Brewers' Guild of NZ and an ex-scientist – the methodical and enquiring mind is a useful one to have in a practice like brewing, and Ralph's won a heap of awards for his consistently top-class beers (especially the Oyster Stout, made with some of the world's best bivalves from Bluff on New Zealand's South Island). Three

Boys is a deliberately small-scale brewery focused on quality rather than global domination, and like all of its brews, this Wheat is true to its roots, being a classic Belgian style with prominent yeast characteristics, a cloud-like head, coriander and citrus. But NZ brewers always leave their own mark on their beers, and here it's through a fully native hop bill (including the fresh and tropical Motueka) and the unique Meyer lemon zest. Wheat in a mash tun can get sticky, so bear that in mind when lautering – you can use rice hulls to keep it loose.

GRAIN
Gladfield NZ Light Lager malt, 2.01kg/4lbs 6.9oz (47%)

Gladfield NZ Wheat Malt, 1.34kg/2lbs 15.3oz (32%)

Gladfield NZ Raw Wheat 670g/1lb 7.6oz (16%)

Gladfield Gladiator Pale Crystal 10L 300g/10.6oz (5%)

MASH
69C/156F for 60 mins

HOPS
Green Bullet 13.9% AA, 7.5g/0.26oz, 90 mins

Motueka 7.5% AA, 3.5g/ 0.1oz, 10 mins

Motueka 7.5% AA,10g/ 0.35oz, 0 mins

YEAST
Wyeast 3994 Belgian Wit

FERMENT
20C/68F

OTHER INGREDIENTS
Fresh Meyer lemon zest, 22g/ 0.8oz, boil for 5 mins

Ground coriander, 33g/ 1.2oz, boil for 5 mins

three boys

Wheat

Three Boys Wheat evokes ancient abbey ales, when yeasts and citrus instead of hops were added for bitterness. We use germinated wheat that with the wheat malt produces the authentic freshly baked cloudiness and huge flavours sought in this wit bier (white beer). The addition of coriander and citrus zest really make this beer special.

Brew By Numbers

Bermondsey, London, England

01|01 CITRA SAISON
HOPPY SAISON

20 L / **5** GAL | ABV **5.5%**
OG **1.044** | FG **1.002**

You've probably realised by now that brewing does involve a lot of numbers, but it means something different here. This innovative London brewery was set up in 2011 by two keen homebrewers, Tom Hutchings and Dave Seymour, who from the very start wanted to do things properly. A trip to the Low Countries opened their eyes to the vast range of idiosyncratic beers produced there, and back in Britain they set about making their own with Belgian rigour and attention to detail, but unlimited imagination. The 'numbers' in the name refers to a unique cataloguing system: the first part denotes style (08 is stout, 14 is tripel, for instance) and the second is the recipe: 05|08 is a Mosaic IPA. And here's where it all started, with Citra Saison. Traditional saisons definitely don't involve Washington hops, but as with Brooklyn's Sorachi Ace (see p60) and 8 Wired's Saison Sauvin (see p63), the style warms to them perfectly. The greengrocer's-basket bouquet of lychee, grapefruit and melon from the Citra is perfect in this light, smooth and sparkling saison.

GRAIN
Low-colour Maris Otter pale malt, 1.35kg/2lbs 15.6oz (36.5%)

Pilsner malt, 1.08kg/2lbs 6.1oz (29%)

Wheat malt, 810g/1lb 12oz (22%)

Flaked wheat, 270g/9.5oz (7.5%)

MASH
65C/149F for 60 mins

HOPS
Hallertauer Magnum 12.9% AA, 5g/0.15oz, 60 mins

Citra 12% AA, 10g/0.35oz, 10 mins

Citra 12% AA, 10g/0.35oz, 5 mins

Citra 12% AA, 50g/1.8oz, flameout. Steep for 10 mins before chilling

YEAST
Wyeast 3711 French Saison, or other saison yeast of your choice

FERMENT
24C/75F, ideally hold for 48 hours then allow to free rise, ideally maintain at 27C/80F

OTHER INGREDIENTS
Dextrose, 180g/6.3oz (5%), added slowly as the wort is coming to a boil to ensure it dissolves and doesn't scorch

Cracked coriander seeds, 10g/0.35oz, boil for 5 mins

Burning Sky Artisan Brewers and Blenders

Firle, Sussex, England

SAISON À LA PROVISION
SAISON

▬

20 L / 5 GAL | ABV **6.5%**
OG **1.052** | FG **1.002**

The British Guild of Beer Writers brewer of the year 2014 Mark Tranter was a founder of Dark Star (see p140). It still makes great beer, but he's transferred his passion elsewhere. Mark set up Burning Sky in 2013 as, literally, a long-term project: its main focus is wood-aged, vatted beer; he uses yeasts that take their time to make a product that's in no hurry to mature. Think of it as slow brewing. Saisons are a particular favourite of Mark's, and this Saison à la Provision is a labour of love. "We have French oak foudres that were built for us and are only used for this beer," he says. "We transfer into them after one week of primary fermentation and age the beer for three months. The 'wild yeasts' are becoming resident in the wood; consequently the beer is constantly developing, batch to batch. For homebrewers, unless you have a wine barrel, try ageing the beer on lightly toasted French oak chips or spirals. Our saison yeast strain, plus the Brett/Lacto, are not commercially available as vials, they were harvested from various sources. For the Brett, choose a gentle variety."

- -

GRAIN
Pilsner malt, 3.9kg/8lbs 9.6oz (85%)

Wheat malt, 220g/7.8oz (5%)

Spelt malt, 220g/7.8oz (5%)

Cara Gold, 220g/7.8oz (5%)

MASH
65C/149F for 60 mins

HOPS
East Kent Goldings 3.75% AA, 25g/0.9oz, 75 mins

East Kent Goldings 3.75% AA, 12g/0.4oz, 15 mins

Saaz, 23g/0.8oz, 0 mins

Celeia, 23g/0.8oz, 0 mins

Sorachi Ace, 25g/0.9oz, 0 mins

YEAST
A saison strain: primary fermentation

Brettanomyces: pitch when SG is 1.015

Lactobacillus: pitch when SG is 1.015

FERMENT
Start at 22C/71F and let rise to 25C/77F for a cleaner, less phenolic beer

Lagunitas Brewing Company

Petaluma, California, USA

LITTLE SUMPIN' SUMPIN'
PALE WHEAT ALE

▬

20 L / **5** GAL | ABV **7.5%**
OG **1.070** | FG **1.016**

Sonoma County is a pretty laidback place. It's got mountains and streams, stunning Pacific beaches, famously mellow residents and that sunny California climate. Lagunitas Brewing Company, founded in 1993, has its home there and used to hold informal taproom get-togethers at precisely 4.20pm every Thursday afternoon. If you understand the significance of that time, you're probably as mellow as a Sonoman yourself. Lagunitas is now a major US brewing operation, but its beers are still perfect to kick back with: its IPA is an unparalleled example of the type of West Coast beer that started the craft revolution all those years ago. This Little Sumpin' Sumpin' has a large proportion of wheat, giving it a silky-smooth mouthfeel – and an explosion of piney, aromatic hops means it smells just as good as it tastes. Avoid a stuck sparge while brewing it by mashing thinly and keeping the liquid flowing freely. Lagunitas filters Little Sumpin' Sumpin', which you can do yourself for a clearer glassful – homebrew stores sell the equipment you'll need. This beer's one for the hopheads (or heads of any sort).

- -

GRAIN
2-row American pale malt, 3.23kg/7 lbs 1.9oz (50%)

American wheat malt, 2.46kg/ 5 lbs 6.8oz (38%)

English torrified wheat, 720g/ 1lb 9.4oz (11%)

German toasted (roasted) wheat malt, 80g/2.8oz (1%)

MASH
65.5C/150F for 60 mins, mashout at 75C/168F

HOPS
Nugget pellet 9% AA, 9g/0.3oz, 90 min

Horizon pellet 12.5% AA, 1.5g/0.05oz, 90 min

Summit pellet 17.5% AA, 1.5g/0.05oz, 90 min

Willamette pellet 5.2% AA, 7g/0.2oz, 45 min

Santiam pellet 5.6% AA, 23g/0.8oz, 15 min

Willamette pellet 5.2% AA, 8g/0.3oz, 15 min

Cascade, Centennial and Simcoe pellets, 20g/0.7oz of each, dry hop

Chinook pellet, 24g/0.85oz, dry hop

Columbus pellet, 13g/0.4oz, dry hop

Amarillo pellet, 15g/0.5oz, dry hop

YEAST
White Labs WLP002 English Ale

FERMENT
17-18C/62-65F for 36 hours, then to 20C/68F for 36 hours, then 21C/70F to end

OTHER INGREDIENTS
Add gypsum if you're in a particularly low-mineral water area

Freigeist

Cologne, Germany

KÖPENICKIADE
BERLINER WEISSE

▬▬▬

20 L / 5 GAL | ABV **3.5%**
OG **1.037** | FG **1.010**

Brewing in Germany has a uniquely regulated history. The medieval Reinheitsgebot purity laws are not enforced now, but the industry remains regionalised: salty gose is brewed in Leipzig, altbier in the Lower Rhine. Braustelle, however, is an innovative little brewery in Cologne that makes beers with reverence for the past and a forward-looking attitude; from its experimental offshoot Freigeist ('free spirit') comes this modern take on a Berliner weisse. These increasingly popular beers are sour (from the Lacto bacteria), refreshing (low alcohol, light malts) and easy on hops. This version replaces the traditional wheat with spelt malt, a gluten-free grain which adds a slight nuttiness. The techniques here are fairly advanced. Make a starter with the Lacto before pitching. Wort pH should be less than 4.5 to ensure optimum conditions for its development. You'll need to maintain a high temperature while it ferments, too. Wort splitting is not a traditional method, but it makes the results more predictable (and still taste great). The style responds positively to fruity additions, and it also ages well in bottle.

GRAIN

Pilsner malt, 1.52kg/3lbs 5.6oz (50%)

Spelt malt, 1.1kg/2lbs 6.8oz (36%)

Carapils, 430g/15.2oz (14%)

MASH

63C/145F for 30 mins, then 72C/162F for 30 mins, then mash out at 78C/172F

HOPS

Saphir, 10g/0.35oz, 60 mins

Saphir, 10g/0.35oz, 0 mins

YEAST

Fermentis K97 German Wheat, and White Labs WLP677 Lactobacillus

FERMENT

Split the boiled wort into two separate fermentation tanks. Pitch Fermentis K97 into one (at 20C/68F), and the Lactobacillus into the other (35C/95F). After primary fermentation, rack both into a secondary fermentation tank. Leave at 20C/68F for 10 days. Condition at 4C/39F for 14 days

Baladin

Farigliano, Piedmont, Italy

OPEN WHITE
BIERE BLANCHE

▬

20 L / 5 GAL | ABV **5%**
OG **1.051** | FG **1.016**

You'd be hard pressed to find anywhere in the world that takes food and drink more seriously than Italy: it seems that every Italian understands the importance of the land and what's produced on it. Think of Baladin as being part of the beer arm of the Slow Food movement. Local cherries, pears, orange blossom, pumpkins and heather honey are used in founder Teo Musso's brews, which often come in magnum sizes for proper dinner-table sharing. He's big on cooperation and collaboration too, hence the Open series of 'crowd sourced' beers. This is where Open White comes in: Baladin's version of a biere blanche uses malted wheat as well as the raw wheat traditional in a Belgian biere blanche, and it's dry-hopped too. The orange and coriander, however, bring things back closer to Brussels, and note the use of gentian, a distinctively bitter root which predates hops as a historical beer flavouring. Don't use finings in this recipe – suspended yeast and cloudiness is an important aspect of the white beer style, plus it should be well carbonated for a big fluffy head, which the wheat helps maintain.

GRAIN
Pilsner malt, 4.17kg/9lbs 3.1oz (87%)

Wheat, 440g/15.5oz (9%)

German weizen malt, 180g/ 6.3oz (4%)

MASH
Mash in at 50C/122F; then 48C/118F for 20 mins; 62C/ 143F for 40 mins; 69C/156F for 20 mins; mash out at 78C/172F

HOPS
Perle 8% AA, 2g/0.07oz, 90 mins

Perle 8% AA, 3g/0.1oz, 45 mins

Mittelfrüh 5% AA, 8g/0.3oz, 45 mins

Perle 8% AA, 3g/0.1oz, 0 mins

Amarillo 8% AA, 12g/0.45oz, dry hop

YEAST
Wyeast 3942 Belgian Wheat

FERMENT
20C/68F, then rack off the yeast and add the dry hops and second lot of spices. Reduce the temperature to 4C/39F for 15-20 days before bottling

OTHER INGREDIENTS
Sweet orange zest, 2g/0.07oz; bitter orange zest, 2g/0.07oz; crushed coriander, 22g/0.77oz, to be added at the end of the boil. Stand for 30 minutes

Crushed coriander, 4g/0.14oz; gentian root, 1g/0.03oz, added with dry hops at the end of fermentation

Crooked Stave Artisan Beer Project

Denver, Colorado, USA

ORIGINS
BURGUNDY SOUR ALE

▬▬

20 L / 5 GAL | ABV 6.5%
OG 1.053 | FG 1.006

As the craft beer world begins to appreciate the power of sour, one name is at the vanguard of this modern expedition into classic Belgian and French styles. Chad Yakobson founded Crooked Stave in 2010 after years of studying the science of fermentation (read his dissertations online for unsurpassed insight). Few brewers have such a knowledge of the mysterious Brettanomyces yeast and its wild relatives, and his beers are sought-after and revered. They're sometimes challenging but always sophisticated, brewed with respect for tradition and a constant desire to progress. This is Chad's recipe for his twist on the classic Flanders red. Stick to a low-profile, low-AA hop like Hallertau or one of its New World relatives (Mt Hood, say) – bitterness is to be avoided. Skill and time is needed from primary fermentation onwards. Flanders reds get their unique sour/fruity/winey notes from long ageing on oak (although you can use glass with oak chips). Then, batches are typically blended to balance extreme flavours and maximise complexity – a process that gets easier with experience!

- -

GRAIN
2-row pale malt, 1.65kg/3lbs 10oz (35%)

Vienna malt, 1.65kg/3lbs 10oz (35%)

Carahell, 660g/1lb 7.3oz (14%)

Caramunich I, 330g/11.6oz (7%)

Special B malt, 330g/11.6oz (7%)

Carafa Special II (dehusked), 90g/3.2oz (2%)

MASH
Mash in at 65C/149F. Rest for 30 mins. Recirculate for 10 mins. Mash out at 75-76C/167-169F for 10 mins

HOPS
(90 minute boil)

6% AA hop, 11g/0.4oz, first wort hops

6% AA hop, 11g/0.4oz, 30 mins

YEAST
For primary fermentation, something clean. Then add a mixed culture of Brettanomyces and Lactobacillus bacteria

FERMENT
For a clean primary fermentation, follow standard ale temperatures. After this, age on oak at 17–19C/ 63–66F for 12–18 months. Particularly long rests in barrel may require more yeast before bottling (something powerful but clean)

Red, amber & rye

Caramel malt gives beer a rich, auburn tone and warm, toasty flavours. Rye in small amounts is recognisably earthy and spicy, and is increasingly given a starring role in craft beers. Amber falls between lager and ale, with conspicuous malt and middling alcohol levels.

Anchor Brewing

San Francisco, California, USA

ANCHOR STEAM BEER
STEAM BEER/CALIFORNIA COMMON

20 L / 5 GAL | ABV **4.5%**
OG **1.050** | FG **1.016**

The story of Anchor Brewing is the story of American craft beer. It was established in California by a German brewmaster in 1896, back when *all* brewing was craft brewing – there was no other way. Prohibition curtailed Anchor's activities from 1920, and the nationwide shift towards macro-produced lagers threatened its existence in the late 1950s, but blessedly it's still here and more popular than ever. Anchor makes several great beers at its loveably old-fashioned San Francisco brewery, many of them in the pioneering spirit of its founders (Liberty Ale was the blueprint for the US IPA that the world can't get enough of these days; the California Lager is faithful to a nineteenth-century pioneer's standard). The beer that made the Anchor name – Steam – is a 1970s revival of the traditional California Common style, which was practically extinct at that time. Nowadays it's venerated, with its own yeast strains and a hop blend that's tailor-made for its profile (US Northern Brewer, with a minty, piney character). Anchor Steam Beer is pure liquid history.

- -

GRAIN
2-row pale malt, 4.1kg/ 9lbs 0.6oz (87%)

Crystal 40L malt, 600g/ 1lbs 5oz (13%)

MASH
65C/149F for 60 mins

HOPS
US Northern Brewer pellets 9.6% AA, 14g/0.5oz, 60 mins

US Northern Brewer pellets 9.6% AA, 7g/0.25oz, 20 mins

US Northern Brewer pellets, 9.6% AA, 14g/0.5oz, 0 mins

YEAST
White Labs WLP810 San Francisco Lager or Wyeast 2112 California Lager

FERMENT
16C/61F for 7 days then 19C/66F for 3 days. Store cold for approximately 2 weeks before serving

Saint Arnold Brewing Company

Houston, TX, USA

BLUE ICON
RYE IPA

▬▬

20 L / 5 GAL | ABV **7.8%**
OG **1.067** | FG **1.013**

Another homebrewer-turned-pro (there are many in this book), Brock Wagner was an investment banker by trade when he founded Saint Arnold in 1994; it's now Texas's oldest craft brewery but its new releases are still anticipated with fervour, especially those that are part of the limited Icon range. Brock brought a business mind to beermaking, taking his start-up statewide then across the Deep South into Florida. However, without good beer, a good business plan is just numbers on a page, and you can hang your hat on the fact that Saint Arnold makes good beer. This one's from that Icon series, and uses two types of rye – Weyermann rye malt and the darker, richer CaraRye – for a rounded spicy flavour. It's not all about the rye though – Briess Victory is a biscuit malt, very lightly toasted, which adds a 'baking bread' flavour without too much colour. The big hop additions (especially the Mosaic at the end) gives a real West Coast character to this beer. Note that it's dry hopped twice – once warm then once in the cold crash stage for even more hop oil retention.

- -

GRAIN
Rahr 2-row pale malt, 5.44kg/ 12 lbs (79%)

Weyermann rye malt, 900g/ 2lbs (13%)

Weyermann CaraRye, 340g/ 12oz (5%)

Briess Carapils, 114g/4oz (1.5%)

Briess Victory, 114g/4oz (1.5%)

MASH
67C/152F for 60 mins

HOPS
(60 minute boil)

Columbus 16.3% AA, 34g/ 1.2oz, first wort hops

Simcoe 13% AA, 8.5g/0.3oz, 15 mins

Chinook 10.5% AA, 6g/0.2oz, 15 mins

Chinook 10.5% AA, 21g/0.75oz, 0 mins

Cascade 6.5% AA, 21g/0.75oz, 0 mins

Mosaic 11.5% AA, 64g/2.25oz, warm dry hop within 2 or 3 SG points of FG

Mosaic 11.5% AA, 14g/0.5oz, cold dry hop 5 days before packaging

YEAST
White Labs WLP007 Dry English Ale

FERMENT
21C/70F, cold crash at 0C/31F for 7 days prior to packaging

Brewfist

Lombardy, Italy

CATERPILLAR
AMERICAN PALE ALE WITH RYE

20 L / 5 GAL | ABV **5.8%**
OG **1.055** | FG **1.011**

Along with Baladin (see p74) and Del Ducato (see p168), Brewfist is proof that Italy deserves its place at the top table of European craft brewers. Brewfist is less immediately Italian than those two: the name suggests something a bit commanding, and indeed it concentrates on US-style ales (like the Spaceman IPA or the X-Ray imperial porter), plus collaborations with craft beer luminaries like Prairie and To Øl. One such hook-up (with Denmark's Beer Here) resulted in this Alice in Wonderland-inspired recipe, and it's a winning combination: punchy malts and a decent whack of hops from the resinous US Columbus and the tropical-citrus Kiwi Motueka. This is a great example of the way that rye, even in small amounts, can add its own personality to a brew: 10% will supply a gentle, earthy, spicy dryness, but in bigger proportions it becomes more assertive. Advice from a caterpillar: this is a great beer to try as one of your first brews, with just two hop varieties used cleverly through the boil, and enough complexity to keep things interesting.

GRAIN
Pale ale malt, 3.96kg/ 11.7oz (80%)

Rye malt, 500g/1lb 1.6oz (10%)

Caramalt, 300g/10.6oz (6%)

Crystal malt 10L, 100g/ 3.5oz (2%)

Wheat malt, 100g/3.5oz (2%)

MASH
66C/150F for 45 mins, 78C/ 172F for 5 mins

HOPS
30g/1.06oz Motueka, 10 mins

8g/0.28oz Columbus, 10 mins

30g/1.06oz Motueka, whirlpool

8g/0.28oz Columbus, whirlpool

30g/1.06oz Motueka, dry hop

15g/0.53oz Columbus, dry hop

YEAST
Danstar Nottingham Ale

FERMENT
20C/68F

Two Birds Brewing

Spotswood, Victoria, Australia

Maybe because of beer's unfortunate former reputation as a bloke's drink, the perception still exists that brewing is a bloke's business. It's not true: all over the world, women are tending their mashes and boils, and the open-mindedness of the craft beer world hopefully breaks down any old-fashioned barriers to entry, for both drinkers and makers. What's still a bit more rare though is a completely female-founded and operated brewery. Jayne Lewis and Danielle Allen set up Two Birds in 2011 after an eye-opening trip to the craft beer heartland of the USA's West Coast, and in 2014 opened The Nest, a dedicated brewery and tasting room in Spotswood, a suburb of Melbourne in Australia. But when you taste their beers, you'll realise that it's not important whether it was made by Aussie birds or Aussie blokes –

it's just great. The brewery's success is built on a core range that includes the flagship Golden Ale, Sunset amber ale (see the next page for the recipe) and Taco Beer, made with wheat, corn, lime and coriander, and every bit as enticing as it sounds. At the brewery tap you might find the more leftfield likes of a rhubarb saison or red ale with vanilla and cacao, but what's experimentation without consistency? It's not the barrel-aged spiced tripel that's going to win over that 99% who don't yet drink craft beer. And after a hard day at work, you're probably not going to reach for that 120-IBU IIPA. Two Birds don't make beer for beer nerds, they make beer for everyone. To do that and win awards and see year-on-year expansion is arguably harder than continually making boundary-breaking beers.

Two Birds Brewing

Spotswood, Victoria, Australia

SUNSET ALE
RED ALE

---

20 L / 5 GAL | ABV **4.6%**
OG **1.048** | FG **1.014**

Sunset Ale is Jayne and Danielle's second-ever creation as Two Birds. It's an American-style red or amber ale (the difference between the two isn't worth getting worked up about), but 'sunset' sums up the colour far better – it would delight a shepherd, that's for sure. It has won stacks of awards in Australia for its rich, biscuity caramel flavour (from the Munich and amber malts) and citrussy combination of US and local hops. Amber/red ales are designed to have a fuller body and more involving maltiness than pale ales, but are still thirst-quenching and balanced – along with the summer ale style, they're perfect for hot Aussie weather. The handful of wheat in the grain bill ensures the head on the Sunset Ale sticks around to the last drop, while the Citra/Cascade/Galaxy trio at the end of the boil makes for a seriously zesty finish. One of the Two Birds, Jayne Lewis, was previously head brewer at Mountain Goat (see p95), and along with their Hightail, Sunset represents all the best things about Australian session ales.

GRAIN
Traditional ale malt, 2.71kg/ 5lbs 15.6oz (63%)

Munich malt, 640g/1lb 6.6oz (15%)

Pale crystal malt, 340g/12oz (8%)

Amber malt, 210g/7.1oz (5%)

Wheat malt, 210g/7.1oz (5%)

Dark crystal malt, 80g/2.8oz (2%)

Roasted malt, 80g/2.8oz (2%)

MASH
67-68C/152F-154F for 40 mins

HOPS
Centennial, 2g/0.07oz, 60 mins

Citra, 7g/0.2oz, 20 mins

Cascade, 7g/0.2oz, 20 mins

Galaxy, 7g/0.2oz, 20 mins

Citra, 5g/0.15oz, end of whirlpool

Cascade, 5g/0.17oz, end of whirlpool

Galaxy, 5g/0.17oz, end of whirlpool

Citra, 13g/0.4oz, dry hop

Cascade, 13g/0.4oz, dry hop

Galaxy, 13g, 0.4oz, dry hop

YEAST
Fermentis US-05 American Ale

FERMENT
18C/65F

Brú

Trim, County Meath, Ireland

RUA
IRISH RED ALE

▬▬

20 L / 5 GAL | ABV **4.2%**
OG **1.044** | FG **1.011**

This brewery's name is pronounced as you'd imagine: by fortunate coincidence it comes from the Gaelic Brú na Bóinne, a prehistoric site of burial north of Dublin in County Meath. In a country with a young but flourishing craft beer industry, Brú keeps one eye on tradition and another on the world at large – look out for its take on the world-beating Irish dry stout (Dubh, meaning black) and this red ale. Irish red ale is a unique style similar to Scottish ales (creamier than most English bitters), gentle enough to enjoy a few pints, with a deep coppery hue from the combination of pale and dark crystal malts. Standard Irish red ales have modest hop bills, but Brú's Rua uses the fruity and flowery tones of the classic US Cascade for a modern twist: maybe it's not by the book, but that's what craft brewing's all about. The brewers recommend four teaspoons of Irish moss (see p33 and p182) with ten minutes to go in the boil to keep the beer bright, and add: "Fermenting at 25C/77F creates a lot of ester formation which brings the hop aroma up and enhances the flavour."

GRAIN
Irish pale ale malt, 3.47kg/7lbs 10oz (86%)

Crystal 150L malt, 280g/ 9.9oz (7%)

Torrified wheat, 280g/ 9.9oz (7%)

MASH
70C/158F for 60 mins

HOPS
Magnum, 27g/0.95oz, 60 mins

Cascade, 20g/0.7oz, 10 mins

Cascade, 20g/0.7oz, 0 mins

YEAST
Danstar Nottingham Ale or White Labs WLP039 Nottingham Ale

FERMENT
25C/77F

BREWERS'RESERVE

LA

RYE IPA

INTENSELY HOPPY

NET CONTENTS 0.33 L   8,5%

Lervig Aktiebryggerie

Stavanger, Norway

RYE IPA
RYE IPA

20 L / 5 GAL | ABV **8.5%**
OG **1.076** | FG **1.013**

Mike Murphy is one of the best-travelled brewers in Europe. First off, he's from Pennsylvania, where the alcohol laws are among the meanest in the US. After starting out as a homebrewer, he worked professionally in Italy and Denmark (including brewing for Mikkeller) before ending up in southwestern Norway as brewmaster of Lervig, now one of the country's biggest and best. In a typically internationalist Scandinavian style, he's collaborated with tons of other breweries (see p154 for Lervig and Põhjala's imperial porter) and is now busy keeping Norway on the international craft beer map with beers that range from the Carlsberg-besting Pilsner to Lucky Jack APA and this Rye IPA. It's just about strong enough to be considered a double IPA, but the high alcohol is there to stand up to the hop bitterness and the uniquely flavoured rye. Rye can be used up to percentages of even more than 50 in some grain bills, but here, with just under 20, it makes its dry spiciness subtly but firmly known. Some people grind rye malt separately from the rest of the grist to get a finer grain size.

GRAIN
Pilsner malt, 4.93kg/10lbs 13.9oz (74%)

Rye malt, 1.27kg/2lbs 12.8oz (19%)

Oats, 200g/7oz (3%)

Crystal malt 10L, 130g/ 4.6oz (2%)

Crystal malt 150L, 130g/ 4.6oz (2%)

MASH
Mash in at 61C/142F, rest at 68C/154F for 45 mins, mash out at 78C/172F

HOPS
A good bittering hop to 65 IBU, ie 65g/2.3oz of 10% AA hop, 60 mins

Centennial, 24g/0.8oz, 30 mins

Chinook, 29g/1oz, 15 mins

Citra, 29g/1oz, 10 mins

Simcoe, 29g/1oz, 0 mins

Simcoe, Citra, Centennial, 29g/ 1oz of each, dry hop

YEAST
An American ale strain

FERMENT
20C/68F

Mountain Goat Beer

Richmond, Victoria, Australia

HIGHTAIL ALE
BRITISH-INSPIRED PALE ALE

20 L / 5 GAL | ABV **4.5%**
OG **1.043** | FG **1.009**

The Aussies have a habit of taking English inventions and effortlessly improving them. Cricket's a prime example, or you could have rugby, and here's another: Mountain Goat's Hightail Ale. The Victoria brewery took the classic British bitter and gave it a full Shane Warne-esque spin, retaining the traditional warm malt and all-important balance that makes the style such a fine session sipper, but adding a heap of floral New World hops (Pride of Ringwood is a quintessential early-addition hop Down Under). It's full-bodied too (from the crystal malt blend and the small portion of wheat). As one of Australia's earliest new-wave craft breweries (founded in 1997), Mountain Goat has had a long time to perfect Hightail and its other laidback beers like the New World Summer Ale or the Fancy Pants Amber ale. If you're ever in inner Melbourne, stop by the Goat Bar in Richmond to try the whole range (plus limited 'Rare Breed' editions) on tap. A final tip from Goat brewer Dave: "Carbonate gently and drink fresh!" Hightail, by the way, is perfect for watching cricket with.

GRAIN
Pale malt, 2.55kg/6lbs 6.3oz (69%)

Munich malt, 510g/1lb 2oz (14%)

Medium crystal malt, 240g/ 8.5oz (8.5%)

Wheat malt, 200g/7oz (5.5%)

Dark crystal malt, 80g/2.8oz (2%)

Roasted malt, 30g/1.1oz (1%)

MASH
67.5C/153.5F for 30 mins

HOPS
Pride of Ringwood, 20g/0.7oz, 60 mins

Cascade, 50g/1.76oz, 0 mins

Galaxy, 10g/0.35oz, 0 mins

YEAST
Wyeast 1056 American Ale

FERMENT
21C/70F

Pale ale, IPA & lager

—

Pale ales are balanced and very drinkable with fragrant hops. IPAs are more hop-heavy (usually with dry hops, originally to keep them from spoiling on long sea journeys) and stronger. Lager is clear and refreshing, and mostly made with bottom-fermenting yeast.

Evil Twin

Brooklyn, New York, USA

BIKINI BEER
AMERICAN IPA

---

20 L / 5 GAL | ABV **2.7%**
OG **1.026** | FG **1.006**

The twin in the name of this pioneering Danish gypsy brewer is Jeppe Jarnit-Bjergsø; the other half of the pair is Mikkel Borg Bjergsø, founder of pioneering Danish gypsy brewer Mikkeller (see p108). There's an ocean between them now, as Jeppe plans all his adventurously brewed beers out of Brooklyn, New York (his phenomenally productive output includes The Talented Mr Orangutan orange stout, and Ryan And The Gosling pale ale). This Bikini Beer is not so much a breakfast beer as a bedside table beer – but its fairly innocent 2.7% ABV hides a huge hop hit, much of it from Falconer's Flight, an expansively aromatic Pacific Northwest pellet blend containing Simcoe, Citra and Sorachi Ace among several others. Bikini Beer is the sort of summery brew you could drink all day. And we could all learn a lot from Jeppe's thoughts on making beer. "My idea of brewing is pretty simple," he said in a 2011 interview. "I don't care too much about the process, about what yeast or if I do it the right way. The only thing I care about is the result." Important advice whether you're on your first brew or your thousandth.

GRAIN
Canadian pilsner malt, 1.75kg/3 lbs 13.7oz (66%)

Thomas Fawcett pale crystal malt 27L, 300g/10.6oz (11%)

Weyermann Carafoam, 250g/8.8oz (10%)

Weyermann or Best Munich malt 10L, 250g 8.8oz (10%)

Flaked oats, 75g/2.6oz (3%)

MASH
67C/153F for 20 mins, 69C/156F for 20 mins, mashout 76C/169F

HOPS
Simcoe 13% AA, 23g/0.8oz, 60 mins

Simcoe, 10g/0.35oz, 15 mins

Cascade, 10g/0.35oz, 15 mins

Falconer's Flight pellets, 20g/ 0.7oz, 5 mins

Falconer's Flight pellets, 10g/0.35oz, 1 minute

Falconer's Flight pellets, 34g/ 1.2oz, dry hop

Simcoe, 17g/0.6oz, dry hop

YEAST
Wyeast 1056 American Ale

FERMENT
21C/70F

EVILTWIN
BREWING

BIKINI
BEER.

12 FL OZ.
INDIA PALE ALE

Gigantic Brewing Co

Portland, Oregon, USA

There's one problem with being a brilliant professional brewer. You make a brilliant beer, and everyone loves it. So you make more. Everyone drinks all that, so you make more. And more. And more… Before you know it, you're brewing the same beer over and over again. This is maybe the reason why brilliant craft brewers love to experiment, pushing the boundaries of what can be called beer. But in Portland, Oregon, a couple of time-served brewers have come up with a solution. Make a few beers, sell them till they run out, then make some different ones. A surefire remedy for brewhouse boredom. It takes confidence to say, "Sure the last beer tasted good, but this one's going to taste even better." And it takes even more confidence to then put the recipe for last week's beer on the website so everyone can share the Gigantic largesse.

After collective decades in the industry, founders Ben Love and Van Havig wanted to get back to basics, opening the manageably compact Gigantic to allow them both to concentrate on the fun part: brewing beer. Their #3 was The End of Reason, a strong, dark Belgian-style ale. And #24, Pipewrench, was an old-tom-gin barrel-aged IPA. Bang On, #16, was an English pale ale. And not only is the beer in the bottles unique every time, the label artwork is too. Gigantic is official beer sponsor of Portland's Design Museum, so you'd expect it to look amazing – and every release is realised by a different artist. This is certainly not the most cost-effective way to label a beer. But it's definitely the coolest.

Gigantic Brewing Co

Portland, Oregon, USA

GINORMOUS
IMPERIAL IPA

——

20 L / **5** GAL | ABV **8.8%**
OG **1.078** | FG **1.012**

This Ginormous American imperial IPA is one of Gigantic's year-round brews. It lives up to its name – this beer is all about the hops, and it brings it with seven assertive varieties all jostling for attention. This is probably not a recipe to try for your first ever brew. There's a lot of malt in weight terms, but it's not really meant to be balanced in flavour. The sugar is there to bump up the ABV and make sure the sweetness of the malt doesn't get in the way – IIPAs are dry. This heavy grain is going to need careful attention. And with so much dry-hopping, you're going to lose a fair bit of wort to absorption. Ben from Gigantic makes an important point about end-of-boil IBUs too: "Note the very low hop weights at the beginning and heavy weights at the end. Large, high-alpha additions at the end of boil give a lot of IBUs – especially if you leave the hops for 45 minutes post-boil before cooling." A 45-minute hop-stand? Ben's a pro – pay attention. Don't skimp on the yeast either. To be on the safe side you can use extra (maybe another half packet) and consider making a starter.

- -

GRAIN
Great Western Northwest Pale Ale malt, 5.7kg /12lbs 9oz (89%)

Weyermann Munich malt I, 270g/9.5oz (4%)

MASH
65C/149F for 60 mins

HOPS
Magnum, 12g/0.4oz, 90 mins

Cascade, 80g/2.8oz, 15 mins

Cascade, 55g/1.9oz, 0 mins

Crystal, Mosaic, Simcoe, 30g/ 1.1oz of each, 0 mins; rest for 45 mins before cooling

Cascade, 40g/1.4oz, dry hop 1 (1 day after reaching FG)

Citra, 20g/0.7oz, dry hop 1

Simcoe, 20g/0.7oz, dry hop 1

Cascade, 40g/1.4ozoz, dry hop 2 (2 days after dry hop 1)

Citra, 20g/0.7oz, dry hop 2

Simcoe, 20g/0.7oz, dry hop 2

YEAST
Wyeast 1728 Scottish Ale

FERMENT
20C/68F

OTHER INGREDIENTS
Raw sugar, 480g/0.9oz (7%), added to the boil

Thornbridge Brewery

Bakewell, Derbyshire, England

KIPLING

SOUTH PACIFIC PALE ALE

—

20 L / 5 GAL | ABV **5.2%**
OG **1.050** | FG **1.011–1.012**

The pretty little Peak District town of Bakewell, right in the middle of England, is famous for two things: the Bakewell pudding (a delicious jam and custard tart), and the incredible beers made by Thornbridge. From humble roots in the grounds of the stately Thornbridge Hall to today's globally exporting state-of-the-art operation, via winning shedloads of awards along the way, the brewery has won fans with beers of just about every style. Kipling is a pale ale with a short list of ingredients: don't make the mistake of thinking it's simple, however. With one malt and only two hops, there's no place to hide; good brewing technique is essential to match the Maris Otter pale malt with the grape-and-gooseberry flavours of the famous NZ Nelson Sauvin hop. To get the bitterness balanced perfectly with the Sauvin, Thornbridge brewmaster Rob Lovatt has a tip: "Keep the Nelson Sauvin constant and alter bittering to achieve 40-45 EBU." (EBU is European Bittering Units: apart from some slight molecular differences, it's more or less the same as IBU.)

GRAIN
Maris Otter pale ale malt, 4.65kg/10lbs 4oz (100%)

MASH
67-69C/152-156F for 60 mins

HOPS
Magnum, 17g/0.6oz, 60 mins

Nelson Sauvin, 50g/1.8oz, in the hopback

YEAST
White Labs WLP001 California Ale

FERMENT
20C/68F

Boneyard Beer

Bend, Oregon, USA

NOTORIOUS
TRIPLE IPA

---

20 L / **5 GAL** | ABV **11.5%**
OG **1.100** | FG **1.012**

A boneyard is a lot where retired aeroplanes, cars, bikes, engines – any sort of metal machinery – goes to be stripped down and reappropriated. It's an apt term for Tony Lawrence's Oregon brewery, opened in 2010 with two co-founders. With a healthy brewing history on his CV (including time at Deschutes, see p150), Tony started making his own beer in downtown Bend with bits of kit collected from all over north America. It was upgraded when he moved to bigger premises, but the magpie spirit remains. Oregon and the Pacific northwest is true hops country, and this raved-about triple IPA gives them a platform to shout loud from: Boneyard hops harder than a one-legged trampolinist. Such perfection in a glass is not easily obtained, as the massive malt bill (including flaked barley) will result in a stuck mash if you don't sparge very carefully, plus the bucketfuls of Citra and Mosaic will mean you'll lose a fair bit of wort from dry-hopping (although the hop oil saves a bit there). Give the yeast a fighting chance too – "pitch very heavy and oxygenate massively!" says Tony.

GRAIN
Pale malt, 6.77kg/14lbs 14.8oz (80.5%)

Munich malt, 250g/8.8oz (3%)

Flaked barley, 250g/8.8oz (3%)

Acidulated malt, 120g/4.2oz (1.5%)

MASH
64–65.5C/148–150F for 60 mins

HOPS
Fuggles, 13g/0.45oz, mash hop

CO_2 alpha hop oil, 1.5g/0.05oz, 60 mins

Citra, 5g/0.15oz, 20 mins

Mosaic, 5g/0.15oz, 20 mins

Citra, 5g/0.15oz, 10 mins

Mosaic, 5g/0.15oz, 10 mins

CO_2 alpha hop oil, 1.5g/0.05oz, 5 mins

Citra, 5g/0.15oz, 0 mins

Mosaic, 5g/0.15oz, 0 mins

Citra, 25g/10.9oz, whirlpool

Mosaic, 25g/10.9oz, whirlpool

Citra and Mosaic, 20g/0.7oz of each, dry hop 1 (pull out yeast first)

Citra and Mosaic, 53g/1.9oz each, dry hop 2 (2 days later, after dry hop 1)

YEAST
Wyeast 1968 London ESB Ale, 2 packs

FERMENT
Start at 20C/68F and allow to rise 0.5C/1F every 24 hours to 23C/73F, if you can

OTHER INGREDIENTS
Dextrose, 980g/2lbs 2.6oz (12%), boil for 30 mins

Mikkeller

Copenhagen, Denmark

—

If somebody was to survey a cross-section of worldwide brewers on their most respected peer, one name might come out on top: Mikkel Borg Bjergsø, a Danish former school teacher who founded Mikkeller in Copenhagen with a friend in 2006. Following the pioneering principles of US microbrewers, Mikkel took an internationalist outlook and practically drew up a blueprint for the current stage of the global craft beer revolution. First off, Mikkeller has made literally hundreds of different bold, innovative beers with resolutely top-class ingredients, from the plain great Stateside American IPA to a oak-barrel-aged spontaneously fermented blueberry sour. Mikkeller's more straightforward beers are just brilliant versions of their type, but the experimental brews are pure imagination in a bottle – they're challenges that demand to be taken up and drunk, but are always enjoyed. Mikkel was more or less the first ever 'gypsy' brewer, having no premises

FFF
4 BLOT OUT THE SUN
PA IMP. STOUT
65kr 10,4%

7 WARPIGS
CHAMPAGNE BRUS
ALE WITH CHAMPAGNE YEAST
100 kr 4% 60kr

11 WARPIGS
MOONBASE OF FILTH
OATMEAL STOUT
6,3% 65kr

15 WARPIGS
LIGHTS OUT, RICK
SMOKED LAGER
6,1% 65kr 1

WARPIGS
5 SUBTLE LIKE AN ATOMIC
GOL BOMB
60kr SESSION ALE 55.-
3,8%

8 MIKKELLER
BEER GEEK COCOA SHAKE
IMP. STOUT
12,10% 60kr

12 WARPIGS
CRY FOR HELP, RICK
ROBUST PORTER
7,4% 70 kr

16 WARPIGS
KILLER KYLE'S
COLA NUT
BROWN ALE 6,5%

WARPIGS
PATCH 6 BIG BLACK BICYCLE
BLACK IPA
65kr 6,3% 65kr

9 WARPIGS
BIG DRUNK BABY 13
DIPA
9% 70kr

WARPIGS
MUSTARD TIGER
BELGIAN PALE ALE
6,9% 70 kr

17 MIKKELLER
SPONTAN TRIPLE BLUEBERRY
SOUR
10% 80 kr 2

☆=Small
Beer

10 WARPIGS
SALMON PANTS 14
HOPPY PILSNER
5,7% 55kr

WARPIGS
SMOLDERING HOLES
IMPERIAL STOUT
9,6% 50kr 18

BOON
2013 FOEDER 78
2 YEAR LAMBIC
6,5% 75 kr 2

but instead designing recipes to be realised remotely. He has a laidback attitude to brewing that emphasises fun, creativity and the social aspect of beer over science and exclusivity. He collaborates constantly with likeminded brewers in Australia, Europe and the US. He puts instantly recognisable artwork on his labels, which is clearly created with as much love as the beer itself (drawn by US artist Keith Shore). He owns several bars in places as far-flung as Bangkok. Mikkeller is a brand, but one that retains an indefinable Scandinavian cool and an anti-establishment ethos, despite the fact the beer is available in 40 countries all over the world. Plus every year it runs the Copenhagen Beer Celebration, perhaps the most welcoming and enlightening trade festival around.

Mikkeller

Copenhagen, Denmark

CREAM ALE
CREAM ALE

———

20 L / 5 GAL | ABV **5.0%**
OG **1.047** | FG **1.009**

This Cream Ale is one of Mikkeller's less experimental beers, but it's a stunner nonetheless, and still a fairly unconventional example of its type. Cream ale is a relatively rare style originating from the US and is best described as a beautifully balanced cross between a lager and an ale. It's top-fermented like an ale, but with light maltiness and a crisp finish. And it uses flaked corn as an adjunct – it's often negatively associated with macro-brewed US lagers, but here's proof that using it is not always a bad thing. It makes the Cream Ale clean and smooth, providing easy passage for the hops, and the Carapils helps retain a full head. The yeast is a blend of lager and ale varieties with high attenuation and faintly fruity aromas. Some brewers practise cold conditioning with cream ales at the end of fermentation for extra clarity and even more smoothness. Finally, Mikkeller's Cream Ale has a distinctive orangey scent from the liberal use of Amarillo hops: not an 'authentic' trait in this style, but that's what craft brewing is all about. Carbonate it well for a super-refreshing fizz.

- -

GRAIN
Pilsner malt, 1.2kg/2 lbs 10.3oz (30%)

Pale malt, 1.2kg/2 lbs 10.3oz (30%)

Flaked corn, 680g/1 lb 8oz (17%)

Carapils, 260g/9.17oz (6.5%)

Flaked oats, 260g/9.17oz (6.5%)

Vienna malt, 200g/7.05oz (5%)

Munich malt, 200g/7.05oz (5%)

MASH
*67C/152F for 75 mins,
74C/165F for 15 mins*

HOPS
*Columbus 13% AA, 20g/0.7oz,
60 mins*

*Amarillo 6.5% AA, 25g/0.9oz,
15 mins*

*Amarillo 6.5% AA, 30g/1.1oz,
dry hop*

*Challenger 7.6% AA, 30g/1.1oz,
dry hop*

YEAST
*White Labs WLP080 Cream Ale
Yeast Blend*

FERMENT
18-20C/65-68F

Camden Town Brewery

Camden, London, England

INDIA HELLS LAGER
HOPPED HELLES LAGER

---

20 L / 5 GAL | ABV **6.2%**
OG **1.060** | FG **1.012**

Camden Town was founded by Australian Jasper Cuppaidge after he brewed in the cellar of the Horseshoe, a pub in Hampstead, north London. This was 2010, making it a relatively early player in London's craft brewery scene. Since then it's expanded at a huge rate, raising millions of pounds of capital through crowdfunding, and conquering foreign markets. But what sets it apart is its devotion to lager, a style whose reputation suffered horribly at the hands of macro brewers and as such is often overlooked. But done well – and at Camden it always is – a good lager is a beautiful thing. Its Hells is a modern classic, and this India Hells is lager with an even bigger personality – there's a massive hop statement but it's still clear, smooth and balanced. Lagering at home (see p22) needs accurate temperature control, either through an immersion-type cooler or a fridge; master making your own lager though and you'll be a very satisfied brewer and popular come summer. And if you're ever in Camden Town itself, the brewery taproom is great fun to visit.

GRAIN
Weyermann pilsner malt, 4kg/8lbs 13oz (75%)

Munich malt, 1.07kg/2lbs 5.75oz (20%)

Carapils, 270g/9.5oz (5%)

MASH
For single-stage, mash in at 66C/150F for 70 mins. For multi-rest, mash in at 50C/122F, raise to 62C/143F and hold for 60 mins, heat to 72C/161F and hold for 10 minutes. Mash out at 78C/172F

HOPS
Magnum 12.7% AA, 17g/0.6oz, 60 mins (to 25 IBU)

Simcoe 13.9% AA, 9g/0.3oz, 10 mins

Chinook 13.9% AA, 9g/0.3oz, 10 mins

Mosaic 11.2% AA, 11g/0.4oz, 10 mins

Simcoe 13.9% AA, 7g/0.2oz, 0 mins

Chinook 13.9% AA, 17g/0.6oz, 0 mins

Mosaic, 11.2% AA, 9g/0.3oz, 0 mins

Chinook, Simcoe, Mosaic, 80g/2.8oz of each, dry hop

YEAST
Fermentis Saflager W-34/70

FERMENT
10-12C/50-54F until halfway through fermentation, then 14C/57F till the end. When active fermentation is complete leave at 14C/57F for another 72 hours to reduce the diacetyl. After the diacetyl rest is complete, rack on to the dry hops in a separate vessel. Beef up with up to another 2g per litre (0.3oz per gallon) of more of the dry hops if you want to boost the aroma. Continue to hold the beer warm for another 24-48 hours. Then lager it in a beer fridge for approximately 2 weeks

Firestone Walker Brewing Company

Paso Robles, California, USA

UNION JACK
WEST COAST IPA

—

20 L / 5 GAL | ABV **7.5%**
OG **1.068** | FG **1.012**

Adam Firestone comes from a California winemaking background; David Walker is his English brother-in-law. This Sunshine State/rainy Blighty alliance is represented by the bear and the lion on the logo, and by the endlessly award-winning beers (there literally isn't enough space on this page to list the plaudits that have been heaped upon Firestone Walker). The brewery uses a unique and historical Burton upon Trent oak-barrel circulation system for fermenting some of its beers, such as its flagship Double Barrel Ale – the wort spends six days on wood before moving into steel to finish it off. This peerless and classic West Coast IPA is fermented on steel, however, so you can give it a go at home. It's bullish with bitter hops and garlanded with high-aroma varieties from the US. This is down to the double dry-hopping, a subject brewmaster Matt Brynildson knows pretty much everything about. "I'm a firm believer in short contact time with the hops," he says, "no more than three days. If it starts to taste vegetal, you are on the hops too long. You want clean, juicy-fruit hop oil notes."

- -

GRAIN
2-row American pale malt, 5.18kg/11lbs 6.7oz (86%)

Munich malt, 360g/12.7oz (6%)

Carapils, 300g/10.6oz (5%)

Simpsons crystal malt 30–40L, 180g/6.3oz (3%)

MASH
63C/145F, then 68C/155F to finish conversion

HOPS
Magnum 15% AA, 35g/1.2oz, 90 mins

Cascade 6% AA, 32g/1.1oz, 30 mins

Centennial, 32g/1.1oz, 15 mins

Cascade, 30g/1.1oz, whirlpool

Centennial, 30g/1.1oz, whirlpool

Centennial, Cascade, Simcoe, Amarillo, 75g/2.6oz total ("equal amounts Centennial and Cascade, a bit less of Simcoe and Amarillo"), dry hop 1 at the end of fermentation

As above for dry hop 2, 3 days after first

YEAST
White Labs WLP013 London Ale

FERMENT
19C/66F, then cold crash

Russian River Brewing Company

Santa Rosa, California, USA

RON MEXICO

EXPERIMENTAL-HOPPED AMERICAN PALE ALE

—

20 L / **5** GAL | ABV **4.5%**
OG **1.045** | FG **1.012**

There are cult beers, and then there's Pliny the Younger. When this triple IPA is served once a year in February at the Russian River brewpub in Santa Rosa, people travel from far and wide to sample 'the best beer in the world'. But to focus on Pliny is to miss what RRBC is really all about: founder Vinnie Cilurzo is a master of souring and ageing, with 600 barrels at his disposal; he's also one of the most selfless, knowledgeable and respected people brewing today. This recipe is down to his relationship with hop growers and home brewers: he created it for the

2015 Homebrewers Conference in San Diego using HBC-438, an experimental hop so new it doesn't have a name (though it's nicknamed 'Ron Mexico'). Uniquely, 438 will only be available in small quantities for the time being, for keen individuals to get creative with. "A brewer could swap out the HBC-438 for any hop and make a single-hop beer," says Vinnie. "We make a similar beer at RRBC called Hop 2 It and we use it to test new hop varieties." So, hunt down some Ron Mexico, or get some #07270 or 527 or 342, and see why every hop deserves its time in the limelight.

- -

GRAIN
Rahr pale ale malt, 2.01kg/ 4lbs 6.9oz (51.5%)

Rahr 2-row malt, 1.66kg/3lbs 10.6oz (42%)

Weyerman acid malt, 120g/4.2oz (3%)

Breiss Carapils, 100g/3.5oz (2.5%)

Simpsons crystal malt 60L, 30g/1.1oz (1%)

MASH
69C/156F for 60 mins

HOPS
HBC-438 15.7% AA, 3g/0.1oz, 90 mins

HBC-438, 14g/0.5oz, 15 mins

HBC-438, 60g/2.1oz, 0 mins

HBC-438, 73g/2.6oz, dry hop 1 (after 10 days)

HBC-428, 73g/2.6oz, dry hop 2 (pull dry hop 1, after 15 days)

YEAST
WLP001 California Ale

FERMENT
18C/64F; pull yeast after 10 ten days; at 18 days drop to 0C/32F; at 21 days use gelatin or similar to fine, before racking off and carbonating

Brewdog

Ellon, Scotland

From a small brewery in Aberdeenshire, northeast Scotland, James Watt and Martin Dickie set out in 2007 with a pretty ambitious aim: to shake the beer world to its core. You'd have to say they succeeded. From the start they've been on a mission against mediocrity in all its beer-related forms, and even if their audacious marketing isn't to your taste, the beers can't fail to be. They're all uncompromisingly flavourful, every one a no-holds-barred celebration of its style, like the hop eruption of Jackhammer IPA or the suave, inky and epic Cocoa Psycho Russian imperial stout. Brewdog has never been afraid to venture to the extremities of craft beer, releasing the better-than-water Nanny State pale ale (0.5% ABV) as well as End of History, a Belgian ale with nettles and juniper which at 55% was stronger than most whiskies and was packaged in taxidermied roadkill. Now there are almost thirty Brewdog bars, from Birmingham to Brazil. Beers exported to more than fifty countries. A brewery in Columbus, Ohio, to send brews in their freshest state all over the States. A record-setting crowdfunding campaign, turning drinkers into investors. One of the fastest-growing brands in the UK. In twenty years' time, the Brewdog story will probably be taught in MBA courses, but more importantly, Brewdog beer will probably still be awesome.

Brewdog

Ellon, Scotland

PUNK IPA
IPA

———

20 L / 5 GAL | ABV **5.60%**
OG **1.054** | FG **1.012**

If you're not drinking a Punk IPA right now, you probably know someone who is. It's sold in shops, supermarkets, off-licences, bottle shops, bars and pubs the world over. This is the beer that started it all for Brewdog back in 2007: not many people in buttoned-up Britain had ever tasted a beer so fresh, so confident, so rammed full of flavour with every sip. Buttoned-up Britain was a bit scared, to be honest, although Punk didn't take long to win them over, and it won over loads of other countries to boot. It's a true craft beer classic: refreshing but involving; strong enough to make itself known but friendly enough to enjoy a few of; gushing with pine, tropical fruit, flowers and citrus, all that's great about hops – a result of the generous handfuls of six strains including the Pacific Northwestern Ahtanum and Cascade, and the peerless Kiwi Nelson Sauvin. The malt backbone is steady but simple enough to give them all a chance to shine. If you can make your own version even 10% as good as the original, you'll be a hero. In a world where bland beer fills most glasses, Punk IPA is still a rebel.

GRAIN
Pale ale malt, 4.4kg/9lbs 11.2oz (92.5%)

Caramalt, 360g/12.7oz (7.5%)

MASH
Mash in at 65C/149F, rest for 15 mins. Raise to 72C/162F, rest for 15 mins (iodine test, see p37). Mash off at 78C/172F

HOPS
Ahtanum, 2g/0.07oz, 80 mins

Chinook, 8g/0.3oz, 15 mins

Ahtanum, 10g/0.35oz, 15 mins

Ahtanum, 6g/0.21oz, whirlpool

Chinook, 4g/0.14oz, whirlpool

Simcoe, 10g/0.35oz, whirlpool

Nelson Sauvin, 5g/0.15oz, whirlpool

Ahtanum, 40g/1.4oz, dry hop

Chinook, 50g/1.8oz, dry hop

Simcoe, 40g/1.4oz, dry hop

Nelson Sauvin, 20g/0.7oz, dry hop

Cascade, 40g/1.4oz, dry hop

YEAST
Wyeast 1056 American Ale

FERMENT
19C/66F for 5 days, dry hop at 14C/57F for 5 days, mature at 0C/32F for 15 days

Siren Craft Brew

Finchampstead, Berkshire, England

UNDERCURRENT
OATMEAL PALE ALE

---

20 L / 5 GAL | ABV **4.5%**
OG **1.044** | FG **1.010**

Within two years of Darron Anley's inaugural mash-in, his Berkshire brewery had been named second-best new brewery in the world in Ratebeer.com's annual drinkers' survey. The love Siren receives is largely down to its commitment to courageously un-traditional beer, open-mindedness and a total disregard for brewing boundaries. Limited-edition releases have included a peach cream IPA brewed with Omnipollo (see p130) and a barrel-aged hopfenweizen with Brettanomyces yeast. Experimentation has to be built on a solid understanding of what works in a brewhouse – and this Undercurrent is a prime example of an overperforming everyday beer. As well as wheat malt and Carahell to add body and colour, it uses oat malt, a not-often-seen grain with a really warm flavour – it works well in all sorts of beers, but in this pale ale it's a revelation. This is also the only recipe in the book that uses the Pacific Northwestern Palisade hop, which brings 'sweet nectar' fruit along with herbs and freshly mown meadow flavours.

- -

GRAIN
Maris Otter pale malt, 2.66kg/5lbs 13.8oz (71%)

Malted oats, 520g/1lb 2.3oz (14%)

Wheat malt, 260g/9.2oz (7%)

Carahell, 260g/9.2oz (7%)

Caraaroma, 40g/1.4oz (1%)

MASH
68C/145F for 60 mins (Siren recommends recirculating for last 45 minutes, if you can)

HOPS
(70 minute boil)

Magnum, 7g/0.3oz, 60 mins

Cascade, 20g/0.7oz, 10 mins

Cascade, 20g/0.7oz, 0 mins

Palisade, 16g/0.6oz, 0 mins

Columbus, 12g/0.4oz, 0 mins

YEAST
Fermentis US-05 American Ale

FERMENT
20C/68F

Oskar Blues Brewery

Lyons, Colorado, USA

DALE'S PALE ALE
AMERICAN PALE ALE

—

20 L / 5 GAL | ABV **6.5%**
OG **1.066** | FG **1.015**

If you're a brewer called Dale then you pretty much have to make a pale ale and then call it Dale's Pale Ale. Oskar Blues founder Dale Katechis did just that with his citrussy hop-loaded signature brew, then he went one step further – he put it in a can. That was in 2002, when canned beer meant gassy, ricey, mainstream and bland. Now, beer crafters the world over are saying "yes we can" and packaging their brews in protective aluminium. Dale's was the first craft beer in a can, a true pioneer, but that's not the only thing that

makes it great. The copious amounts of classic US craft beer 'C' hops (Cascade, Centennial, Columbus) brings a recognisably grapefruit/ flowery/herbal flavour, but without the dry-hopping present in more aggressive American IPAs; the relatively complex malt bill provides a sweet body that sits side-by-side with them in perfect harmony. It's everything an American pale ale should be: balanced and crisp, charismatic and friendly, there for you any time of day. DPA is the perfect toast to a real revolution in beermaking.

- -

GRAIN
North American 2-row pale malt 2L, 4.68kg/10lbs 5.1oz (80%)

Crystal malt 25L, 590g/ 1lb 4.8oz (10%)

Munich malt 10L, 470g/ 1lb 0.6oz (8%)

Crystal malt 85L, 120g/ 4.2oz (2%)

MASH
69C/156F for 60 mins

HOPS
(90 minute boil)

Columbus 14% AA, 14g/0.5oz, 80 mins, to 25 IBU

Cascade, 14g/0.5oz, 25 mins

Columbus, 17g/0.6oz, 10 mins

Centennial, 45g/1.6oz, whirlpool

YEAST
Wyeast WLP001 California Ale

FERMENT
Primary at 18C/64F, then cold condition for around 10 days

SPECIAL INSTRUCTIONS
Dale's is brewed with soft water with a target wort Chloride:Sulfate ratio of 1:1

The Celt Experience

Caerphilly, Wales

SILURES
MUNICH PALE ALE WITH SPRUCE

—

20 L / 5 GAL | ABV **4.6%**
OG **1.044** | FG **1.008**

Celt Experience is not a normal brewery. Founder Tom Newman takes inspiration from the mythology of the Welsh Celts and has a deep connection to the land. His beers include the brilliant Tailless Black Sow, a herb-infused pale ale named after a ghostly pig of folk legend. Wild yeasts are harvested from sites of spiritual significance; mugwort and yarrow foraged from forests. Silures (after an ancient tribe from southeast Wales) uses what Tom calls his hop druid: "It eats hops for dinner," he says. You probably don't have a hop druid. But you could buy a percolator, or make one – it's a vessel with a sealed lid which allows wort to flow through and it extracts huge amounts of aroma from steeped hops within (similar to a hopback: see p24). 'Generous' amounts are called for – about as much as you can fit in. A note on spruce tips: pick them locally if possible. You can buy them online, and if you don't live near a native forest it may be your best option. It won't have the same magic, but you'll still appreciate their uniquely resinous, floral character.

GRAIN
Pale ale malt, 3.6kg/7lbs 15oz (92%)

Munich malt, 160g/5.6oz (4%)

Wheat malt, 160g/5.6oz (4%)

MASH
64.5C/148F for 60 mins

HOPS
(60 minute boil)

Magnum or similar bittering hop, 25g/0.88oz, 40 mins, to hit 36 IBU

Centennial, 67g/2.4oz, 5 mins

Citra, 17g/0.6oz, 5 mins

Simcoe, 34g/1.2oz, 0 mins

Citra, Centennial and Simcoe in the hop druid (see above!)

Simcoe, 34g/1.2oz, dry hop

YEAST
Fermentis US-05 American Ale

FERMENT
20C/68F

OTHER INGREDIENTS
Foraged spruce tips, 17g/0.7oz, at flameout, steeped for 5 mins

Trouble Brewing

Kildare, Ireland

HIDDEN AGENDA
PALE ALE

—

20 L / 5 GAL | ABV **4.5%**
OG **1.043** | FG **1.009**

There's a joke about drinking in Irish pubs. You've got two choices: a pint of Guinness, or a half-pint of Guinness. It's true that the black stuff flows like water in Ireland, and thanks to its ubiquity Irish beer has a bit of a one-dimensional reputation worldwide. But a growing band of brewers all over the country are looking beyond stout to give beer lovers something to get excited about. Trouble, based in County Kildare (and just down the road from Arthur Guinness's birthplace), is doing just that by making classy beers ranging from a relaxed golden ale to a cherry chocolate stout. Hidden Agenda isn't especially Irish in outlook but is a deadly drop all the same. It's a relaxed and supremely drinkable sunny-day pale ale, with a fairly simple objective: crisp and complex malts provide a launchpad for a faceful of fruit-salad Aussie hops. The relatively new Vic Secret strain and its compatriot Summer are all about apricots, peaches, melons and citrus; melanoidin is a speciality grain which in small quantities adds a subtle red colour and a malty taste. Who needs Guinness?

- -

GRAIN
Pale ale malt, 2.75kg/6lbs 1oz (72%)

Munich malt, 760g/1lb 10.8oz (20%)

Melanoidin, 150g/5.3oz (4%)

Carapils, 80g/2.8oz (2%)

Crystal malt 57L, 80g/2.8oz (2%)

MASH
66C/150F for 60 mins

HOPS
Magnum 12.7% AA, 9g/0/3oz, 60 mins

Summer 5.3% AA, 26g/0.9oz, 10 mins

Summer 5.3% AA, 26g/0.9oz, 5 mins

Vic Secret 15.8% AA, 39g/ 1.4oz, 0 mins

Vic Secret 15.8% AA, 39g/1.4oz, dry hop

YEAST
Fermentis US–05 American Ale

FERMENT
20C/68F

Omnipollo

Stockholm, Sweden

With a team made up of a talented graphic designer (Karl Grandin) and a talented brewer (Henok Fentie), it was pretty much inevitable that Omnipollo would produce beer that looked as good as it tastes. See the labels below for proof of the first bit, see your local bottle shop for proof of the second. What wasn't inevitable, but is the result of tireless creativity and hard work, is that their beers are some of the most sought-after in the world. Omnipollo, like so many in Scandinavia, is a gypsy brewery: many are made at the high-tech

De Proefbrouwerij in Belgium, others are born of collaborations (with Siren, Evil Twin and Stillwater, among others); the imagination, though, is all theirs. Nathalius is an 8% imperial IPA brewed with rice and corn, ingredients usually shunned by craft brewers: all the more reason to use them. Yellow Belly, brewed with Buxton Brewery, is a 'peanut butter biscuit stout' without peanut butter or biscuits, one of the most sought-after beers in the world. Mazarin, the one with the covetable candle bottle, is simply a pale ale, but maybe the best one you'll ever try.

Omnipollo

Stockholm, Sweden

4:21
DOUBLE RASPBERRY/VANILLA SMOOTHIE IPA

—

20 L / 5 GAL | ABV **6%**
OG **1.054** | FG **1.010**

Along with the likes of Mikkeller and To Øl, Omnipollo represents everything that's exciting, nonconformist and forward-thinking about Scandinavian brewing. It's run by homebrewer-turned-pro Henok Fentie and graphic designer Karl Grandin, who's responsible for perhaps the coolest beer art in the world – the bottles are so smart you'll want to hang on to them long after the last sip. There's no actual Omnipollo brewery, but instead the pair's creations are made all around the world, with plenty of collaborations along the way. This 4:21 is part of Omnipollo's Magic Numbers series, a set of small-batch, limited-edition beers which blast off even further into the unexplored reaches of brewing. It's super-fruity and sharp from the raspberries and wheat, but the vanilla and lactose gives it a creamy, almost thick character – hence the 'smoothie' in the name. Lactose is almost completely unfermentable with beer yeast, so won't increase the ABV; it does increase the gravity of the wort though. And the late, heavy hop additions add a ton of flavour and even a fair amount of IBUs. A genuinely groundbreaking beer!

- -

GRAIN
Pilsner malt, 2.65kg/5lbs 13.5oz (60%)

Wheat, 880g/1lb 15oz (20%)

Flaked oats, 440g/15.5oz (10%)

MASH
67C/152F for 75 mins

HOPS
(60 minute boil)

Mosaic, 27g/1oz, 10 mins

Mosaic, 67g/2.4oz, whirlpool

Mosaic, 200g/7oz, dry hop for 3 days

YEAST
Fermentis S-04 English Ale

FERMENT
19C/66F

OTHER INGREDIENTS
Dextrose, 440g/15.5oz (10%), in the boil

Lactose, after the boil, to raise the OG by 3P (about 12-13 specific gravity points); around 700g/1lb 8oz

Fresh raspberries, 1.3kg/2lbs 13.9oz, and 2.5 vanilla pods sliced down the middle, after primary fermentation, before dry hopping

Yeastie Boys

Wellington, New Zealand

DIGITAL IPA
NZ-HOPPED IPA

———

20 L / 5 GAL | ABV **5.7%**
OG **1.056** | FG **1.013**

There might be a better-named brewery in the world than Yeastie Boys, but it's hard to imagine. It started as a part-time project for Stu McKinley and Sam Possenniskie in Wellington, but such was the quality of their beers that they were soon the toast of the NZ brewing scene. Their Pot Kettle Black (the most-awarded Kiwi beer) doesn't just blur the lines between black IPAs and hoppy porters, it pretty much proves there needn't be any lines there in the first place. The Yeasties' lean business model sees them planning their beers from a Wellington base while the brewing is done elsewhere. Stu relocated half a world away to London in 2015 to kick off the brand's operations in the Northern Hemisphere – resulting in fresher beer which is somehow still Kiwi through-and-through, despite being made over 10,000 miles away (look for the Gunnamatta earl-grey-infused IPA). Their story is a paradigm of modern craft brewing, and this Digital IPA is a paragon of modern IPAs: a balance between caramel malts and lots and lots of lovely NZ hops.

- -

GRAIN
Pilsner malt, 2.48kg/5lbs 7.5oz (52%)

Vienna malt, 2.06kg/4lbs 8.7oz (43.5%)

Gladiator malt (or Carapils), 210g/7.1oz (4.5%)

MASH
66C/151F for 60 mins

HOPS
Pacific Jade pellets 13.4% AA, 35g/1.2oz, 60 mins

Motueka pellets 7.3% AA, 8g/0.3oz, 10 mins

Nelson Sauvin pellets 12.1% AA, 8g/0.3oz, 10 mins

Southern Cross pellets 13.6% AA, 8g/0.3oz, 0 mins

Motueka pellets 7.3% AA, 40g/1.4oz, 0 mins

Nelson Sauvin pellets 12.1% AA, 8g/0.3oz, 0 mins

Southern Cross pellets 13.6% AA, 17g/0.6oz, dry hop 1

Nelson Sauvin pellets 12.1% AA, 8g/0.3oz, dry hop 1

Motueka pellets 7.3% AA, 17g/0.6oz, dry hop 1

Southern Cross pellets 13.6% AA, 8g/0.3oz, dry hop 2, 4 days after first

Nelson Sauvin pellets 12.1% AA, 4g/0.14oz, dry hop 2

Motueka pellets 7.3% AA, 17g/0.6oz, dry hop 2

YEAST
Fermentis US-05 American Ale

FERMENT
18C/65F

Young Henrys

Newtown, New South Wales, Australia

NATURAL LAGER
KELLERBIER

—

20 L / **5 GAL** | ABV **4.2%**
OG **1.042** | FG **1.010**

A kellerbier is an ancient German style, fairly rare outside the country, which can be top- or bottom-fermented, but is also unfiltered and boldly loaded with aromatic hops. NSW brewery Young Henrys stays true to the tradition, including Munich malt to give this Natural Lager an authentic amber tint. Instead of Hallertauer or Mittelfrüh, however, they've used Summer, Helga and Sylva – all relatives of classic European strains that emigrated Down Under and grew extra fruity under the Aussie sun. The result is unpretentious, gently citrussy and perfectly refreshing, hazy too from the wheat and lack of filtering. It also uses Cry Havoc yeast, which works at lager and ale temperatures. Young Henrys was founded by two friends in 2012 – it *is* still young, but something of a prodigy: a consistently exacting core range (which also includes Real Ale English best bitter) is brewed alongside out-there creations like a witbier made with mussels (really), and I Should Coco, a chocolate truffle stout. There are now YH breweries in two more Australian states, so the beer's as fresh in Sydney as it is in Perth.

GRAIN
Pilsner malt, 3.2kg/7lbs 0.9oz (86%)

Pale wheat malt, 250g/ 8.8oz (7%)

Munich malt, 250g/ 8.8oz (7%)

MASH
67C/152F for 50 mins

HOPS
(60 minute boil)

Summer, 15g/0.5oz, first wort hops

Summer, 20g/0.7oz, 5 mins

Sylva, 20g/0.7oz, whirlpool

Helga, 20g/0/7oz, whirlpool

YEAST
White Labs WLP862 Cry Havoc

FERMENT
16C/61F until gravity reaches 1.020, then let temperature rise naturally to 22C/71F. Wait 2 days after final gravity is reached then chill for 7 days before priming and packaging

Stout, porter & black

—

The difference between stout, porter and black IPA is a source of debate, and craft brewers love blurring the lines. Save yourself the arguments, and just make and drink them. Heavily roasted malts give a midnight-black colour and chocolate, coffee, and dark fruit notes, which stand up well to high alcohol, big hops and complementary added flavours.

Dark Star Brewing Company

West Sussex, England

ESPRESSO
DARK COFFEE BEER

▬

20 L / 5 GAL | ABV **4.2%**
OG **1.048** | FG **1.014**

Reasons to love Sussex brewery Dark Star:
1) It sponsors the British National Homebrew Competition and every year brews the winning beer for commercial release. 2) It contributes to all sorts of pub and beer-related charities through the Dark Star Foundation. 3) Since 1994 it has brilliantly combined the best of British brewing traditions (plenty of cask ale) with New World ingredients and attitudes. 4) All its beer is just great, including this Espresso black beer. It's maybe not quite hefty enough to be called a stout, as the only really dark grain involved here is the roasted barley. It's a very useful and distinctive grain to use in heavier beers, and is highly baked in a drum, giving it almost coffee-like characteristics. Roasted barley adds a beautifully sweet aspect to cushion the bitter jolt from the ground coffee. Other coffee-based beers may use more ground beans by weight, but in Dark Star's version it's more of a background brew within a brew. In other words, maybe not a substitute for your morning cup of joe, but a fine beer with layers of subtle blackness.

GRAIN
Pale ale malt, 3kg/6lbs 10oz (70%)

Wheat, 690g/1lb 8oz (16%)

Roasted barley, 470g/1lb 1oz (11%)

Caramalt, 130g/4.6oz (3%)

MASH
67C/153F for 60 mins

HOPS
Challenger, 30g/1.1oz, 60 mins

Challenger, 11g/0.4oz, 0 mins

YEAST
Danstar Nottingham Ale or White Labs WLP039 Nottingham Ale

FERMENT
20C/68F

OTHER INGREDIENTS
Freshly ground Arabica coffee, the best you can get your hands on, 22g/0.8oz at the end of the boil. Leave as you would aroma hops before transferring to fermenter. Best to use a fine bag – coffee grounds are messy to clean up!

Beavertown Brewery

Tottenham, London, England

In the few short years since Beavertown Brewery was founded by Logan Plant in a London bar, it's come a long way. Out of the basement of Duke's Brew & Que, his barbecue restaurant, into dedicated premises in nearby Hackney Wick; then outgrowing them and moving into an even bigger space in Tottenham. And instead of just making beer for the pulled-pork-munching diners in Duke's, Beavertown exports to twenty countries around the world from its north London base. One thing has remained the same and fuelled its expansion – a range of amazing beers unfettered by convention and founded on fearless experimentation. A few were brewed in the pub cellar and went on to form the core range (the spicy 8-Ball Rye IPA, say, or Smog Rocket); others are collaborations with some of the world's most

innovative brewers or limited-release one-offs (a bramley apple saison, for example). Some redefine 'cult' beer: the annual arrival of Beavertown's 7.2% blood orange IPA is heralded by a stampede towards the bars and bottle shops lucky enough to have some in stock. There's also a canning line for the core beers: a commitment to freshness and lower environmental impact. And central to the Beavertown success is the identity, which has been clear since the start. Nick Dwyer worked in Duke's and presented Logan with a few sketches inspired by his brews: "If you ever need labels for them, here are some ideas." Now Nick is the brewery's creative director and his much-lauded designs are seen on cans by eager Beaver lovers in markets as diverse as Australia, the US and Hong Kong.

Beavertown Brewery

Tottenham, London, England

SMOG ROCKET
SMOKED PORTER

—

20 L / 5 GAL | ABV **5.4%**
OG **1.057** | FG **1.014**

This is one of Beavertown founder Logan Plant's original homebrew recipes, and it has survived the journey from kitchen kit to 50 hectolitres pretty much intact. Smog Rocket's hugely diverse grain bill – nine varieties! – creates a complex and involving porter, with an enveloping darkness that allows the smoke to curl in and out among the roasted coffee, burnt toffee, smouldering peat and dark chocolate flavours. Too much smokiness in any brew recipe could lead to an overpowering ashtray sensation rather than a gently welcoming wisp of campfire, but the proportion of smoked malt here is carefully balanced by its mash mates. The combination of crystal, brown, chocolate, cara and black, even in low quantities, all bring something unique to the mix. Hops in this beer are there mainly for equilibrium (the IBUs are fairly low), although the delicately smoky notes sometimes picked up in Chinook make themselves known too. Beavertown cans almost its whole range and they're available around the world now, so if you see a Smog Rocket, snap it up.

- -

GRAIN
Pale malt, 1.53kg/3lbs 5.6oz (30%)

Beechwood-smoked malt, 1.53kg/3lbs 5.6oz (30%)

Munich malt, 560g/1lb 3.75oz (11%)

Flaked oats, 410g/14.5oz (8%)

Dark crystal malt, 310g/ 10.9oz (6%)

Brown malt, 310g/10.9oz (6%)

Chocolate malt, 310g/10.9oz (6%)

Caramalt, 100g/3.5oz (2%)

Black malt, 50g/1.8oz (1%)

MASH
66C/150F for 60 mins

HOPS
Magnum, 8g/0.3oz, 60 mins

Chinook, 14g/0.5oz, 30 mins

YEAST
Fermentis US-05 American Ale

FERMENT
19C/66F

Brouwerij de Molen

Bodegraven, Netherlands

SPANNING & SENSATIE
SPICED IMPERIAL STOUT

▬▬▬

20 L / 5 GAL | ABV **9.8%**
OG **1.102** | FG **1.028**

The brewing of the Netherlands might be historically overshadowed by its neighbours Belgium and Germany, but under these conditions a microbrewing industry thrives, free from any need to even pretend to compete with the likes of Heineken. De Molen ('the Windmill') is the most consistently eclectic, bold and brilliant, notable not just in Holland but across the world for an enormous roster of rarely repeated beers with inspiration from classic European and US styles. Spanning & Sensatie ('Thrills & Spills') is described as 'Imperial Stout-ish', and it's certainly strong, panther-black and loaded with roasted malts; such turbo-charged porters are never short of flavour, but this is enhanced daringly with cacao nibs, chilli and salt. The result is something like a molten Aztec dark chocolate bar, with liquorice and coffee undertones, a warming current of alcohol and spice and an intriguing tang at the end. However, the additions are nothing without a good beer, and imperial stout isn't easy to brew, so take your time: vorlauf slowly, sparge slowly, run off slowly, pitch yeast heavily, then age… slowly.

GRAIN
Belgian pilsner malt, 4.03kg/ 8lbs 14oz (43%)

Smoked malt, 1.22kg/2lbs 11oz (13%)

Brown malt, 940g/2lbs 1oz (10%)

Crystal malt 60L, 940g/2lb 1oz (10%)

Flaked oats, 840g/1lb 13.6oz (9%)

Acid malt, 750g/1lb 10.5oz (8%)

Chocolate malt, 520g/1lb 2.3oz (5.5%)

Roasted barley, 140g/4.9oz (1.5%)

MASH
69C/156F for 60 mins

HOPS
Columbus, 60g/2.1oz, 90 mins

Saaz, 8g/0.3oz, 10 mins

YEAST
Fermentis US-05 American Ale, 2 packs

OTHER INGREDIENTS
Cacao nibs, crushed lightly, 100g/3.5oz

½ Madame Jeanette chilli pepper

Sea salt, 10g/0.35oz

Put all in a sanitised bag and add after primary fermentation for up to a week

Odell Brewing Company

Fort Collins, Colorado, USA

CUTTHROAT PORTER
PORTER

20 L / 5 GAL | ABV **5.1%**
OG **1.050** | FG **1.015**

Doug Odell was making beer at home back when most of today's craft brewers were drinking nothing stronger than milk. Now he's one of the most respected brewers in the country, and his canny expansion from Colorado across the world is based on a foundation of great beer with a perfect balance between experimentation and consistency. His take on a 90/- Scottish ale has been an Odell constant since 1989 and is a modern classic; so too this creamy Cutthroat Porter, named after an endangered Coloradan trout. Technically speaking, it's more of a 'brown' than a robust porter, having a lower percentage of the highest-roast malts than some other examples. The mash temperature is high to create a full body in the beer, and the English ale yeast is low in esters and clean, but leaves a mild sweetness that suits the style. It's deep and dark, with plenty of coffee, chocolate, tobacco and burnt flavours; this, along with its English East Kent Goldings and Fuggles at flameout (hops are meant to be subtle in this style) plus easygoing ABV, makes it an accessible and sessionable porter.

GRAIN
Pale ale malt, 3.78kg/8lbs 5.3oz (79%)

Caramalt, 270g/9.5oz (5.5%)

Chocolate malt, 220g/ 7.8oz (4.5%)

Crystal malt 53-60L,170g/6oz (3.5%)

Amber malt, 170g/6oz (3.5%)

Munich malt, 110g/3.9oz (2.5%)

Roasted barley, 60g/1.8oz (1.5%)

MASH
68C/154F for 60 mins

HOPS
Nugget, Cascade or any good bittering hop, 24g/0.85oz, 60 mins, to hit 40 IBUs

East Kent Goldings, 12g/0/4oz, 0 minutes

Fuggles, 10g/0.35oz, 0 minutes

YEAST
A clean, low-ester yeast, such as WLP002 English Ale

FERMENT
20C/68F

Deschutes Brewery

Bend, Oregon, USA

BLACK BUTTE PORTER
PORTER

▬▬

20 L / **5** GAL | ABV **5.2%**
OG **1.057** | FG **1.019**

Deschutes is a beacon of righteous Oregon brewing. Named after the local river, it's been based in Bend since 1988, when it opened as a humble brewpub. Bend is a town surrounded by place names familiar to brewers the world over thanks to the state's famous hops, including the Cascade Mountains and Willamette National Forest; Deschutes is now one of the biggest craft breweries in USA. Forming a solid base to a series of experimentals and seasonals (including the much-anticipated fresh-hopped IPA in winter) is a core range that includes this Black Butte Porter, a tribute to an extinct volcano in Deschutes National Forest. For a long-established Pacific Northwestern brewery to have a porter as its flagship brew is brave, but this rich, sweet and creamy beer is every bit as drinkable as a pale ale. Bravo is a fairly new (2006) hop from local breeding fields which brings high alpha acid levels and a lightly fruity aroma; it's augmented with the most-used craft hop variety in the US (Cascade) plus Tettnang. A weeknight porter with enough character to see you through to Saturday.

- -

GRAIN
2-row pale malt, 2.8kg/ 6lbs 2.8oz (63%)

Chocolate malt, 450g/1lb (10%)

Wheat malt, 400g/14oz (9%)

Crystal malt C75, 400g/14oz (9%)

Carapils, 400g/14oz (9%)

MASH
Mash in at 54C/130F and hold for 10 mins. Raise temperature to 69C/157F and rest for 30 mins. Mash off at 75C/168F and hold for at least 5 mins

HOPS
Bravo 14% AA, 14g/0.5oz, 60 mins

Cascade 6% AA, 14g/0.5oz, 30 mins

Tettnang 5% AA, 28g/1oz, 5 mins

YEAST
White Labs WLP002 English Ale or Wyeast 1187 Ringwood Ale

FERMENT
17C/63F

Ninkasi Brewing Company

Eugene, Oregon, USA

OATIS
OATMEAL STOUT

▬▬

20 L / 5 GAL | ABV **7%**
OG **1.072** | FG **1.020**

Oregon is a pretty good place to be a craft beer fan, as you can tell from the dozens of breweries dedicated to keeping the Beaver State flush with good things to drink. And although Portland may have more breweries per head, Eugene is a pretty good city to be a craft beer fan too. As well as Ninkasi, beermakers here include Hop Valley, whose cans burst with the flavours of the region's precious hop crop, as well as Oakshire and a whole load more. Ninkasi is a refreshing alternative to the skulls-and-heavy-metal-asskicking that typifies a lot of brewing: it's named after the Sumerian goddess of beer, its 'Beer is Love' programme supports charity in a big way, its spent grain goes to feed some (lucky) naturally reared cows. And it makes fine beer: Oatis is a tribute to the brewery's mascot dog Otis, and while he might not be able to enjoy it, the rest of us can appreciate the silky smooth mouthfeel, the deep dark roastiness and the balance of sweet malt and mildly bitter Nugget hops. Ninkasi also makes a Vanilla Oatis, which has an extra creamy depth.

- -

GRAIN
2-row pale malt, 4.86kg/10lbs 11.4oz (74%)

Chocolate malt, 390g/13.8oz (6%)

Crystal malt, 390g/13.8oz (6%)

Flaked oats, 390g/13.8oz (6%)

Vienna malt, 330g/11.6oz (5%)

Roasted barley, 130g/4.6oz (2%)

Rice hulls, 70g/2.5oz (1%)

MASH
67C/152F for 40 mins

HOPS
Nugget, 23g/0.8oz, 60 mins

Nugget, 23g/0.8 oz, 30 mins

YEAST
White Labs WLP005 British Ale

FERMENT
20C/68F for 3-7 days; hold for 2 days at final gravity; chill to 0C/32F for 7-10 days

Põhjala

Tallin, Estonia

ODENSHOLM
IMPERIAL PORTER

▬

20 L / 5 GAL | ABV **9%**
OG **1.083** | FG **1.019**

For most people outside the country, Estonian beer means Viru, a pilsner whose unusual tower-shaped bottle somewhat overshadows its contents in terms of interest. Not now: there's a real craft scene, with young breweries across the Eastern European state producing memorable beers. Põhjala is based in the capital Tallinn and headed up by Christopher Pilkington, a Scottish brewer once of Brewdog (see p118). Põhjala teamed up with another northern powerhouse, Norway's Lervig (see p93), to create this midwinter-black imperial porter. Such supercharged stouts are often described in terms of 'size', and this one's so big it has dark corners to get lost in. The rye and chocolate rye give it a spicy kick, while the long maturation at low temperature take the warming alcohol and bitter hops into deep new dimensions. Make sure your yeast is healthy – it will have a lot of work to do. Christopher gives his beer a further rest in a pinot noir barrel, which if you can do you should: "It makes the dark berry flavours of the carafa malt and chocolate rye merge perfectly." One to get you through a cold night.

- -

GRAIN
Viking pale malt, 4.84kg/ 10lb 10.7oz (62.5%)

Rye malt, 1.55kg/3lb 6.7oz (20%)

Carafa Special Type-II malt, 500g/1lb 1.6oz (6.5%)

Chocolate rye malt, 390g/13.8oz (5%)

Special B malt, 390g/13.8oz (5%)

MASH
68C/154F for 45 mins

HOPS
Magnum or CTZ, 50g/1.76oz, 60 mins

Chinook, 20g/0.7oz, 0 mins

YEAST
White Labs WLP090 San Diego Super

FERMENT
19C/66F, then 4 weeks maturation at 0C/32F

OTHER INGREDIENTS
Demerara sugar, 80g/2.8oz (1%), halfway through boil

The Kernel Brewery

Bermondsey, London, England

EXPORT INDIA PORTER
EXPORT INDIA PORTER

20 L / 5 GAL | ABV **6%**
OG **1.060** | FG **1.016**

This is not subjective, it's true: the Kernel makes incredible beer. Everything about it speaks of simplicity: brown hand-printed labels with minimal information (no tasting notes or boasts of how the contents will change your life); a concise range of beers, ever changing but always true to their style and perfectly crafted. They're mainly heartily hopped IPAs and pale ales, plus the easy-drinking Table Beer, sours and reinventions of historical London styles like mighty stouts and porters. This Export India Porter is free with the hops, just as they would have been in the nineteenth century. And the varieties aren't specified. That's not secrecy, it's because there are no fixed recipes. "We like to experiment with different hop varieties," says founder Evin O'Riordain. "They can create very different flavours when combined with darker malts, which is fascinating. Bramling Cross is our favourite for a more traditional British character. Columbus works very well for a brasher, New World character." Use the recipe here as an inspiration, aim for about 48 IBU. The Kernel uses hard London water, with extra calcium chloride.

GRAIN
Maris Otter malt, 3.96kg/ 8lbs 11.7oz (75.5%)

Brown malt, 370g/13oz (7%)

Chocolate malt, 370g/13oz (7%)

Dark crystal malt, 370g/13oz (7%)

Black malt, 180g/6.3oz (3.5%)

MASH
Around 69C/156F for 60 mins

HOPS
12% AA, 10g/0.35oz, first wort hop

12% AA, 10g/0.35oz, 15 mins

12% AA, 14g/0.5oz, 10 minutes

12% AA, 20g/0.7oz, 5 minutes

12% AA, 40g/1.4oz, dry hop for 3 days before bottling/kegging

YEAST
Kernel uses a house yeast, but you could use something locally appropriate like White Labs WLP013 London Ale

FERMENT
20C/68F, then condition for 10-14 days at 15-20C/59-68F for the beer to carbonate properly

To Øl

Copenhagen, Denmark

BLACK BALL
PORTER

---

20 L / 5 GAL | ABV **7.1%**
OG **1.084** | FG **1.024**

Non-Danish speakers – it's pronounced 'too eul' and translates into one of the best phrases in any language: 'two beers'. In 2005, founders Tobias and Tore, then at school, had a cool science teacher who just happened to be future Mikkeller supremo Mikkel Borg Bjergsø (see p108). United by a disillusion with mainstream Danish beer (you surely know which one), the trio began brewing in the school kitchen after hours. The school was presumably totally fine with this arrangement, and it's worked out pretty well for beer lovers too. If you were ever in any doubt that Denmark is probably the best place to live in the world, that story has doubtless convinced you. In the progressive way, To Øl has no premises – it's a gypsy brewery – but still manages to make an increasingly adventurous range of beautifully designed beers. And this Black Ball is no ordinary porter: the multifarious malt bill is nuanced and involving, the unrefined sugar adds further intrigue, and the plentiful hops illuminate the dark depths. Hoppy porter, black IPA or India stout? When it tastes this good, who cares.

- -

GRAIN
Pilsner malt, 4.15kg/9lbs 2.4oz (57%)

Roasted barley, 700g/1lb 8.7oz (9.5%)

Smoked malt, 610g/1lb 5.5oz (8%)

Flaked oats, 530g/1lb 2.7oz (7%)

Chocolate malt, 440g/15.5oz (6%)

Caramunich, 350g/12.4oz (5%)

Brown malt, 210g/7.4oz (3%)

MASH
67C/152F for 60 mins, 72C/ 161F for 15 mins

HOPS
Simcoe 13% AA, 26g/0.9oz, 60 mins

Simcoe 13% AA, 20g/0.7oz, 15 mins

Centennial 10% AA, 20g/0.7oz, 10 mins

Cascade 6.5%AA, 30g/1oz, 1 min

YEAST
White Labs WLP002 English Ale

FERMENT
20-21C/68-70F

OTHER INGREDIENTS
Demerera, cassonade or similar dark sugar, 210g/7.4oz (4.5%), added at mash stage

Brown, Belgian, bitter & strong

—

Brown ales are malty, mahogany-coloured and deep. Belgian beer is often fruity with distinctive yeast strains and a light body but high alcohol content. English bitter is easygoing and light on hops. Strong ales have heavy grain bills for high ABV and warming alcohol.

Nøgne Ø

Grimstad, Norway

#100
BARLEYWINE

▬▬

20 L / 5 GAL | ABV **10.1%**
OG **1.092** | FG **1.015**

The first commercial barleywine was Bass No 1 in 1903. More than 100 years later, Nøgne Ø has created its own version, and it's a worthy successor to the Burton upon Trent trailblazer. When made well barleywine stands shoulder-to-shoulder with the grand vintages of Bordeaux, but it's challenging to make. It's difficult to work with such a large volume of grist, and to get all the desired sugars out. The grain bed will be heavy, making filtering tough. If you don't hit the OG then the ABV won't be high enough and you simply won't have barleywine. This is an occasion when bumping the pre-fermentation OG up with malt extract is not a bad idea, should you need to. Other methods to ensure a strong barleywine include making two smaller worts then combining. Plus, yeast is key: without proper attenuation, you'll be left with a super-sweet and undrinkable syrup. A liquid yeast is advisable, probably two packs' worth. It's also best to rack it off the yeast after primary fermentation has finished, then again after three or four weeks, before thinking about priming and bottling. Nothing about barleywine can be rushed.

GRAIN
Maris Otter, 6.85kg/15lbs 1.6oz (88%)

Wheat malt, 800g/1lb 12.2oz (10%)

Chocolate malt, 160g/5.64oz (2%)

MASH
63C/145F for 90 mins

HOPS
Chinook, 70g/2.5oz, 90 mins

Centennial, 50g/1.8oz, 15 mins

Centennial, 50g/1.8oz, 5 mins

Columbus, 50g/1.8oz, 0 mins

Chinook, 50g/1.8oz, dry hop

YEAST
White Labs WLP007 Dry English Ale or Danstar Nottingham Ale

FERMENT
20C/68F

SPECIAL INSTRUCTIONS
This is a beer for the future. It needs long and gentle bottle ageing to reach full potential. (Even carbonation will take one or two months.) Six months' rest isn't an exaggeration; longer will be even better. Store the bottles somewhere dark and peaceful, and open one now and again to appreciate the developing characteristics

Renaissance Brewing

Blenheim, New Zealand

STONECUTTER SCOTCH ALE
SMOKED SCOTCH ALE

---

20 L / 5 GAL | ABV **7%**
OG **1.074** | FG **1.021**

Marlborough, at the northern tip of New Zealand's South Island, is winemaking country. All that viticulture is thirsty work, but luckily the award-winning Renaissance is on hand to give those toiling farmers something decent to drink. Like many New World beers, Stonecutter takes its inspiration from a classic European style – in this case, the Scottish 'wee heavy', a strong, hearty ale originally from Edinburgh. Malts are in charge here – nine varieties provide roasty, toasty, chocolate-and-toffee complexity, and the smoked malt,

even in a tiny proportion, floats up in a delicate wisp. But this being New Zealand, locally grown hops feature too. Stonecutter is a big, big beer, and will gladly rest on wood for a while to let its flavours develop: Renaissance head brewer Andy Deuchars recommends oak chips, 15g/0.5oz, in the fermenter for three to five weeks. Put them in a sterilised bag and add to secondary, from where you can sample the beer every week or so to check how much oakiness the beer has taken on. This is a good method for those who don't have a barrel.

GRAIN

Pale ale malt, 2.5kg/5lbs 8.18oz (68%)

Amber malt, 500g/1lbs 1.6oz (6.8%)

CaraAmber, 500g/1lbs 1.6oz (6.8%)

Biscuit malt, 250g/8.8oz (3.5%)

Medium crystal malt, 250g/ 8.8oz (3.5%)

Pale crystal malt, 250g/8.8oz (3.5%)

Vienna malt, 250g/8.8oz (3.5%)

Wheat malt, 250g/8.8oz (3.5%)

Smoked malt, 60g/2.1oz (0.9%)

MASH

Mash at high temperature to get the required attenuation, 68C/154.4F, 60 mins

HOPS

(60 minute boil)

Southern Cross 14% AA, 20g/ 0.7oz, first wort hops

Pacific Jade, 16g/0.6oz, hopback or whirlpool

YEAST

Wyeast 1968 London Ale

FERMENT

20C/68F

Weird Beard Brew Co

Hanwell, London, England

BORING BROWN BEER
IMPERIAL BEST BITTER

20 L / 5 GAL | ABV **7.2%**
OG **1.069** | FG **1.013**

The 'boring brown beer' of the name is supposedly craft beer's absolute antithesis: interchangeably conservative beers served in pubs up and down the land, offering drinkers zero excitement and zero adventure. Weird Beard's Boring Brown Beer, however, is anything but boring. It's a range of American-style brown ales or 'imperial best bitters' featuring a single hop to impressive effect – here it's the turn of Chinook, which brings enough herbal aroma, spice and even grapefruit to stand up to the dark caramel of the Special B malt. Two malts,

one hop, loads of character – it's a simple recipe, but leaves nowhere to hide, and your brewing techniques have to be sound. Weird Beard is another inspiration for homebrewers: founders Gregg and Bryan started brewing professionally after years of amateur experimentation. Their hirsute skull logo adorns every bottle label, from the Little Things That Kill 3.8% hop-heavy session ale to the Sadako barrel-aged imperial stout. 'No gimmicks, no crap and never knowingly underhopped' is the slogan: a mantra we could all take to heart.

GRAIN
Pale malt, 5.3kg/11lbs 11oz (84%)

Special B malt, 1.1kg/2lbs 6.8oz (16%)

MASH
64C/147F for 75 mins

HOPS
Chinook 13%AA, 50g/1.8oz, 60 mins

Chinook 13%AA, 20g/0.7oz, 30 mins

Chinook 13%AA, 20g/0.7oz, 15 mins

Chinook, 13%AA, 20g/0.7oz, 0 mins

YEAST
White Labs WLP007 Dry English Ale

FERMENT
19C/66F for 4 days primary, 10 days secondary

Birrificio del Ducato

Soragna, Emilia-Romagna, Italy

WINTERLUDE
TRIPEL

▬

20 L / 5 GAL | ABV **8.8%**
OG **1.079** | FG **1.012**

For a beer to be certified Trappist, it must be made by one of a select few monasteries (mostly in Belgium, although there are others in the Netherlands, Italy and even Massachussets), and all profits from sale must go to charitable causes. Tripel is a strong pale ale from the Low Countries and a classic Trappist brew: devotion to an abstemious life is not required to make or drink Del Ducato's delightful Winterlude, although with its classic European hops, Belgian yeast and candi sugar, it's faithful to the style. Kaleidoscopes of complex flavours come from these simple ingredients. Giovanni Campari's brewery, in the town of Soragna near Parma, creates beers with an elemental link to the land and heartfelt stories behind their inception: "Winterlude is a tribute to a friend who went missing, who we may meet again one day, just like the sun that is hiding behind the hill." This is a beer to age – tripels benefit from a secondary fermentation off the yeast and then a couple of months in the bottle, when it can be savoured with all the lip-smacking and pontification associated with a fine wine.

- -

GRAIN
Pilsner malt, 5.95kg/13lbs 1.9oz (86.5%)

Acidulated malt, 290g/10.2oz (4%)

Carapils, 190g/6.7oz (3%)

MASH
66C/152F for 60 mins

HOPS
Herkules, 4g/0.14oz, 70 mins

Marynka, 13g/0.45oz, 5 mins

Whitbread Goldings Variety, 25g/0.9oz, 0 mins

YEAST
Wyeast 3787 Trappist High Gravity

FERMENT
20C/68F

OTHER INGREDIENTS
White candi sugar, 450g/15.9oz (6.5%), added during the boil. Stir till it's properly dissolved to avoid it burning on the kettle

Stillwater Artisanal

Baltimore, Maryland, and Brooklyn, New York, USA

OF LOVE & REGRET
BOTANICAL FARMHOUSE ALE

20 L / 5 GAL | ABV 7%
OG 1.058 | FG 1.004

Of Love & Regret (also the name of the Stillwater Artisanal bar in the Brewers Hill district of Baltimore, Maryland) is described as a 'botanical farmhouse ale', and it doesn't need to be pigeonholed beyond that. From the first sip you'll realise this is no ordinary brew. Belgian beers often have spices, fruits and natural additions, and this is a particularly inventive take on that tradition. The heather, camomile, dandelion and lavender steeped in the boil add subtle garden flavours as they intertwine with the grassy, spicy Sterling and Styrian Golding: imagine a Low Countries hop field overgrown with summer wildflowers and you're somewhere near the intensely floral character of this beer. The French saison yeast brings out the herbal notes and provides the high attenutation needed for a dry finish. Aromatic malt is a speciality grain which adds a distinctive maltiness and a deep copper colour (and there's no substitute for it). These sort of open-interpretation Belgian ales really allow the imaginative brewer to become an artist. Get creative!

GRAIN
Pilsner malt, 4kg/8lbs 12oz (78%)

Wheat malt, 510g/1lb 2oz (10%)

Vienna malt, 510g/1lb 2oz (10%)

Belgian aromatic malt, 100g/3.5oz (2%)

MASH
63C/146F for 45 mins,
75C/167F for 15 mins

HOPS
Magnum 14% AA, 7g/0.25oz, 75 mins

Sterling 7.5%, 15g/0.53oz, 10 mins

Sterling, 28g/1oz, 0 mins

Styrian Golding, 14g/0.5oz, 0 mins

YEAST
Wyeast 3711 French Saison

FERMENT
Pitch at 23C/70F then allow to rise to 24C/75F. Crash cool when activity is complete

OTHER INGREDIENTS
Heather (Calluna vulgaris), 20g/0.7oz
Dandelion (Taraxacum officinale), 12g/0.42oz
Camomile (Matricaria chamomilla), 8g/0.28oz
Lavender (Lavandula x intermedia), 4g/0.14oz

At flameout, steep all botanicals in a mesh bag for 10 mins

Marble Brewery

Manchester, England

MANCHESTER BITTER
BITTER

20 L / 5 GAL | ABV **4.2%**
OG **1.040** | FG **1.008**

Manchester in the north of England is a proper brewing city, and Marble is Manchester through and through. It's committed to cask as well as keg and bottle, and the no-nonsense Northern branding of its logo hints at the honest and sturdily dependable beers within. Almost every style of beer has left the brewery gates, from a German latzenbier to the bourbon-barrel-aged Russian Imperial Stout, but Marble also makes the traditional sort of ales that made the city great and fuelled the Industrial Revolution in the nineteenth century. So there's the Best, English IPA, hearty Stouter Stout and Pint, an everyday bitter that really would be welcome every day. Plus the classic bitter-with-a-twist showcased here: it features the solid malt base you'd expect (Maris Otter with a smaller proportion of darker roasted crystal grains), but updates the hop bill with the Kiwi Waimea and Motueka, leaving a dry, slightly fruity and, of course, bitter finish. It's a Mancunian classic up there with the Smiths, football rivalry and rain.

GRAIN
Maris Otter, 3.2kg/7lbs 0.9oz (94%)

Caramalt, 140g/4.9oz (4%)

Crystal malt 150L, 70g/2.5oz (2%)

MASH
66C/151F for 50 mins

HOPS
Herkules 16.1% AA, 3g/0.1oz, 70 mins

Goldings 3.4% AA, 20g/0.7oz, 15 mins

Waimea 18% AA, 25g/0.9oz, 0 mins (steep for 20 mins)

Motueka 8% AA, 25g/0.9oz, 0 mins (steep for 20 mins)

YEAST
Something very neutral and appropriate to the style

FERMENT
18–21C/64–70F

Rogue Ales

Newport, Oregon, USA

HAZELNUT BROWN NECTAR
AMERICAN BROWN ALE

20 L / 5 GAL | ABV **6.2%**
OG **1.057** | FG **1.016**

Nut brown ale is a traditional English-style ale, the deep burnished colour of chestnuts, with a mildly nutty taste from a complex blend of roasted malts. What it doesn't usually have is actual nuts in it, but Rogue's classic Hazelnut Brown Nectar takes things to the next level with a delicate infusion of real nut extract (Northwestern's high-quality flavourings mean the brewer can control exactly how much 'nuttiness' makes it into the beer). It also uses the Rogue strain Pacman yeast, which can be bought through Wyeast. The Oregon brewery has a history of pushing the boat out with its experimental yet always drinkable beers (Sriracha Hot stout with chilli sauce really works), but its standard range is anything but standard. Dead Guy Ale is undoubtedly the best-known heller bock in the USA (okay, probably the only known heller bock) and the Shakespeare oatmeal stout is a rated favourite the world over. Rogue also has its own farms in the Pacific Northwest growing ingredients for its brews (pumpkins, rye) as well as some that hopefully don't make it anywhere near beer (turkeys, for instance).

GRAIN
Great Western 2-row pale malt, 3.5kg/7lbs 12oz (59%)

Great Western Munich malt 10L, 0.9kg/2lbs (15%)

Great Western Crystal malt 75L, 680g/1lb 8oz (11%)

Baird Brown malt, 312g/11oz (5%)

Great Western Crystal malt 15L, 255g/9oz (4%)

Great Western Crystal malt 120L, 255g/9oz (4%)

Franco-Belges Kiln Coffee malt, 113g/4oz (2%)

MASH
67C/152F for 60 mins

HOPS
(70 minute boil)

Perle pellets 9% AA, 17g/0.6oz, 60 mins

Sterling pellets 5%AA, 14g/0.5oz, 0 mins (ten-minute hop stand)

YEAST
Wyeast 1764 Pacman

FERMENT
16-18C/60-65F

OTHER INGREDIENTS
Northwestern hazelnut extract, ½ tsp, to be added at bottling stage

Williams Bros Brewing Co

Alloa, Scotland

80/-
SCOTTISH ALE

20 L / 5 GAL | ABV **4.2%**
OG **1.043** | FG **1.012**

Scotch ale is known to most people worldwide as something strong, sweet-ish and richly mahogany in colour. It often has an embarrassing name like 'Big Tam's Kilt Lifter'. It's not, unsurprisingly, what most Scots drink day-to-day. A more appropriate contender for a national pint would be 80 shilling (called '80 bob' or even just '80' by locals – it's named after an old system of taxation on a barrel, whereby the strongest and best-quality beer commanded keener interest from the exciseman). Scott and Bruce Williams, based in the historical Central Belt brewing hub of Alloa, have done more than anyone to revive and maintain ancient Scottish styles; as well as their Fraoch heather ale, a resurrection of a beer that predated hop use by a good few centuries, is this updated 80/-. Its generous malts and English bittering hops are faithful to a traditional version, but then the Northwestern US aroma hops and orange peel infusion give it a modern flourish (although those ingredients still tread quietly – this is a malty beer). Drink with a *slainte* (Gaelic for cheers).

GRAIN
Pale malt, 2.87kg/6lbs 5oz (75%)

Wheat malt, 380g/13.4oz (10%)

Crystal malt 115L, 250g/8.8oz (6.5%)

Chocolate malt, 170g/6oz (4.5%)

Milled oats, 150g/5.3oz (4%)

MASH
70C/158F for 50 mins

HOPS
First Gold, 14.5g/0.5oz, 60 mins

Savinski Goldings, 11g/0.4oz, 45 mins

Amarillo, 10g/0.35oz, 0 mins

Cascade, 10g/0.35oz, dry hop

YEAST
White Labs WLP039 Nottingham Ale

FERMENT
20C/68F

OTHER INGREDIENTS
Sweet orange peel, 40g/1.4oz, boil for 15 mins

	DEN TOWN	HELLS LAGER	4.6%	£
		PIVO 12°	5%	£5
	MDEN TOWN	PALE ALE	4.0%	£
KEG	BEAVERTOWN	GAMMA RAY	5.4%	£.
KEG	TO ØL	GARDEN OF EDEN	6.4%	£
KEG	WEIHENSTEPHANER	HEFEWEISSBIER	5.4%	£
KEG	ANCHOR	SPRING ALE	7.2%	£
KEG	CAMDEN TOWN	INK STOUT	4.4%	£
KEG	MIKKELLER	IT'S ALIVE	8%	£
KEG	TROUBADOUR	IMPERIAL STOUT	9%	
		OLIVER'S CIDER	AND PERRY	MEE

KEG	TROUBADOUR	WESTKUST			LF
KEG	LERVIG	KONRAD'S STOUT			
KEG	FOUNDERS	CURMUDGEON	9.8%		
NT	CASK	DARK STAR	HOPHEAD	3.8%	£3.80	PINT
T	CASK	WILD BEER	BIBBLE	4.2%	£3.90	PINT
T	CASK	BAD	WILD GRAVITY	5.2%	£4.20	PINT
NT	CASK					PINT
T	CIDER	LILLEY'S	STARGAZER CIDER	4.5%	£4.20	PINT
LF	CIDER	BARBOURNE	STRAWBERRY CIDER	4%	£4.40	PINT
ALF	CIDER	OLIVER'S	DRY CIDER	6%	£4.40	PINT

KER | & TAP TAKEOVER | ON THURSDAY | JUNE 18TH

Glossary

—

As befits a centuries-old practice, brewing comes with its own often pleasingly medieval-sounding vocabulary, many of it borrowed from German and Old English, including the witchy-sounding 'wort' (properly pronounced 'wert', if you're being pedantic), and 'copper', a traditional name for the boil kettle.

ADJUNCTS
Unmalted grains added to a mash;
sometimes other additions too (spices
or flavourings).

ALPHA ACIDS (AA)
Acids in hops which contribute towards
the overall bitterness of the beer.

AERATING
Oxygenating boiled wort to allow yeast
to thrive.

AROMA HOPS
Hops added after the first half-hour or so
of the boil: they are usually low in alpha
acids and provide aroma.

ATTENUATION
Conversion of sugar to CO_2 and alcohol
(by yeast).

BITTERING HOPS
Hops added at the start of the boil:
after an hour of boiling they give up their
desired bitter flavours.

BOILING
The process of infusing wort with the
bitterness, flavour and aroma of hops.
Done in a boil kettle, aka a copper.

BOTTLING/KEGGING
Transferring beer to a receptacle suitable
for convenient consumption.

CONDITIONING
Resting beer in a bottle, barrel, cask or
keg to allow it to carbonate and develop
in flavour.

FERMENTING
The process by which yeast converts
fermentable sugars into alcohol and CO_2.

FINING
A substance added during the brewing
process to clarify the beer (Protofloc or
Irish moss).

FLAMEOUT
Literally, the moment when the heat under
the boil is extinguished: also refers to
the moment when hops are added to the
wort to impart maximum aroma. See also
whirlpool.

FLOCCULATION
The act of clustering or clumping
together, in the case of brewing, yeast
solids in the fermenter.

GRAVITY, SPECIFIC
The density of liquid (in brewing, the
concentration of sugar in liquid).

GRIST
Ground grain for mashing.

KRAUSEN
A foam of proteins and yeast that forms
on the wort during primary fermentation.
Looks disturbing, is actually a reassuring
sign that all is going well.

LAUTERING

The process of rinsing the grains of all their fermentable sugars and taking the wort to a pre-boil volume. It involves two stages: recirculation (aka vorlauf), using the existing water in the tun, and sparging: sprinkling fresh water over the grain bed.

LIQUOR

Water used directly in a brew. The total volume needed is split into strike water (used to mash) and sparge water (in the sparging process).

MASH HOPS

Hops added in the mash for bittering. An uncommon practice.

MASHING

The process of soaking grains and adjuncts in hot water in the mash tun to extract sugars. Can be done at one temperature (single-rest) or variable-temperature stages (multi-rest). Mashing out is the process of raising the temperature sharply at the end of the infusion to halt enzyme action.

PITCHING

Adding yeast to wort.

PRIMING

Adding sugar (or malt extract, or occasionally yeast) to wort before bottling to facilitate the creation of carbonation in the bottle.

RACKING

Transferring wort from one vessel to another, typically from a primary fermenter to a second, or from a fermenter to a priming vessel.

TRUB

Unwanted sediment in the boil kettle and fermenter, consisting mainly of hop matter, proteins and dead yeast cells.

WHIRLPOOL

When brewers spin the post-boil wort at high speed to form a mound of undesirable solids in the middle. 'Whirlpool hops' are sometimes added at this stage.

WORT

Sweet liquid taken from the tun after the mash, containing fermentable sugars.

Index

_

Acknowledgements

Firstly, a huge thanks to my brilliant commissioning editor Zena, who made this book a hundred times better in every way. Thanks to Ashleigh for her amazing illustrations and book design, and to Charlie for his great photographs. Also, the technical expertise of Talfryn Provis-Evans was indispensable.

Thanks to all the breweries that I cajoled, encouraged and hassled to share their recipes with me. They're all world-beating, but for extra distinction, special mention to James at Brewdog, Evin at The Kernel, Logan, Jenn and Nick at Beavertown, Vinnie at Russian River, John at Brouwerij de Molen, Henok at Omnipollo, Brian at Stillwater Artisanal, Jayne and Danielle at Two Birds, Tony at Boneyard, Chris Pilkington at Põhjala, Chad at Crooked Stave, Scott Williams at Williams Bros, Doug Odell, Stu at Yeastie Boys and all the NZ Craft Beer Collective, Fabio at Baladin, Andrew Bell and Benjamin Weiss at Bruery Terreux, and Ben Love at Gigantic.

Thanks to everyone who helped me assemble an incredible collection of beers from around the world to take pictures of: Splandos, Rob, Tina, Benjamin, Ben, Fabio, Chris, and Jules at Hop Hideout. And for allowing me to invade their premises and turn them into photographic studios: everyone at the Kings Arms, Bethnal Green, the Three Johns, Islington, and Ubrew, Bermondsey.

Big thanks to Will and Tom at Clapton Craft, the best craft beer shop in the world!

COLOURS!

CANCER
(June 21-July 21)

YOUR LUCKY COLOUR

Your true colour is gold. Pure yellow
[gol]d, not greeny-gold or reddish-gold or
[any] other mixture. Steer clear of the very
[bri]ght daffodil and sunshine golds —
[the]y're too outgoing for you to wear all the
[tim]e.

Your special colour is a lovely pale gold that
[m]akes you think of moonlight. It's for clinging
[and] floating tops and skirts, not for practical
[th]ings like trousers and socks! When you
[w]ear it this year you'll bring out the best of
[yo]ur sympathetic, sensitive nature
[wh]ich is a Cancer characteristic. Friends
[w]ith problems will turn to you because you're
[a] good listener. And wearing pale gold, you'll
[di]scover that your own difficulties won't drag
[yo]u down so much, either. It's not easy to be
[d]own in the dumps for long when
[y]ou're wearing gold!

YOUR ROMANTIC COLOUR

And just the right kind of boys will fall
for you in your golden glory. Not the noisy,
pushy boys who go in for girls in knock-
out colours (that's not your style anyway),
but nice romantic boys who'll want to hold
your hand and walk with you on the beach —
and then take you back to the party to show you
off to all their mates!

COLOURS TO AVOID

Go easy on any of the very vivid
colours and especially easy on red.
Red's really too forceful a colour for you.
You won't feel comfortable wearing it
and it'll attract boys who are too
aggressive for you.

LEO
(July 22-Aug. 21)

YOUR LUCKY COLOUR

You can ring the changes of all the colours
in sunlight! The delicate reds of sunrise
— the almost-white intensity of high noon —
the mellow gold of late afternoon — the
blazing scarlet of sunset — you can wear
them all, because the Sun is your ruling
planet. Wear them separately, wear them
together (just be careful they don't clash!) —
either way they'll help you to think positively.

Your truest colour is a *clear yellow* that's
like a really ripe lemon. It helps you feel
sympathetic and helpful towards other
people. It gives you a natural vitality
and determination — and makes sure you
tackle life with a smile! Wearing lemon
yellow means you should be both hopeful
and realistic.

YOUR ROMANTIC COLOUR

The effect of lemon yellow on your love-
life can only be good, whatever happens.
If you find your dream-boy is looking your way
(and he should be!) you'll intrigue him by just
being there and not taking any notice of him —
until the moment comes for you to make your
play! While the romance lasts, you'll be his
special girl, faithful but always fun to be
with — but if it comes to an end (and

especially if you find he's a two-timer!) you
won't shed any tears over *him!* You'll have
your eye on the next boy, instead . . . .

COLOURS TO AVOID

Colours to avoid in 1981 are grey,
brown and black – though you can get
away with these if you wear your
sunlight colours too. Otherwise they'll
give you a fit of the miseries!

VIRGO
(Aug. 22-Sept. 21)

YOUR LUCKY COLOUR

The colour for you to wear this year
is delicate, pale green — the colour of
young grass or newly-opened leaves.
When you wear it, you'll be in a gentle
mood. You'll enjoy being out in the open,
just sitting watching the flowers grow, or
taking the dog for a walk. It'll give
you serenity.

If you've never worn light green before,
though, go easy on it to begin with. Mix it
in with your "everyday" colours — grey, navy
and brown — so that you keep your feet well
on the ground. Green can be a very
heady colour, full of life and excitement and
high hopes — which is just great, as long as
you remember to be practical about it all! So
try some navy with your green to bring out your
strength and reliability.

YOUR ROMANTIC COLOUR

When it comes to your love-life, most
boys can't resist a girl who knows how to wear
pale green — so invest in at least one light,
floating, dress in green for summer! And wear
white sandals with it — just so you'll remember
what Dad said about being in by half-past
ten! Green will bring out all your romantic

depths — and you'll be your boy's dream-girl,
sweet and tender without being silly or
sentimental.

COLOURS TO AVOID

Colours to avoid are the really bright
ones like shocking pink, electric blue,
and daffodil yellow. They'll make you feel
restless and edgy, all keyed up without
knowing what you should be doing about
about it.

LIVING

QUIZZES

FEATURES

POP

BEAUTY

ASTROLOGY

FUN

FICTION

FASHION

Season's Greetings

Hello again! And welcome to your Jackie Annual 1981! We've got all your favourites here — including everyone's favourite bumbler, Leonard J. Watkins. Mind you, he always seems to end up with Myrtle, so he can't be *that* much of a bumbler! But — can he wrest (or wrestle) her away from the amorous clutches of the Fiend from France this time? We're not telling, so you'll just have to turn to page 10 to find out!

There are lots of other exciting things to find out in this year's annual, too. We tell you what your true colours are according to your star sign, and what colours you should avoid at all costs. We told Danny he should avoid wearing puce and green together, not because it's particularly unlucky for him, but because it makes everyone else go green and puce when they see him.

He ought to take a few lessons from Marjie, though. You can see what (tasteful and nice!) colour combinations Marjie's come up with in her special fashion spread on page 68.

As well as fashion and all the super new looks, though, your Jackie Annual also has all your favourite features plus lots of super fiction. As well as Leonard J. Watkins, there's a full-length Reader's True Experience in Pictures, a super-scary full-length picture story set in 19th-century Bavaria, and lots more super stories.

There's loads more goodies in this year's annual too, of course. We've got pop specials, fun features, beauty, quizzes and lots, lots more! So enjoy your Jackie Annual 1981, have a super Christmas and don't forget, we're around in Jackie every week to make your life a whole lot more fun!

Love,

The Ed.

YOU KNOW YOU'RE A WINTER WINNER WHEN . . .

. . . you're safely snuggled inside your boyfriend's overcoat with him.

. . . your St Bernard dog has just rescued the most fanciable boy you've ever set eyes on.

. . . two rival football teams have asked you to be their mascot.

. . . your snowman lasts until June!

. . . he tells you you're just like a cuddly little puppy — cold nose and warm heart!

. . . you've got a date with the most handsome Eskimo around!

. . . it's blowing a gale outside, the frost's an inch thick on the windows and you don't even need to set foot outside because it's the first day of your holidays!

. . . you're the only person around with a gorgeous bronze tan. (It's out of a bottle, of course, but who cares?)

. . . you're clad in your thermal undies, electric blanket coat, insulated wellies and double-glazed specs.

. . . you're curled up in front of the fire with a huge plate of hot, buttered toast, a giant mug of hot chocolate and an enthralling book.

. . . you're the only girl in the class with a mink-lined school uniform.

. . . the pull-on hat that Grandma knitted for you stretches right the way down to your toes!

. . . you've fallen madly in love!

. . . you can fall on your backside on an icy, busy High Street pavement and come up laughing.

. . . you're lying on a sun-soaked beach in far-off Hawaii writing postcards to all the folk back home.

. . . you've knitted matching legwarmers for the whole family — Mum, Dad, Grandma, your little brother, the cat, the dog and the budgie.

. . . you commute to school on ice skates and pass all your friends, cold and shivering at the bus stop.

. . . you've built the biggest and best snowman in the street.

. . . he tells you you're the only girl he knows who still looks lovely with cold sores, cracked lips and a red nose.

. . . you've bought every single piece of mistletoe in town — and there's none left for any of the other girls!

. . . you've got yourself all lovely and slim so you can afford to eat whatever you like over the holidays!

. . . you bought all your Christmas presents in July!

. . . you bought twenty tickets for the Christmas draw and so far you've won the first nineteen prizes.

. . . you traded in your bike for a pair of snowshoes in the summer holidays.

. . . your smile generates warmth wherever you go!

. . . you've cleverly switched to roll-on deodorants and cream perfumes to avoid being knocked out by icy blasts from aerosol containers.

. . . you "accidentally" glide into the arms of the best-looking ice skater at the rink.

. . . you're part-time Santa at the department store and all the children are bringing along their big brothers.

. . . the B.B.C. have asked you to knit another two miles on to Dr Who's scarf.

. . . you buy every Jackie Annual in the local shop, then sell them to your friends at a profit of ten pence for each one.

. . . you've got a temporary job as hot-water-bottle sales representative — and you're on commission!

. . . you give up your boring boyfriend (who only has a draughty moped) for an equally boring boyfriend (who has a car with sheepskin seat covers and a really good heater).

. . . you have a mum who gives you a big cooked breakfast every morning. It's great to have your own internal combustion.

. . . you've practised skating on a polythene sheet in the garden all summer, so now you can impress everyone with your dinky pirouettes performed on the duck pond.

. . . you're one of those rotten skinny people who can go all winter on a diet of steam pudding, chips and crumpets and not put a rotten skinny ounce on.

. . . some crummy kid pelts you with snowballs and you can turn round and get him on the back of the neck, first throw, at thirty yards.

. . . it's the January sales and you've saved yourself a fortune doing next year's Christmas shopping.

. . . you really love sledging, 'cos there's this grotty creep who's so besotted with you that he pulls your sledge back up the hill every time — with you still on it.

. . . you come home with the downhill slalom prize when you only went along to the ski club to watch, but lost your balance.

. . . you pass out from fatigue during the Inter-County snowball fight, and this amazing medical student just happens to be on hand with the longest, most delicious kiss of life ever known to man.

. . . you knit tea-cosies for the local sale of work, and a girl sees them there and offers you £10 for each to sell as hats in her London boutique!

. . . Santa drops in to ask how much you want for your reindeer.

. . . you don't take a bath from October onwards, then by the time winter really arrives, you have a lovely two-inch layer of dirt all over.

. . . you build an igloo in your garden and live in it until it melts!

. . . you save pounds on blusher because it comes naturally at this time of year!

Roll up! Roll up — for all the fun of the fair! Because this year we've decided that what we need to get things started is a completely captivating, colossal Christmas carnival! So what we've done is to pick a few of our favourite stars — and some of our not so favourite ones as well! — and match them up with the sorts of carnival jobs we think they'd be best at. Of course you may not agree with everything we have to say, but we *can* assure you that we've tried to be (groan!) fair-minded . . .

FIRST, let's introduce you to our very own fairground barker (Lassie *did* audition for the part, but we turned her down . . .) and what better person for the job than John Cleese! His description of the delights in store for you will be so tempting — or confusing! — that you'll feel you couldn't possibly walk on by. So take his advice, count out your pennies and come on in . . .

No carnival would be complete without a Big Heel — oops! Sorry . . . Big Wheel — and we couldn't think of anyone more talented at making your head spin, your heart race, and your stomach re-position itself somewhere at the back of your throat, than the delicious David Essex! But, Dorothy — why are you lying on the ground rolling your eyeballs when you haven't even paid your 30p yet . . . ?

After a spin like that, how about a nice easy ride on the roundabouts run by the best people we know at going round in circles and producing monotonous music — ABBA! Or you could test your strength at superhero Christopher Reeve's stall — em . . . you're actually supposed to use the hammer, Jackie . . . not challenge him to a quick wrestle!

BUT what's this? Fran and Dave are heading towards the Tunnel of Love . . . we might have known! Well, they'll just have to take their place in the queue behind Debbie Harry and Chris Stein — such a romantic couple!

Wait a minute, they're being turned away by James Hazeldine who's showing them a big notice saying "Me and Paula only"! Wonder how much she paid him for that . . .

Now it's time for a hair-raising ride on the ghost train, featuring Vincent Price, Christopher (don't forget your garlic!) Lee and Boris Karloff — and if you can manage to survive that, you'll be glad to hear that the next stall is full of candy floss, sold by none other than sickly, sugary Charlie's Angels!

Then you can choose between a fantastic ride on the helter-skelter run by the deplorably dizzy Aimi MacDonald, and a giggle a minute in the Hall of Mirrors which is run by Bob Geldof — when he opens it up, that is! At the moment he's probably in there admiring himself . . .

Or how about trying out Clint Eastwood's famous rifle range — poncho and half-smoked cigar provided free! The trouble is, the Ed's hands are shaking so much she's liable to blow Lena Martell's head off . . .

Christmas Carnival!

before she gets a chance to open up her Howling Alley. Oh, sorry . . . it says Bowling Alley, does it? So she can't write either . . .

We know a lot of you will be heading towards the coconut shy where Nicholas Ball is being shyer than ever! Or why not join Woody Allen and Spike Milligan on the Dodgems? They're the dodgiest pair we could think of — guaranteed to give a crooked answer to a straight question!

YOU'RE probably feeling pretty thirsty by now so it's time to stop for a cup of tar (em, char, we mean, of course!) from our very own tea-lady Olive, who's kept us going all year (Olive's tea's a bit like that . . .) — before you move on to the mini-circus!

We've nominated actor John Hurt as ringmaster because no matter how awful everyone else is, we *know* he'll make the show a success! And if that sounds a bit silly, just wait till you see who we've got lined up for you . . .

First in the ring are the clowns — alias the Radio 1 DJs! Rotten eggs and tomatoes are provided in case Tony Blackburn tries to tell a joke, and we've had a special custard pie made which is big enough to shut even Dave Lee Travis's mouth!

Hey, don't tell me Marjie's actually *laughing* at them! No . . . Legs & Co are the ones who're making her giggle. They've just tripped into the ring behind the DJs as our only choice for circus ballerinas. (Best place for them, too — Dave.)

AS soon as they've finished prancing around, we'll be presenting Peter Sellers as the only lion-tamer in the world to use domestic cats, as well as Elvis Costello who'll be juggling away with music and words to come up with some of the best songs around.

What's this? I didn't know we'd booked midgets for the show! Pardon? Oh . . . well nobody told *me* Racey were making a guest appearance . . . When they're finished, you'll be stunned and amazed by the antics

of the dancing bear (which is actually Barry Gibb sporting his customary coconut matting) and our favourite contortionist Gary Numan — anyone who can get to No 1 as quickly as he can *has* to be a bit of a contortionist!

Moving on from the mini-circus, the first stall you'll come to is the hoop-la, run by none other than Larry Grayson and Isla St Clair. The trouble is, all the prizes are on a conveyor belt so it's not all that easy to win . . .

Now let's see, what have we got left . . . Hey, it's Sting! The Police are here, girls — isn't that great! What was that you said . . . Licence! You mean, you need a licence to hold a carnival? But that's ridiculous! I mean, this is supposed to be the season of goodwill and . . .

THE JACKIE CHRISTMAS CARNIVAL IS CLOSED UNTIL FURTHER NOTICE . . .

ARE YOU NIC

THERE are two sides to human nature — the nice, kind, good side and the nasty, mean, bad side. Most of us are a mixture of both good and bad — but what kind of mixture are *you*? Are you a goodie or a baddie? Nice or nasty? Just how do you see yourself and, more important, how do *other* people see you? Well — now's your chance to find out! Just try our fun quiz and find out how nice (or nasty!) you are — and what that means about your relationship with boys!

1. Before an important interview, would you . . .
a. be so nervous you'd feel positively sick,
b. make sure you have a good night's sleep and a good breakfast beforehand so you'll be at your best,
c. keep your fingers crossed and carry your good luck charm with you,
d. say a quick prayer as you go in, and then leave it all in the hands of Fate?

2. If you were visiting an old church while on holiday, what would you be most likely to think?
a. It's got a really weird atmosphere.
b. Just think of all the people who've been here over the years.
c. Gosh! It's freezing cold in here.
d. What beautiful colours those stained-glass windows are.

3. There's a market in the town where your friend lives, and you like going there. Which stall would you find most interesting?
a. The second-hand clothes stall.
b. The antiques stall.
c. The flower and plant stall.

d. The pets and petfoods stall.

4. If you're watching TV with your family, and a sexy statue of a naked woman is shown, would you think . . .
a. what a lovely body! Wish I looked like that!
b. gosh, this is a bit embarrassing,
c. I wonder what Mum and Dad are thinking . . .,
d. that statue is a really beautiful work of art?

5. While your steady boyfriend is away on holiday, you're asked out by a boy you've fancied for ages. Do you . . .
a. feel it's wrong, but go anyway, unable to resist him,
b. indulge your feelings and have without feeling guilty,
c. say no, with a lot of regrets, and think about him,
d. say no, but go on feeling guilty being tempted?

6. When you say hello and goodby family and friends, do you . . .
a. give them all big hugs and kisse
b. feel you want to kiss them, but be shy,
c. give your mum and dad a peck on cheek, but that's all,
d. not kiss or hug anybody: it f wrong and you don't want to?

7. How would you most like to spen summer afternoon?
a. Swimming and sunbathing or deserted beach.

b. Having a picnic on a riverbank friends.
c. Lying on your back in a sunny listening to the sounds all around y
d. Taking a neighbour's children to park to give her a break.

8. What do you think of poetry?
a. It's OK sometimes — when funny.
b. It's a load of old rubbish.
c. You like reading it; it fills you ideas and feelings.
d. You even *write* it sometimes! like expressing your feeli in this way.

9. Music's something you probably en But what's the thing you like most about
a. The great, foot-tapping rhythm o
b. The sheer exhilarating noise.
c. The patterns you can hear in it.
d. The words of the songs and feelings they express.

10. You're at a party where most pe seem to be kissing and cuddling. Is y reaction . . .
a. to blush all over,
b. to think it's embarrassing but a exciting,
c. to want to join in,
d. to wonder why they're all beha like that?

OR NASTY?

1. Which of these would be your favourite smell?
 a. Roasting coffee.
 b. The smell of expensive perfume.
 c. The smell of honeysuckle by a cottage door.
 d. The cool fresh smell of lemon eau de cologne.

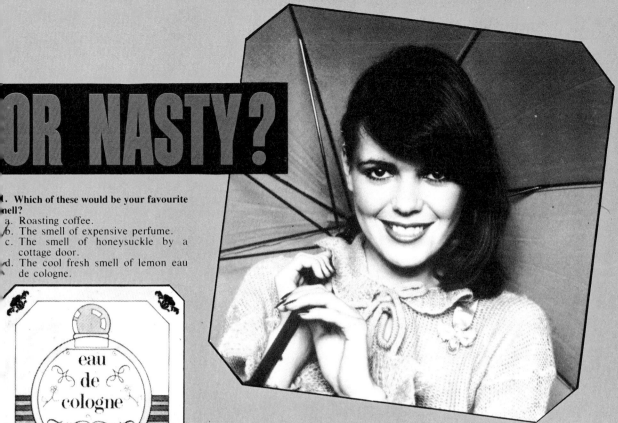

2. Are you attracted to . . .
 a. mainly good-looking boys,
 b. ugly boys sometimes — if they're interesting,
 c. only interesting boys — and you don't always fancy them, either!
 d. ugly boys quite often, 'cos they're usually nicer?

13. You're at a posh dinner and you want to go to the loo. What do you do?
 a. Quietly ask the nearest person where it is, and feel embarrassed.
 b. Go off and look for it on your own, too shy to ask.
 c. Announce, "I must go to the loo!" in a loud voice.
 d. Wait till you get home, even though you're bursting, rather than ask.

QUIZ CONCLUSIONS

Now count your score and turn to the conclusions.

SCORES

1. a-4, b-3, c-2, d-1.
2. a-1, b-2, c-4, d-3.
3. a-3, b-1, c-2, d-4.
4. a-4, b-3, c-2, d-1.
5. a-3, b-4, c-2, d-1.
6. a-4, b-3, c-2, d-1.
7. a-4, b-3, c-2, d-1.
8. a-3, b-4, c-2, d-1.
9. a-3, b-4, c-1, d-2.
10. a-3, b-2, c-4, d-1.
11. a-3, b-4, c-2, d-1.
12. a-4, b-3, c-2, d-1.
13. a-3, b-2, c-4, d-1.

If you scored 40-52:

You're much more of a baddie than a goodie! But don't worry — all it means is that you're very basic and down-to-earth. You like to enjoy yourself, and your pleasures are eating, drinking, looking at beautiful things — in short, all the pleasures of the senses, including touching! This makes you very affectionate and warm. You probably come from a very cuddly, happy family — you're a lucky girl and a lovable one, too!

Your feelings are all very immediate, and even violent sometimes. You're quite hot-blooded really! You tend to fall suddenly and passionately in love, but you do find it hard to stay loyal for long. The trouble is, you just can't resist your feelings and get swept along by them. In fact, you haven't really got much self-discipline. You probably find it hard to concentrate on work for long!

You're a very physical person. Looks matter to you, you make the most of your own, and go for good-looking guys. You're also active — you enjoy the sheer sensation of swimming, dancing, and bounding around. In fact, you're a real bundle of fun! If people might whisper behind your back that you're a weeny bit empty-headed, or can't control yourself, what do you care?

If you scored 30-39:

You're mostly bad but with one or two good qualities thrown in! Which means you're a straightforward, pleasure-loving, warm person, but occasionally you are plagued by doubts or guilt or ideas which upset you. However, you're still much more likely to be swamped by your feelings than able to reason them away or rise above them. The result, more often than not, is a feeling of conflict — torn between the desire to do something and the feeling that you mustn't. And you usually go ahead and do it, but feel guilty afterwards! Boys find you a warm and friendly girl. As far as being faithful is concerned, you'd be capable of it if the boy was really your type. Try to find a boy who's fond of sports, dancing, and who has a good sense of humour. An intellectual type probably wouldn't suit you so well, and you'd fly off at the first chance — and feel guilty about it!

If you scored 20-29:

You've got your life pretty well sorted out! You understand yourself and your motives. You know how to enjoy yourself, and in some quite sophisticated ways sometimes. But you'd hardly ever let pleasure get in the way of duty. Which means that you're a very nice girl to know: reliable, loyal, and very considerate of other people's feelings. You think before acting and would be unlikely to commit yourself to a relationship with a boy who didn't suit you. And the sort of boy who wouldn't suit you would be a tearaway, irresponsible and wild, even though he might be really attractive. Boys find you a bit shy but once they discover your warm, balanced personality, they find you pretty irresistible!

You don't chase after boys. In fact, though you like people a lot, you're also happy just being on your own. Peace and quiet, and a chance to feel your own feelings and think your own thoughts, is what you need.

What you really need to do is work out what pleasures you're going to allow yourself, and enjoy them to the full. And be really firm with yourself about the ones you know you should resist! (Be they jam doughnuts or other people's boyfriends.) If you work hard to develop a bit more self-discipline, you'll be a really well-balanced person!

If you scored 13-19:

Where are your wings and halo? 'Cos you're the nearest thing to an angel we've ever heard of! (Unless you cheated?!) This means that you're very highly disciplined, you have incredibly high standards for yourself and other people, and you take a fairly detached, cool and calculating attitude to life. Your sense of duty is strong — so strong, often interferes with your pleasures. And your pleasures are pretty intellectual — you like reading, art, and learning more about life. You're the girl who can be totally faithful to her chosen boy. But that boy had better be pretty wonderful, 'cos you've got such high standards for him that he's almost bound to disappoint you. When he does, though, you'll forgive him. You're an angel, after all! The thing that's real missing from your life is good, strong, spontaneous feelings. You've never swept off your feet. (Have angels got feet, anyway?) Even when a really attractive, interesting boy comes along, you're very wary of losing your heart too quickly. A little tiny bit of you wants to — and it would do you good to indulge that little tiny spark from time to time. Go on, let yourself go and really enjoy yourself for once in your life! Otherwise, you end up just too good to be true!

Occasionally your shyness gets the better of you, and it could lead you to miss a lot of what's out there waiting for you. It might be a good idea to work at losing it a bit — for example, that there's a boy who fancies you a lot and is just too shy to do anything about. He needs encouragement and you might need to encourage him. So try and become a bit more outgoing and confident!

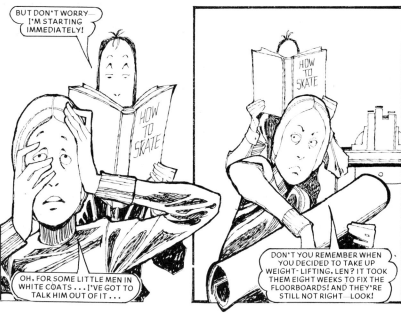

So much for my ideal Christmas . . .

PIERRE, HOW WONDERFUL! I DIDN'T KNOW YOU COULD SKATE!

MAIS, OUI! ALWAYS I AM TAKING THE PART IN THE WINTER OLYMPICS AT GRENOBLE . . .

THE GREAT LIAR! HOW CAN HE BE IN THE OLYMPICS IF HE ALWAYS LANDS ON US AT CHRISTMAS?

BUT LEN CAN SKATE TOO, YOU KNOW, PIERRE!

HE IS LEADING YOU UP THE GARDEN POLE, MYRTLE—HE CANNOT SKATE!

WHAT IS THIS GARDEN POLE? IS IS LIKE THE MISTLETOE?

That Pierre . . . you just have to mention mistletoe and he's away . . .

BUT, MYRTLE . . .

COME, MY LEONARD— KISS ME UNDER THE MISTLETOE! I LOVE THESE CUSTOMS OF THE ENGLISH . . .

It was only later that I realised . . .

AND JUST WHERE HAVE YOU BEEN ALL EVENING?

I HAD TO GET A STOP-WATCH FOR THE SKATE-IN, REMEMBER?

IT TOOK YOU TWELVE HOURS? YOU'VE JUST BEEN AVOIDING PIERRE AND NICOLE!

NEVER MIND THAT—WHY ARE YOU MAKING UP A BED ON THE COUCH? DON'T TELL ME PIERRE'S TAKEN OVER OUR ROOM AGAIN . . .

AND JUST WHAT ARE YOU DOING, LEONARD?

LALA SAID I HAD TO PRACTISE MY SPIN TURNS . . .

It was a long, hard night . . .

AT TWO O'CLOCK IN THE MORNING?

WELL, I CAN'T SLEEP. YOU WON THE TOSS FOR THE COUCH, REMEMBER? THIS FLOOR'S SO COLD I DREAMED I WAS BACK IN THE ICE-RINK, SO I THOUGHT I'D GET IN SOME PRACTICE . . .

PIERRE'S SLEEPING IN MY BED, NICOLE'S DEMOLISHING THE LARDER AND LEN'S PRACTISING SPIN TURNS ALL NIGHT . . . IT MUST BE CHRISTMAS . . .

It must have been the exercise, but I was starving in the morning . . .

LEONARD, THERE'S SOMETHING YOU OUGHT TO KNOW ABOUT YOUR BACON AND EGGS . . .

YES, I HAVE HAD THE SMALL SNACK. WHAT TIME IS THE BREAKFAST?

That did it! I was never going to get to be a champion skater without adequate nourishment. So what I needed was a way to outwit Nicole—in short, a plan to save my bacon . . .

GREAT! EVEN NICOLE WOULD NEVER DREAM OF LOOKING ON TOP OF THE WARDROBE FOR BACON AND EGGS . . .

...OR UNDER THE CUSHIONS FOR A TREACLE TART...

...OR IN RUSS'S BED FOR AN APPLE PIE...

But of course I'd forgotten that there were other people to worry about besides Nicole...

AH, MYRTLE, I ADORE YOU FOR ALL THE TIME. I SHALL NEVER WISH TO LET YOU GO...

YOU MAY NOT BE ABLE TO... WE APPEAR TO BE STUCK TO THE SOFA...

THERE'S A TREACLE TART STUCK TO MY SKIRT! LEONARD, HOW COULD YOU?

I SEEM TO HAVE THE ELBOW IN A BOWL OF SPAGHETTI BOLOGNESE...

I'VE HEARD OF AN APPLE PIE BED BUT THIS IS RIDICULOUS!

I DON'T KOW WHY YOU'RE ALL MAKING SUCH A FUSS. IF IT HAPPENED TO ME, I'D TAKE IT MORE...

...PHILOSOPHICALLY!

WHY, LEONARD, OLD PAL, I DIDN'T KNOW YOU WERE AN EGG-HEAD!

It looked as if I was in trouble again...

BUT MYRTLE...

I HATE YOU, LEONARD! YOU'VE JUST RUINED MY NEW VELVET SKIRT!

COME WITH ME TO THE ICE-RINK, MYRTLE, AND I WILL DEMONSTRATE THE GREAT SKILL...

DON'T YOU BUT MYRTLE ME! GO AND SKATE WITH YOUR PRECIOUS LALA!

NO—SKATE WITH ME, MY LEONARD! I WILL HOLD YOU VERY TIGHTLY!

YOU'VE GOT TO HELP ME, RUSS...WE'VE GOT TO GET RID OF PIERRE AND NICOLE AND MAKE MYRTLE REALISE THAT I'M THE ONE SHE LOVES...

WHAT YOU NEED IS A PLAN...

So...

LOOK, MYRTLE—I BET I'VE GOT MORE SPONSORS FOR THE SKATE-IN THAN ANYBODY ELSE!

LEN! HOW ON EARTH DID YOU MANAGE TO GET THAT MANY?

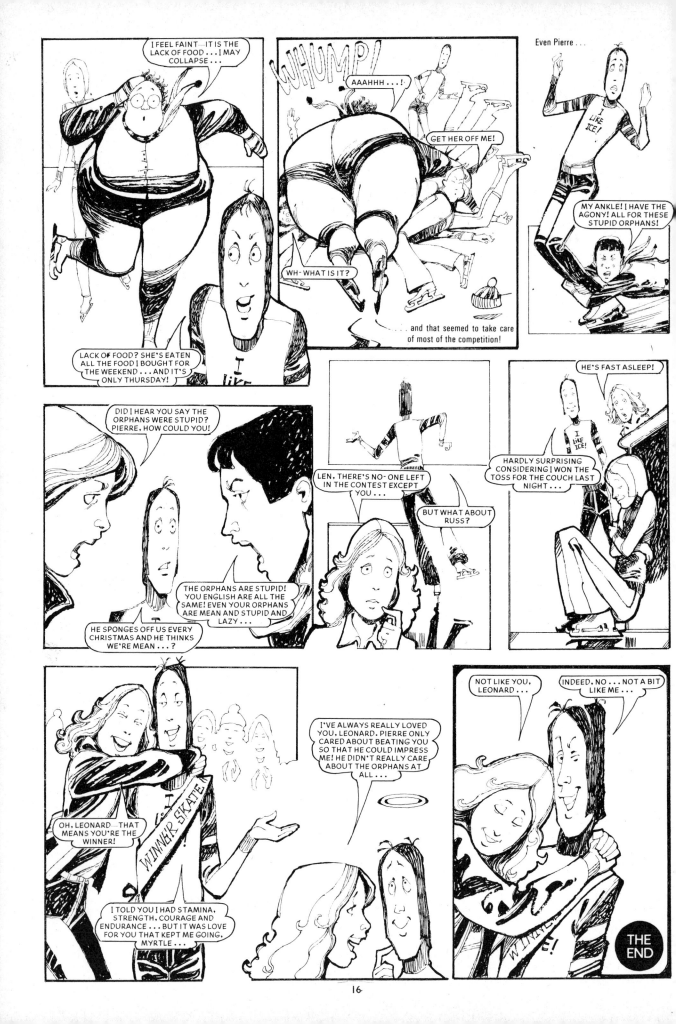

Sometimes it can be hard to settle for a look that's exactly you — moods change, styles change, and occasions vary so much you could end up feeling you *never* get it right. But don't despair if you're having trouble perfecting a natural look, or painting eyes to look their best for a big occasion — here we've created four very definite but very different looks to see you through just about anything you'll ever have to cope with. Follow these basic rules and you'll be coping at your very best!

The Look For You! Beauty Box

It's Only Natural!

For some people, the terms looking natural and wearing make-up just don't mix — they feel make-up has got to be seen to be worthwhile, and aren't at all sure how to achieve a subtle look. But lightly and cleverly applied, a few simple touches of colour can do wonders for your looks and your morale. So for casual, relaxed occasions, we show you how . . .

Firstly, make-up artist Patti dotted foundation all over model Pam's face, then carefully blended it over half the face, to even skin tone and cover any spots or marks. While applying foundation, care should be taken to blend well along the hair line and along the chin, for a natural effect. One tip from Patti is to try foundation colour on the neck when buying a new colour, to pick the shade that's closest to your own colouring. After applying foundation, dust over with translucent powder, to set the base and get rid of any shine.

Brushes for blusher should be chunky, and if you can afford to, invest in a good sable brush, as this is what all the professionals recommend. A soft pink blusher was used for Pam, for a naturally healthy look, and was stroked along the cheekbones, with a touch under the brow.

Patti applied a soft plummy/brown powder shadow under brow and along brow bone, and carefully blended with a medium-sized sable brush. Pink highlighter was used just at the brow, and along the lid. Sky blue crayon was used at the other corner of the eye, close to lashes. Finish off with two coats of black or brown/black mascara. For the finished look, transparent pink gloss was slicked over lips.

T-shirt from Top Shop.
Earrings from Baggage & General.

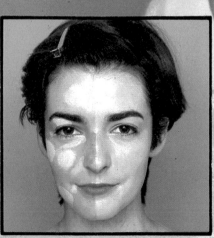

Day by Day!

If you want to look your best during the day, the look you're aiming for has to be light and pretty, without being too bold or overdone. Make-up has to be easy to apply, but individual enough to make a definite statement about your whole personality. Choose shades and colours to blend with the clothes you're wearing, and accessorise to match.

As before, apply foundation and then a dusting of translucent powder. To tone in with Pam's top, Patti used an orangy blusher stroked just under the eyes, just under the brow, stroked from the temple and on the lid, with all strokes meeting and blended to – gether.

Yellow powder was used on the inside of the eyelid, blended towards the bridge of the nose. Orange was stroked on the brow-bone and just under brow. Lime green shadow was dusted on lower part of the upper lid, close to lashes, with bright green eye-liner drawn close to lashes and underneath the eye. Finish off again with two coats of mascara.

Lips were outlined with an orangy/red pencil, and filled in with tangerine lipstick. Hair was softly curled at the front, and Pam slipped on an Alice band to tone with the clothes and make-up shades used.

Blouse from Top Shop.
Earrings and hairband from Baggage & General.

19

Evening All!

Special evening dates are the time to splash out on colour and special effects. Create a sensation by being clever with colour and basic brush work, for a million-dollar look to brighten up anyone's night! Take a few tips from Patti and find out how it's done . . .

Shader is used very effectively alongside blusher for evenings, to shape the face and highlight cheekbones. Wear it under cheekbones, and choose a browny shade, brushed lightly towards the centre of the face and right in at the temples.

Blusher is blended along the cheekbones, slightly overlapping onto the shader. Use highlighter here too, on the very top of the cheekbones, just under the eyes, this time overlapping onto the blusher. Use a touch also above the brow. Then carefully blend shader, blusher and highlighter, to ensure no harsh lines are visible.

Bright blue eye pencil was drawn inside lower lashes, under lower lashes, and very finely along the lid, close to the upper lashes, so that the whole eye is lined in blue. Bright blue shadow was then blended to follow the natural contour of the eye, and accentuated at the outer corner. A lighter, yellow shade was applied to the inner corner of the eye. Hair was clipped back with slides at the side, and lips were painted red — and juicy!

Top by Jeff Banks.
Earrings and hair-slide by Baggage
& General.

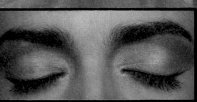

A Touch Of Drama!

Go on — dare to be different! For special parties, and the most exotic evenings, be bold with colour, dramatic in shading and shaping, and confident enough to carry it all off with style! Hide behind your new look if you must, but enjoy being different — just for a change!

Shades of purple, blue and yellow were cleverly blended on the eye. Use the darkest colour to extend the line down from the brows, and the line from under the eye towards the temple, and blend where they meet. Carefully paint a thin line of black eyeliner close to upper lashes, and gradually build up mascara by letting it dry between coats.

Cheek colour is picked to match up with lip colour, and is softly blended to dramatise eyes and lips.

Lips are strong and iridescent, and blotted between coats for longer lasting colour.

Top and shirt, part of matching suit by Jeff Banks.
Earrings by Baggage & General.

MAKE-UP BY PATTI BURRIS

A to Z OF HOW TO MAK

A is for ACCIDENTS

Which *will* happen, and they aren't necessarily anyone's fault! So if you're freaking out at the disco, someone trips, and a glass of Coke suddenly pours itself down your new white dress — do *not* scream and collapse into tears! Also, do not immediately punch the offender on the nose! Soak the stain in cold water in the "Ladies," sponge yourself off, pin a smile on your face — and keep on dancing!

B is for BOYS

Without whom, frequently, life wouldn't be worth living! But if you haven't got a boyfriend, don't despair! It could be you just haven't found anyone you fancy enough yet. Boys need to be handled with TLC (tender loving care)! They must *always* be given the impression *they're* the ones doing the chasing! They must *never* be made a fool of in front of their mates! And you've got to remember that most of the time they're just as worried and scared as *you* are!

C is for COSMETICS

In other words, lipsticks, eye-shadows, cleansers, etc. Do not get conned into believing something in terrific packaging costing three times as much as anything else is the best thing out! Quite often own-make brands, like Boots, are *far* better — as well as cheaper! Basic rule to follow with cosmetics is find a make that suits *your* skin, find colours that compliment your own colouring, and stick with them for a bit. Who *needs* 50 different lipsticks, anyway?

The one thing there is never any point in doing is slobbing around thinking you're a failure! If you want that boy you fancy to notice you, if you want to be pretty, witty and full of personality, well, you can get halfway there at least by making the very most of things – including yourself! If you want to get the very best out of your life, make a start right now by following our extra-special A - Z which tells you all about how to make the very most of yourself!

D is for DAYDREAMS

Which everybody has, but never get so involved in a daydream you can't be bothered with the reality! Daydreams are great for getting you through boring moments at work or at school or on the bus. They're not so great if you drift off into one when your boy's whispering sweet-nothings in your ear and expecting you to answer him!

E is for EYES

Eyes can send a wealth of different messages from, "I love you" to "Get lost, you creep!" Make the most of yours by using complimenting eyeshadows, lashings of non-run mascara, and lots of fluttering! For tired, dull eyes, first rub a little cold cream round them. Dip some cotton wool in witch-hazel water. Lie down. Close your eyes and put the cotton-wool pads on the eyelids. Relax for ten minutes. If you haven't any witch-hazel, a couple of slices of cucumber will do the same trick!

F is for FASHION

And whether you follow it or not is entirely up to you! Always, though, buy clothes that actually suit *you*, and if they're really fashionable but look hideous — forget them! Keep watching Jackie fashion pages, too, for the brightest and best of what's around.

G is for GROWING-UP

Which is frequently a painful process. Try to remember, though, when Mum gives you a lecture for the 50th time, that *she* had to grow up once, too, and that she wasn't always such a nag! Once, *her* mum nagged *her*! All sorts of things happen when you're growing-up. Your body starts changing . . . you're happy as a lark one minute — in the depths of gloom and doom the next. Relax! You're normal! We've all gone through it!

H is for HAPPINESS

Which means different things to different people, so if you find you're at your most ecstatic catching falling leaves or cutting your toenails — ignore anybody who says you're a twit! Just go on being happy! Happiness brings a sparkle to your eyes, a bounce to your step, and generally makes you *feel* like a million dollars. And if you feel that way — there's a good chance you'll look it, too!

I is for INVITATIONS

And they're great things to get! But a quick word of warning. If, for example, you're invited back to *his* place to meet his folks — *do not* turn up looking like a Punk crossed with a Mod. This will only terrify his mum and worry his dad! So whenever you receive an invitation — try to find out about where you're going. You'll feel a right nanna turning up at a disco that doesn't allow jeans in your newest shrink to fits, won't you? And an even *bigger* nanna appearing on a cross-country ramble in footless tights and stilettos!

J is for JEALOUSY

Unfortunately, it's one of those feelings we all experience at some time or another. You can get pangs when you see your boyfriend grinning at his old girlfriend. You can be furious when your best friend starts going out with the dishiest boy in town and suddenly can't meet you every night. Panic not! Just try not to let it get on top of you, because if you're feeling jealous you can say, and do, things you'll later regret. So take deep breaths, think twice before you open your mouth, and *try* not to turn green. (It's a lousy complexion colour, anyway!)

THE MOST OF YOURSELF

K is for KEEPSAKE
In other words, that wilted daisy he gave you on your first date and that you've kept ever since! Keepsakes are great sentimental souvenirs — but they do have snags! If you keep *every* wilted daisy he ever gave you in your underwear drawer, you may not have room for your tights! And if you happen to stumble across one of these daisies two days after you've split from him, you'll just burst into tears. Face it — keepsakes will bring back memories, and they'll also be classified by your mum in sarky moments as "all that rubbish!" So clear them out occasionally!

L is for LOVE
Never underestimate the strength of it. Never play about with it. If you're *not* in love with a guy — don't tell him you are. And don't, either, ever fall for the old line of, "If you loved me, you would . . ." If he loved you, he wouldn't have said *that* in the first place!

M is for MONDAYS
And there is *nothing* good to say about them! They are vile, endless, dreary days, and the only thing you can do with them is get through them without screaming or killing someone! Try, therefore, to make Monday nights special nights, somehow. (Even if you only stay in, have a luxurious smelly bath, then nip early to bed with Jackie and a mug of cocoa-it's *something* to look forward to, isn't it??)

N is for NOTHINGNESS
That awful feeling quite often associated with Mondays! It's a sort of "ugh" where you don't think anything's going to be the same again, and you *know* nobody'll ever understand you — sniff! sniff! Rubbish! That is a very unpositive attitude and you've got to *do* something about it. Nothingness is a frame of mind, so go and spring-clean your wardrobe immediately, or bake a cake, or take the cat for a game of tennis! As long as you stay active — you'll keep the "ughs" at bay.

O is for OPPORTUNITIES
Which should always be grasped firmly with both hands. People who mumble, "I had the opportunity once . . ." are the saddest people around. Don't be like them! If the chance to do something, or go somewhere, or *be* something, crops up — grab it! It doesn't matter how nervous you feel. What *does* matter is that you don't just sit there thinking, "No, I could *never* do that!" That's just soggy! How d'you know anyway — if you don't try!

P is for PEOPLE
Of whom there are all sorts of different types — nice, nasty, and nothing-very-much. If you don't *know* many people — what're you *sitting* here reading this for? Go forth *immediately* and join a club full of the species! Or find a pen-friend! Or start a "People Need People" Society! The more you know, the more fun you'll have — and the more friends you'll make.

Q is for QUARRELS
Not nice things to have. Somebody's granny once said, "Never let the sun set on a quarrel" — and she had a point! If you walk off in the middle, still yelling at each other, it's that bit more difficult to kiss 'n' make up. So avoid quarrels where humanly possible. If you really can't, have a violently spectacular yelling match and get it all out of your system as fast as possible! Then you can start to calm down — and find out what you're *really* arguing about!

R is for RAIN
Which is very damp, we know, but also does wonders for the complexion! All that soft water trickling down your nose may turn it a delicate shade of purple for an hour or two — but think how soft your skin'll feel! And if you don't believe us — try talking to the plants in the garden. They couldn't survive without the stuff!

S is for SLEEP
Which we all need in order to recharge our batteries. About eight hours a night is average, but some people get by on as little as six — while some need ten! Always have your bedroom window open a bit at night — if you go to sleep in a fugged-up room you'll wake up feeling *ghastly*! Don't have too many heavy bed-clothes — you'll just be uncomfortable. And never have a really heavy meal just at bedtime. Apart from stopping you sleeping, it'll very probably give you indigestion!

T is for TALK
Not the every-day, "How are you? Isn't the weather awful?" kind. More the kind when you're really worried or upset and need help. Finding someone you can talk to, and who'll actually *listen* to you, is worth a great deal, because once you've actually started to put what's on your mind into *words* — the worries and anxieties will seem that bit less.

U is for UGLY
Which you're *not* — even if you *think* you are! You may not have the most spectacular face and figure in the world, but d'you have a nice laugh? Are you good fun? Kind? Sincere? Willing to help people? Kind to dumb animals? Then you're *not* ugly!

V is for VICES
Like stuffing yourself with cream-cakes when you're supposed to be on a diet! Buying *another* pair of jeans when you really need a dress! Playing disco sounds at top volume and giving the budgie a headache! Vices, little ones, anyway, are sort of self-indulgent things that don't really matter unless they directly affect someone else. But try never to let the *little* vices grow into *big* ones — or you could be in a whole heap of trouble!

W is for WEATHER
Or rather it's for feeling under it, the weather, that is — and if you're feeling ill, for heaven's sake tell someone about it! Don't be afraid to speak to Mum or go to your doctor — they are there to help, you know. And don't think it's smart struggling on with a streaming cold — it's not, especially when you infect everyone else . . .

X is for XMAS
Or one of the times of the year when you will *certainly* eat too much, drink too much, and have *far too many* late nights! If you want to make the most of yourself — don't accept the third slice of Xmas pudding (unless you want to make the most of yourself in a very *large* way!); do go on a diet on Boxing Day; don't go to parties *every* night of the week; but *do* have a thoroughly good time!

Y is for YOGA
And Yoga exercises are very good for trimming flabby figures, helping you relax, and generally easing aches and pains. Join a class and try. At least you'll meet a load of new people that way!

Z is for ZIP
Both the variety you find on the front of jeans — and the variety that means you're full of get-up-and-go! If the first variety doesn't meet — you *need* those Yoga classes! And if you've got plenty of the second kind — then you already *are* making the most of yourself!

HOW TO PUT HIM OFF YOU!

If you've fancied a certain boy for a while and you want him to start noticing you, it's up to *you* to take the first step — and here's just how *not* to go about it!

AT THE DISCO

Boys are at discos to eye up the talent basically, and, if there's plenty of other female talent around, you have to be *very* careful about what you do and say. Don't dress up outrageously just to catch his eye. You'll catch his eye, all right, and he'll probably have a good laugh at how stupid you look in your leopardskin leotard and orange wig. Don't make an exhibition of yourself by jumping about like a kangaroo on hot desert sand while grinning insanely at him as you jump above the crowd. He *won't* be impressed!

On the other hand, don't stand there trying to look so cool that ice wouldn't melt in your mouth. It may be OK for Clint Eastwood to chew gum and wear shades — but you'll look out of place in downtown Barnsley. And don't stay with your friends for *every* dance — he'll be frightened to approach you! If you *must* be with your mates, don't keep getting the giggles and pointing at him as if he was some prize ape in a monkey house. If you're desperate for him to notice you, don't pretend to fall over in front of him (that's too obvious), and don't walk up and say, "Don't I know you from somewhere?" (that's even more obvious).

Suppose he actually asks you to dance. Try not to ignore him. You know how it is — you *really* fancy the guy so you look at the floor, other people, the ceiling — anywhere but at *him* while you're dancing! On the other hand, don't grin at him with a fixed smile like a finalist in Miss World, and don't for goodness' sake hang around his neck murmuring, "Oh, this means so much to me."

If he offers you a drink, ask for diluted orange, because most boys don't like expensive girls. Above all, don't try to be something you aren't or you're not going to get very far before he sees that you've tried to fool him. Remember that whatever you do he still won't think you're a patch on Hot Gossip, and if he does come over to ask you to dance, don't run to the loo first to fix your face. He won't be there when you get back!

AT SCHOOL

Either he's a new boy or he's been around for ages and is suddenly, quite gorgeously, different and grown-up. Whatever the reason, you fancy him like mad and you know you've got to do something about it. Try not to let your friends know, or they'll make your life a misery. Despite all their promises not to tell a soul, Anne'll tell Mary, who'll tell her brother, whose best mate's Jim, who lives next door to Brian — and HIS name is Brian, then your secret love's no secret any more.

If you travel on the same bus, and you get on first, don't keep the other half of your seat covered with your bag, only to whip it off and smile charmingly at him

when he gets on. Don't deliberately fall on top of him going down the bus stairs, either. He'll just wish you'd drop dead when you arrive in Ward 7 with your stupid smile and a bunch of grapes.

Don't drop your schoolbooks in front of him. He'll either step over them, or pick them up thinking what a clumsy fool you are and he's never even *likely* to fancy you. It's not a good idea to write *I love Brian* all over your bag, the desk, or the blackboard either, because besides being terribly unsubtle, *he'll* be mortified.

Don't change your whole timetable just so that you can sit next to him in Maths or Physics either — this could ruin your whole future career. Also he'll think you're a banana when you say circumference was one of the knights of the Round Table! Don't do stupid things like joining the same clubs as him if you're hopeless at badminton, shocking at swimming, or you don't know which way up to hold the cricket bat — you don't want him laughing as you crash into the net, drown, or knock yourself, rather than the cricket ball, for six!

AT THE LAUNDERETTE

Launderettes are very boring places, where a lot of deep thinking goes on — simply because there's nothing to do but watch the washing go round or fall asleep! Staring at the washing swirling around is conducive to deep thought, so there he is, thinking about tomorrow's home game, not really seeing anything.

Don't disturb him until he sighs deeply and turns to the newspaper or starts chewing his nails. This means he's done

with the thinking — maybe his brain was starting to hurt. So don't start slamming things about, throwing your washing all over, crashing money into the machine, singing "I Got The Washday Blues" and generally being a noisy nuisance.

Don't take along your grottiest undies, mum's tea-towels with half a pot of soup over them and your dog's blanket. He'll think you're a slob and that the dog's blanket is actually *your* blanket.

If, or rather when, you get fed up, don't let him catch you picking at your nose, ears, etc. If you do need change for the machine or the powder dispenser, don't be so obvious as to ask him for it when the woman in charge is in front of you! He'll know straightaway that you're after him.

But don't pretend to be a big know-all about how everything works. If you're lucky, he'll show you how to put the powder in, if you're not, he'll ignore you. Don't for goodness' sake sit down next to him and say, "Nice 'ere, innit?" For one thing, you probably don't look the slightest bit like Lorraine Chase . . .!

THE BOY NEXT DOOR

There's something quite sweet about fancying the boy next door — it's sort of, well, homely.somehow, and *nice*. But unless you go about things the right way and have him fancying you, too, just think how awful it'll be for the poor bloke if he can't get away from you because his house is stuck on to yours!

Don't be too obvious. This means *not* brushing your teeth at the bathroom window every morning when he goes out to feed his rabbit, undressing behind the net curtains in your bedroom every night, or hanging over the garden fence looking for your earring every time the poor guy sets foot outside the back door.

Don't do up your bedroom window to look like a Barbara Cartland boudoir, i.e. single red roses, heart mobiles, volumes of love sonnets, or teddy bears with arms outstretched to next door's drying green — he'll just think you're a soft weedie, or a weedy softie. It's a waste of time spending every free minute gardening for your dad hoping that he'll notice you because it'll only make your hands rough, you'll get cold and fed up, and it's very likely that he'll just think you're a mad keen gardener and the two of you have nothing in common.

Playing blaring pop music, screeching along with The Skids, bellowing to The Boomtown Rats and other such raving

things might convince him that you're a raver, but he'll want you to rave off and do it elsewhere. (This could also make you unpopular with his parents.) Also, don't peer into his parents' lounge window on every one of the hundred occasions you just accidentally-on-purpose happen to be walking past every day. The family, including him, will hate you for being a nosey, gawping ninny, and they'll probably complain to your parents.

AT THE LIBRARY

It could be that you have to use the library for a school project, or even for your own amusement. So one day you stroll in, and there's this lovely guy absorbed in a book at one of the tables. So what don't you do? You *don't* make a noise — not even a discreet little cough, or you'll be *most* unpopular.

Dropping the Encyclopaedia Brittanica is a bit risky — and dangerous. He'd notice you all right, but the thing might land on your foot, and if it gets damaged you'll have to fork out (for the book, not your foot!). He'll also think you're a clumsy oaf with no respect for books (presumably he's fairly keen on the things, or he wouldn't be there).

Don't walk up to him and say, "Excuse me, but I think you have the book I want." He's bound to ask politely how long you've been into agricultural engineering or nuclear physics.

If he's obviously studying and taking notes, don't offer to sharpen his pencil, clean his glasses, turn the pages, etc. He's probably feeling quite irritable enough without your kind offers to interrupt him. If you do manage to get a seat opposite him, don't drop things on the floor just so that you can have the thrill of getting near his feet under the table! He'll soon twig to what you're doing, and you might get kicked. Likewise, don't tie his shoelaces together in the hope that he'll see the funny side of it all when he stands up and falls flat on his face. Studious types often aren't too hot on the humour.

Try not to get into a heavy situation you can't cope with. That is to say, pick books with care before you sit opposite him. It's no good getting involved in a literary discussion over the selected works of Tolstoy that you picked off the shelf, when the nearest you've ever been to "War And Peace" is fighting your kid brother for the last piece of chewing gum — and losing.

Make the most of the long winter evenings by knitting yourself this super threequarter-length, cuddly coat and neat roll-brim beanie, designed exclusively for Jackie by Alan Dart.
We've chosen to knit our coat up in a super tweedy, heathery shade which contrasts well with the pinks, lilacs and blues around just now.

BE A COVER GIRL!

WOOL — Of Patons Husky: 19 (20, 21) x 50 g balls.
NEEDLES — A pair of 6½ mm (No. 3).
PLUS — Five 2.5 cm diameter buttons, a pair of covered shoulder pads and two safety pins.
MEASUREMENTS — To fit 32 (34, 36) in. bust; length 31 in.; sleeve seam 17½ in.
TENSION — 15 sts and 21 rows to 10 cms (4 in.) square measured over pattern.
ABBREVIATIONS — K — knit; P — purl; sts — stitches; dec — decrease by working two stitches together; inc — increase by working into front and back of stitch; tog — together; beg — beginning.
Instructions for larger sizes in brackets.

BACK
Cast on 68 (72, 76) sts and work 8 rows garter-stitch (every row K).
Continue in pattern thus:
1st and every alternate row — Knit.
2nd and 4th rows — (K2, P2) to end.
6th and 8th rows — (P2, K2) to end.
These 8 rows form the pattern.
Work 116 rows in pattern.

Shape armholes — Keeping continuity of pattern cast off 4 sts at beg of next 2 rows 60 (64, 68) sts.
Dec 1 st at beg of next and every following row until 56 (58, 58) sts remain.
Continue without shaping until 166 rows of pattern have been worked from top of garter-stitch hem.

Shape shoulders — Cast off 15 (16, 16) sts at beg of next 2 rows.
Cast off remaining 26 sts.

RIGHT FRONT
Cast on 38 (40, 42) sts and work 8 rows garter-stitch.
Next row — K8, slip these sts on to a safety pin. Working on the remaining 30 (32, 34) sts work 117 rows pattern, commencing with the 1st row.
Shape armhole — Cast off 4 sts, work to end 26 (28, 30) sts.
Next row — Work to end.
Dec 1 st at beg of next and every following alternate row until 24 (25, 25) sts remain.
Continue without shaping until 144 rows pattern have been worked.
Shape neck:
Next row — Cast off 4 sts, work to end 20 (21, 21) sts.
Next row — Work to end.
Next row — Dec 1, work to end.
Repeat the last 2 rows four more times 15 (16, 16) sts.
Work 11 rows without shaping.
Cast off.

LEFT FRONT
Cast on 38 (40, 42) sts and work 8 rows garter-stitch.
Next row — K to last 8 sts, slip these sts on to a safety pin (1st row of pattern).
Working on the remaining sts, and commencing with the 2nd row of pattern, continue without shaping until 116 rows of pattern have been worked.
Shape armhole — Cast off 4 sts, work to end 26 (28, 30) sts.
Next row — Work to end.
Dec 1 st at beg of next and every following alternate row until 24 (25, 25) sts remain.
Continue without shaping until 143 rows pattern have been worked.
Shape neck:
Next row — Cast off 4 sts, work to end 20 (21, 21) sts.
Next row — Work to end.
Next row — Dec 1, work to end.
Repeat the last 2 rows four more times 15 (16, 16) sts.
Work 12 rows without shaping.
Cast off.

SLEEVES (All sizes)
Cast on 44 sts and work 8 rows garter-stitch.

Continue in pattern, commencing with 1st row, thus:
Work 12 rows.
Inc 1 st at beg and end of next and every following 12th row until there are 56 sts on the needle.
Continue without shaping until 90 rows pattern have been worked.
Shape sleeve head — Cast off 4 sts at beg of next 2 rows (48 sts).
Dec 1 st at beg of next 2 rows.
Work 2 rows.
Repeat the last 4 rows until 38 sts remain.
Dec 1 st at beg of next and every following row until 12 sts remain.
Cast off.

POCKETS (2 alike)
Cast on 24 sts.
Work 32 rows patterning, commencing with 1st row of pattern.
Work 8 rows garter stitch.
Cast off.

BUTTON BAND AND COLLAR
Join shoulder seams.
Left button band: Pick up 8 sts from safety pin, rejoin yarn and work 170 rows garter stitch.
Break yarn and slip sts back on to safety pin.
Right button band: Pick up 8 sts from safety pin, rejoin yarn and work 57 rows garter stitch.
*1st buttonhole row: K3, cast off 2 sts, K3.
2nd buttonhole row: K3, cast on 2 sts, K3.
Work 28 rows garter stitch*.
Repeat from * to * two more times.
Repeat buttonhole rows once more.
Work 20 rows garter stitch.
Do not break off yarn, slip the 8 sts on to safety pin.
Pick up neck thus: Pick up left button band 8 sts, 22 sts from left side of neck, 26 sts from back neck, 22 sts from right side of neck and 8 sts from right button band (86 sts).
Work 8 rows garter stitch.
Make buttonhole thus:
Next row: K3, cast off 2 sts, K to end.
Next row: K81, cast on 2 sts, K3.
Work 6 rows garter stitch.
Cast off.

HAT
Cast on 78 sts and work 32 rows garter stitch
Next row: (K2 tog, K9, K2 tog) to end.
Knit 3 rows.
Next row: (K2 tog, K7, K2 tog) to end.
Knit 3 rows.
Next row: (K2 tog, K5, K2 tog) to end.
Next row: Knit.
Next row: (K2 tog, K3, K2 tog) to end.
Next row: Knit.
Next row: (K2 tog, K1, K2 tog) to end.
Next row: Knit.
Next row: (K3 tog) to end.
Next row: Knit.
Break wool, thread through sts on needle an draw up.

MAKE UP: Press all pieces lightly on th wrong side. Join button bands to fronts. Jo side and sleeve seams. Sew sleeves int armholes. Position pockets and sew o Position buttons and sew on. Sew in should pads. Join hat seam. Press all seams lightly

WE'RE GONNA MAKE YOU A STAR.

Well, that record certainly worked wonders for David Essex, but then things went a bit down hill when he started sporting this moody, gypsy look. Thankfully David has now shaved this lot off and we can all see his cute features once again . . .

Silver Dream

WANT TO DO A SWAP?

Just take a look at Noel here in his hippy days. What a difference a few years make. Take a close look at the lace-up shirt and faded jeans—really trendy. Now Mr Edmonds has cultivated a totally different look. We hardly recognised him when we found this old shot of him minus his famous streaks.

GUESS WHO?

Do you ever cringe with embarrassment when your mum produces the holiday snaps from a few years ago and you see exactly how you used to look? We bet you do! And the stars are no exception to this! So, just for fun, we decided to cause a few red faces by digging through our archives for old shots of some top stars to see how they looked ' then ' and how they look ' now ' . . .

MESSAGE IN A BOTTLE.

The message must have come in a bottle of peroxide for the top cops. In our photograph, which is bound to have front man Sting blushing to his dark roots, we think they've all overdone things just a little with the bleach. We prefer the slightly more rugged look the band have now.

DO YA THINK I'M SEXY?

No, not here we don't, Rod. Just a glance at your Lurex top is enough to send shivers up our spines—it's awful! We're glad that the above single wasn't on release when you looked like this, otherwise it probably wouldn't have sold a single copy!

IN THE MOOD FOR DANCING!

Note the natty white suits, platform shoes and clean wholesome look that The Nolan Sisters were sporting a few years ago.
Now The Nolans have not only changed their name, but their image as well. These days the girls have got a much more sultry look and go through a bucketful of lip gloss at each performance.

Fly Me To The Moon

Specially written by Mary Hooper

good job it was after six and cheap rate. As she rattled on about who did and who didn't fancy her, I turned round, ever so slightly, so that I could see the boy, next door out of the corner of my eye.

He was still looking in my direction, or maybe he was just gazing past me and into the distance where his true love was.

"I have long 'admired you from afar...' he was saying, and I would have liked to listen to more but Sara said. "Patty! Aren't you listening to me? Who d'you think I should choose?"

"Oh, the first one." I said, hoping I sounded as if I knew what she was talking about.

"Peter? But I thought you said he sounded big-headed?" "Not... not madly big-headed..." I said hastily.

"Y OUR eyes are like emeralds," the boy in the telephone box next to mine was saying clearly. "Your hair is as black as the raven's wing, your lips are like..."

I giggled down the phone. "You should just hear this boy in the next phone box!" I said. "The patter he's giving some girl!"

"What's he like?" my friend Sara said on the other end of the phone.

"Hang on, I'll look," I said, and I made a pretence of fiddling in my purse for more money and dropped it on the floor. When I turned round to pick it up, there he was, staring at me.

"Not bad!" I said to Sara in a low voice. "Quite dishy, in fact. I haven't seen him round here before."

"What's he saying now?"

I strained to hear him. It wasn't very hard because there were two panes of glass missing at the bottom of the booth.

"Your legs are like twin marble columns!" I whispered to Sara, and snorted with laughter.

"Twin marble columns indeed!" Sara said. "Fat and white, in other words. The bloke who said that to me would be in trouble, I can tell you!"

We giggled for a while and then I went on to tell her about what had been happening round the place since last week — which wasn't a lot. Sara was away on a college course for three months and I'd promised faithfully to ring her every Friday so that she could keep up with all the gossip.

"It's really quite boring," I said. "I mean, no-one's fallen madly in love with me, or anything like that."

"So what else is new?"

"And no-one seems to be pining away for love of you, either," I added.

"I expect they are — they just don't like to mention it to you," she said.

She was probably right. Sara was really pretty and got all the attention when she was home.

"What about up there, then?" I asked. "There must be lots of fanciable

"Oh, all right, then," she said reluctantly, "though I actually preferred Mike."

Then the pips went and I'd run out of coins. I suppose it sounds disloyal but — I did get ever so slightly fed-up with helping my best friend choose between boys when there never seemed to be anyone for me to choose between.

"Ring me next week?" she shouted. "Same day, same time," I said, and she was gone.

W HEN I'd picked up my bag and purse, the boy in the phone box next door had gone, too, which was a pity because I'd have liked to have had a good long look at him. Boys who quoted poetry — well, practically poetry — were pretty rare animals. Almost extinct, I would have said.

Yet he hadn't looked at all peculiar. He'd looked fun — as if he'd been saying all those things tongue in cheek and the girl had known it was a joke.

I couldn't stop thinking about him for several days after that, and the funny thing was, even though I'd only looked at him for a split second, his face was kind of printed on my mind. It was all quite ridiculous, but it seemed I had a little bit of a crush on him.

It was ridiculous because I'd only seen him for a moment and probably would never see him again, and it was madly in love with this wonderful girl he'd been speaking to — this Greek Goddess with the emerald eyes and raven hair.

I sighed to myself when I thought about that. It would be nice to have a boy think I was a Greek Goddess, even if it was only in a joking sort of way.

I told myself that I'd probably never see him again, and that it would do me absolutely no good at all if I did anyway, but that didn't stop me washing my hair as soon as I got in from college on Friday and doing it in a few plaits at the front to make it more interesting, and

then putting on my newest dress and borrowing my sister's pink stilettos, I felt really quite acceptable when I'd finished. Not up to Sara's standard, perhaps, but at least better than normal.

I held my breath as I approached the corner where the two telephone boxes were, but they were empty. I let my breath out in a sigh of disappointment and then whistled a little whistle as I opened the door to the first one — just to let anyone who might be interested see that I wasn't in the least bit put out because he wasn't there.

I DIALLED Sara's number and she picked up the phone almost immediately. "The most marvellous thing has happened!" she shrieked. "James wants me to go home and meet his mum and dad!"

"James?" I said, mystified. "What happened to Peter and Mike?"

"Oh, them!" she said, and she proceeded to tell me exactly what had happened to them, not leaving out any details.

I suppose my mind must have wandered again, for suddenly I heard, "I long to soar with you through a jet-black sky studded with diamond stars, to feel your arms around me..."

Before I could stop myself I'd turned and was staring into the eyes of the boy in the next phone box. I blushed and turned away.

"Are you listening?" Sara said crossly. "I said what shall I take James's mother when I go to visit?"

"Flowers?" I said weakly. He had the most gorgeous eyes framed with long, thick lashes.

"Flowers?! I've just told you — she's allergic to flowers!"

"Handkerchieves!" I said. "If you're allergic to things you need lots of hand-kerchieves."

It wasn't fair. The most interesting, delectable boy I'd ever seen and he was pouring out his

love to some girl miles away. How could life be so cruel to me?

"Y OUR neck is like that of a swan — white and smooth as silk to the touch..."

I shivered just as the pips went. "I've got to go!" I said to Sara. "I'll ring next week."

"Your toes are like... like..." the boy went on.

He'd run out of words — he was actually struggling!

I turned round to look at him. "Little piggies?" I supplied, and we both burst out laughing.

"Sorry!" I said through the glass. "It just came out. I didn't mean to be rude."

He replaced the receiver slowly and came out of his phone box. I picked up my bag and did the same.

"You didn't say goodbye to her," I said.

"That's because she wasn't there," he said.

I stared at him stupidly. Either he was mad or I was.

"No-one there?" I repeated.

"I'd better explain," he said. "I've seen you down there before ringing your friend, but you never seemed to notice me. I thought if I said some outrageous things, you'd be sure to..."

"Well!" I said, and then I said "Well!" again. "So you weren't talking to anyone, really."

"Only you," he said a bit shyly.

"Me? Eyes like emeralds?" I said.

"Eyes like cornflowers, then?" he said.

"Tell me more," I said, and walked into the park and sat there talking until the sun went down. Until in the dark my hair looked as black as the raven's wing, actually.

After that he walked me home and kissed me goodnight quite deliciously. When I meet him tomorrow I must remember to ask him about the bit about legs like twin marble columns. Though I dare say I shall forgive him anyway.

FASHION for 1981 looks exciting and original, but you'll probably have to adapt the styles to make up for shrinking finances!

You must use your imagination when it comes to choosing a "look." Don't try to copy faithfully every fashion page style, but use them to inspire you and help you to develop your own special look.

Basically, you'll find styles which fall into four *general* categories — sporty, elegant, soft and pretty, and practical chic.

Our two main photographs show really stylised outfits, which, if you can put them together, make definite statements about fashion, rather than reflecting a mood or a way of life.

The great thing about fashion just now is that you *can* wear anything you want to, but remember, it's not *what* you wear, but the *way* that you wear it. Don't be a slave to fashion, but dress to suit *your* personality, *your* lifestyle and *your* pocket.

Always wear the clothes, don't let *them* wear *you* — remember to dress in whatever you feel most comfortable, and those styles which you know suit you. It's originality that counts!

1. Elegant

Take a plain V-necked, button-up T-shirt dress, and transform it by wearing it back to front. Add a thin belt, toning or contrasting shoes, and make the look extra special by wearing a pair of pretty gloves.

The flat shoes could be worn with the same dress, too. Add a pair of ankle socks and you'll have a casual look.

2. Practical chic

Down-to-earth, but stylish clothes are acceptable just about anywhere (except, perhaps, at a coming-out ball!). Colours can be bright, contrasting, but never dull.

You have to be quite adept at co-ordinating, but if you keep up with current trends, you'll be able to adapt your basic wardrobe, and add accessories in the latest colours and styles.

3. Sporty

If you're not terribly interested, or just don't have the time for fashion (high fashion, at least), you'll still want to look good. A basic, colourful and sporty look is your line.

Make plain, practical jackets brighter by wearing fun scarves, brightly-coloured patterned jumpers, and brilliant socks. Smaller items like the latter, and bags, shoes and belts come in colourful, sporty styles, so you know that whatever your particular outdoor craze, you'll be looking and feeling good!

4. Soft and pretty

All the new candy pastels can be worn anytime, anywhere, but they do lend a much more cuddly, soft touch to your look! If you want to be a femme fatale, steer clear of the baby colours!

You'll find ski pants and soft tops, like these, easy to wear and quite adaptable. Dresses look really pretty in pastels – ice-cream pinks, mint and lemon suit most people, whatever the colouring, and you can dress them up or down to suit your lifestyle.

1

2

3

4

Something In The Way He Looks

Does he love you? Does he hate you? Do you bore him, drive him wild, or simply send him to sleep? You can find out all these things and more with the help of our extra special feature on body language! Here's everything you need to know about all those mysterious facial expressions of the boy in your life — and what they *really* mean!

1. THE DAZZLER
A dazzling smile, dancing eyes, not a trace of shyness or second thoughts about anything . . . If this is the way he looks when he meets you, well, you've got absolutely nothing to worry about! He's well and truly hooked. There's nothing false about the smile, so count your blessings — and smile back, of course!

2. THE DOUBTER
Oh, dear, what have you done? Let him down in some way, that's what! Could be he thinks you're lying; could be that you're saying or doing something he disapproves of. The under-the-eyebrows look shows that he's signalling to you to come clean, and his pursed lips show he's none too pleased!

3. LITTLE BOY BLUE
Downcast eyes are a sure sign of depression — and that he can't face looking you in the eye. There's a downward-turning, discontented look to his mouth, too, that shows all too clearly how cheesed off he is. If it's about you — put it right! And if it's about something else, force him to tell you.

4. LOVER BOY
He fancies you, all right, and what's more, he's pretty sure you ought to fancy him. His eyes have a thoughtful look — he's giving you the once over. He's looking confident and is obviously very sure of himself. You've certainly made an impression on him, and within 5 minutes he's going to make a pass, so . . . watch out!

5. THE SNEERER
This guy's feeling pretty superior. See the sneering half-smile playing around his lips and nose? And those sarcastically-raised eyebrows? He may be feeling hurt, angry, or just malicious, but whatever it is, somebody's going to get a mouthful of sneer any minute! If it's you, make a quick exit. You've got nothing to lose but a few insults!

6. THE GIGGLER
This guy's feeling absolutely fine — the way he's thrown his head back, showing all his teeth and opening his mouth means he's totally relaxed. Bright, sparkling eyes show he's feeling really good — and the whole impression is one of terrific happiness. Could you be the cause of this insane joy? If so, you're laughing, if you see what we mean!

7. THE THINKER
Touching his nose is always a sign of doubt. Basically he's pretty interested in something (or someone). You can tell that by the way his eyes are looking sideways into space. He has his doubts, though he's not too put off. He's likely to make a grab for whatever it is (Doughnut? Job? Girl?) pretty soon!

8. THE DOZER
Eyes closing, face slumping . . . either he's practising meditation, or yoga, or he's so bored with you, he's dropping off! So sharpen up your small talk quick, before he nods off completely! It could just be lack of sleep. Was he up all night writing love poems to you?!

9. SHY GUY
He likes you, he really does. But do *you* like *him*? He's not at all sure how you feel about him. He's smiling, but it's not a proper smile. His eyes are alert, open for any tell-tale signs that you don't really like him. Put the poor guy out of his misery — give him a great big hug, or tell him to go!

As winter settles in, and the party season looms into view, isn't it about time you stopped hiding all that flab under these winter woollies? Squeezing your bulk into clinging party outfits isn't going to be easy, so, it's *desperation* time . . . and here are a dozen *extremely* desperate measures for shaping up . . . *fast!*

To Get Yourself Into Shape...

1. The Buddhist Special

Fast! *Fast* for *fast* results! Take a leaf out of the mystical Eastern religions books and have a day's fast once a week.

Method:
Be sensible, and read up about this one. Drink fruit juices so you don't dehydrate, and don't play a game of squash or something daft like that, or you'll faint. Then watch your diet carefully for the rest of the week.

Result:
You should feel spiritually and physically a *lot* better.

2. Scare The Inches Off

A good way of seeing lots of horror movies and keeping on your toes.

Method:
Own up to yourself what really scares you, and then embark on a good diet of Boris Karloff, ''Lives Of Snakes'' films, or whatever turns you off. Think about it all at meal-times, or fasten your eyes on your little brother's caterpillar collection.

Result:
You might end up with grey hair, but you *should* be thinner . . . !

3. Think Revolting Thoughts

This one is *not* unlike the scarifying method. It's a case of mind over fat matter.

Method:
At meal-times, gaze at that delicious pile of crispy, golden chips and imagine them as a pile of worms. Then reckon how slimy worms would feel when you bit them, and then *try* and stop there before you have to leave

the table and rush for the loo.

Result:
You don't eat anything because you keep thinking of wiggly, slimy — 'scuse me . . . !

4. The Studious Way

This is for the logically-minded, who like to know *exactly* what's what.

Method:
Arm yourself with information. Slimming leaflets, calorie counters, weight charts, a book with your ideal weight and measurements written down, etc. Then work out how much you can eat per day, write it down with your weight loss and have a lovely time drawing little graphs in different - coloured pens.

Result:
You'll bore your friends to death with calorie talk, and drive boys away when you recoil at the calorific content of a half pint of beer, but you'll end up annoyingly thin and smug!

5. Jog It Off

Another measure best suited to the organised person.

Method:
Draw up a plan of how much free time you have during the day, i.e. an hour before work, lunch-time, two hours in the evening, etc. Then work out which forms of exercise you like best and get to it. A swim first thing every morning would be the most beneficial.

Then do a course in badminton, or tap dancing or even *ballet*.

Result:
Provided you're not so hungry afterwards you fall into a large plate of fry-ups, you'll look and feel 100 per cent. better.

6. Clock Watching

This is for those of us who nibble because we're bored. Because we're sitting around near some food, waiting for a meal, or waiting for work to end, or waiting for a boy to arrive, etc., etc.

Method:
If you can sit down and be honest with yourself, and admit when and how often, and *how* much you do this, you're halfway there. Make sure you're somewhere else at those times, reading, or talking on the phone, or doing some sewing or tidying that really needs doing, and you'll find the eating urge passes.

Result:
A tidier, more informed, more literate, *thinner* you!

7. The Points System

This is basically for the zany-minded who just *love* playing games.

Method:
Devise your own rules of reward and punishment — something like every time you sneak a Mars bar you have to run twice round the block and do fifty jumps. Or for every time you walk past the corner shop without sneaking in for a little snack, buy a new lip-stick or a glittery hair comb, or simply keep tabs on the money you're saving.

Result:
A lot of very startled neighbours as you speed guiltily past the windows!

8. Face The Ghastly Facts Time

This is own-up time for those of us who won't own-up, but stand in front of mirrors at special angles breathing in hard and pretending all's well.

Method:
Buy the most beautiful bikini you've ever seen. Buy it in the size you'd like to be. Go home

and wriggle into it. Stand in front of the mirror without breathing in and have a box of Kleenex ready for the hysterics. If you're really going to torture yourself, swear your mum to secrecy and get her to take a picture of you in it. Carry it around, plus the bikini if it makes you feel even more strong-minded, and sneak glances at them when you're about to reach out for a biscuit or crisp.

Result:
You'll be able to get into it one day. But make sure that photograph doesn't reach enemy hands!

9. The Self-Embarrassment Special

You need a strong personality and ego to bear up to this one. If you're very sensitive, *don't* try it.

Method:
Make a habit of jumping on to those ''I Speak Your Weight'' machines in crowded shopping areas, sea fronts or stations. Stand unflinchingly as the machine bellows the ghastly news to the assembled throng. Do it in front of your boyfriend if you think he's strong enough to cope with the facts. Force yourself to read ideal weight charts . . . and take *action!*

Result:
You'll probably lose one very embarrassed boyfriend — but you'll also lose ten very embarrassing pounds.

10. The Photo Special

Start a huge picture collection of all the slim, glamorous stars you *most* envy.

Method:
Cut out all the pictures, plus really lovely clothes you'd like to wear if you were three stone thinner, and paste them in a huge collage on a board. Intersperse pictures of you looking really ghastly, and prop it up in your bedroom or

somewhere reasonably private where you can look at it a lot. Memorise all the good and the bad things on it. Think about it a *lot* at meal-times.

Result:
You'll get a much clearer idea of how you'd like to look, and if you're sufficiently dedicated you should end up looking that way, too!

11. Safety In Numbers

Go on a diet with a friend. This is a mini-weight watchers method, which relies on the fact that it's much easier to be with people in a similar plight who have to suffer alongside you.

Method:
Compare notes with your friend *meticulously*. It would be good if you both needed to lose the same number of pounds, because then the competition is even keener. Ruthless honesty is needed, weighing in in front of each other every week. It's much more fun moaning when there's two of you!

Result:
You can go on a joint shopping spree for your lovely new clothes.

12. Sponsored Slim

This is a good way, as it makes it known you're slimming, and involves other people, so you'll feel doubly feeble if you fail.

Method:
Pick your favourite charity (it's better not to consider yourself a charitable cause, or you may find people less eager to sponsor you!) and then get as many friends and acquaintances as you can to put money on each pound you lose. With all that money pinned to your efforts, you're gonna have to try, because you'll feel a terrible twit handing 25p over to Dr Barnardo!

Result:
Lots of good feelings all round.

Boy Talk

Father Christmas may have forgotten Danny — but he still has high hopes for the New Year . . .

ALTHOUGH I still believe in Father Christmas, I think he's stopped believing in me. Maybe I said something to upset him. Whatever the reason, he hasn't been around to fill up my stocking for the last few Christmases.

I suppose this Christmas will be just the same. In spite of all my wishing, I bet I don't wake up on Christmas morning to find Debbie Harry dangling in my stocking on the bedpost. Oh, well . . .

Still, Christmas is a great time, isn't it? Even when the old guy with the white beard and red coat has forgotten you. I mean, there's mistletoe, turkey, parties, mistletoe, Christmas pud, gifts from the family, and more mistletoe.

I just hope the parties I go to this year are as good as some of last year's. Come to think of it, all the parties I went to last year were fantastic — except one. And that *was* a drag.

It just didn't take off for some reason. But I made the best of a bad job and chatted up the best-looking girl in the place.

After a while I said, "This is just about the worst party ever. Why don't we sneak away and go somewhere else?"

She said OK and we slipped away to the disco and had a terrific time.

"Who's throwing that party, anyway?" I asked.

"I am," she said. "It's my party."

I got a bit big headed, then. I mean, not many guys could charm a girl away from her own party, could they? But I wasn't quite so pleased with myself at 4 a.m. as I staggered homeward suffering from a bad case of dish-pan hands. I'd let her talk me into taking her home after the party and helping her clear up the mess.

Did you know that when you kiss someone under the mistletoe you're supposed to pick off one of the berries? When all the berries are gone — no more kissing.

I'm glad that particular custom seems to have died out. I wouldn't like the idea of dragging some poor girl around all over the place looking for a piece of mistletoe that hadn't used up all its kissing power. I'd have to carry a supply of spare berries and a tube of glue around with me.

I WAS haunted a bit last Christmas by a girl called Janet. I went to three different parties and each time she was there. And she kept hanging around me. She fancied me but I didn't go for her.

Sad when that happens, isn't it? Usuall it's the other way round. I go for som unbelievable doll and she freezes me out.

This time it was me doing the freezing. Onl Janet didn't freeze easy. Every time I tried t chat up another girl she'd be hovering clos by, joining in the chat and generally slowing me down.

At the third party she came up to me an said, "I know. I'll go and hide, and if you car find me I'll let you kiss me."

I think she was under the impression I was bit shy and that's why I hadn't kissed he before.

"If you have any trouble finding me," she said, "I'll be behind the sofa."

I went back out on to the landing to take up with Jeannie where I'd left off. Come to think of it, I didn't see Janet again. You don' reckon she's still crouched down there behind that sofa, do you?

The nice thing about Christmas, apart from the mistletoe and the fun and genera whoopee, is that we're just about to star another year.

It's called 1981; better make a note of i before you forget. A whole new year, absol utely untouched. All those days lying ahead waiting to be lived in.

This could be the year when everything goes right. That's what I keep telling myself anyway.

I'm going to win on the Premium Bonds and buy myself that Ducati 900 SS. What a bike 864 cc, overhead cam, V-twin engine, with top speed of 131 m.p.h.

Makes your mouth water, doesn't it? I doesn't? Well, it does mine.

And I'm going to meet some fabulous girls You may not know this but girls and moto bikes are my two weaknesses. The chances are you've already noticed.

1981 might just turn out to be *the* great year. Hope it is for you, too.
Love,
Danny

CONTAIN YOURSELF!

Take some pretty boxes and tins, a little imagination, and you're on the way to organising and brightening up your room!

Is your room littered with bits and pieces? Do you find yourself scrabbling through piles of make-up, kirby grips, old letters, notes and junk just to get hold of a pencil? If so, take a tip from us, and start boxing everything away in easily accessible containers like the ones we've got together here . . .

JUNK SHOP FINDS

Visit markets, jumble sales and junk shops for boxes and tins of all shapes and sizes. You're bound to come across both large and small wooden boxes and old tins which would make ideal containers for letters, important papers and photographs. Some may need to be cleaned, and you might also like to try re-varnishing the more battered finds. This can be done relatively cheaply, too.

DUAL PURPOSE CONTAINERS

Tins which once contained Ovaltine, cocoa, tea, syrup, biscuits, etc., are really very pretty, and well worth buying for use after the contents have been consumed.

Tall tins are ideal for storing pens and pencils, and look great on a desk. Smaller, attractive sweet tins are super for keeping fiddly things like earrings together.

Have a look round your local supermarket — you'll be surprised at the number of brand-name tins which can be used in this way. Many manufacturers are bringing back the original containers for their products — perhaps with re-use in mind?

BRAND NEW

Most good gift and craft shops stock an amazing number of boxes and tins, which, although not exactly inexpensive, make nice present ideas, and are attractive to own.

You'll find many Indian-design, carved wooden boxes, and all sorts of tins bearing brand names. These are often copies of Victorian product containers such as Sunlight Soap, Camp Coffee, etc.

If you browse around some of the places we've suggested you're sure to come up with a selection of useful and decorative containers. You'll probably end up with a valuable collection!

34

Graphology is the science of writing, and by looking at someone's writing you can tell an awful lot about them — things that they don't even know themselves! By studying graphology, you can tell if you're liable to get on well with someone, what sort of personality they have, if money is more important to them than relationships — and lots of other little secrets they're giving away without even realising it! So if you want to find out exactly what the people in your life are really like, just read on!

Get It Write!

First of all, look at this word:

lung

← UPPER ZONE
← MIDDLE ZONE
← LOWER ZONE

There are three zones in writing, as you can see, and if unlike the example here, your zones aren't equally balanced, this means your interest in life lies in the zone which is the largest.

UPPER ZONE

If this is very tall and looped, this means you're intelligent, have high ideals and a good imagination. Loops signify emotion — the wider the loop the more emotional you are.

MIDDLE ZONE

This is the social zone. If this part of your lettering is large it means you enjoy the present, being among and talking to people. If there is very little upper or lower zone and the letters are rounded, then this is a sign that you're a little lazy and immature. You enjoy all the little luxuries in your life.

Thick, heavy strokes mean you love loud music, bright colours, warmth, food and drink. If your middle zone is small and you can hardly read it then this means you are shy and a little self-conscious. You may be very clever, but you find social occasions a bit of a strain.

LOWER ZONE

Down-to-earth people always have a long, full, lower zone — and this means that they're also very interested in money. Look at your g's — if they're long like this *g* this is a sign that you are happy and emotionally satisfield. A g like this *g* means you're unwilling to get emotionally involved.

If all the lower zone letters are long and looped then you have an interest in sport and are physically fit. Interest in money can also be seen by the way you write certain letters. For instance, if I is written l, or the letter g like this q, or y like this y, or even more obviously an L like this £ then this person spends a good deal of time thinking about money!

If all the ends of the words stop short and the writing has a leftward slope then this, like very small writing, is a sign of meanness. However, a right slant and long loops at the end of words signify generosity. This is usually a sign of an extrovert too, as long as the writing is broad. Right slant people are ambitious and look to the future, whereas a left slant is the opposite. It signifies an attachment to the past, and a cautious, reserved nature. People with left slanted writing are very loyal to a few friends but often selfish and shy.

Someone who writes with an upright style often thinks carefully before they act. They're a bit cool and aloof — especially if there are no loops in their handwriting. Independence and stubborness are two of their traits, especially if the ends and beginnings of the words slope down, or if there are little hooks on some letters.

If the writing is angular the person could be aggressive, e.g., y or g especially if the pen is pressed into the paper. Also if the cross of the t comes to a thick end, e.g., t then this is a sign of a quick temper.

Gentle, kind people usually write with a thin pen, and have a right slant, no angles and lots of rounded loops.

A mixed slant is a person who is moody, and keeps changing their ideas but who is very versatile and gets on with almost everybody.

If all the letters are joined together, then this is a sign of strength, especially if there's also a right slant. This writer is practical, logical and has an indifferent attitude to most people. They'll never act on impulse — everything has to be clearly thought out. If you and your boyfriend have linked writing then you'll get on well, but if one of you has breaks in it, then watch out!

Look at the little a's and o's to find out if someone is trustworthy. If they're quite wide at the top and slanting to the right, this is an open, honest, but talkative person who finds it difficult to keep a secret and loves a good gossip. If they're open to the left this signifies a deceitful streak and a person with writing like this may not be a good friend. However, if the o's and a's are closed at the top with no loops inside, this shows the person is reliable, can keep a secret, and isn't very talkative. If someone's a's look like this a or æ they're to be watched and not completely trusted.

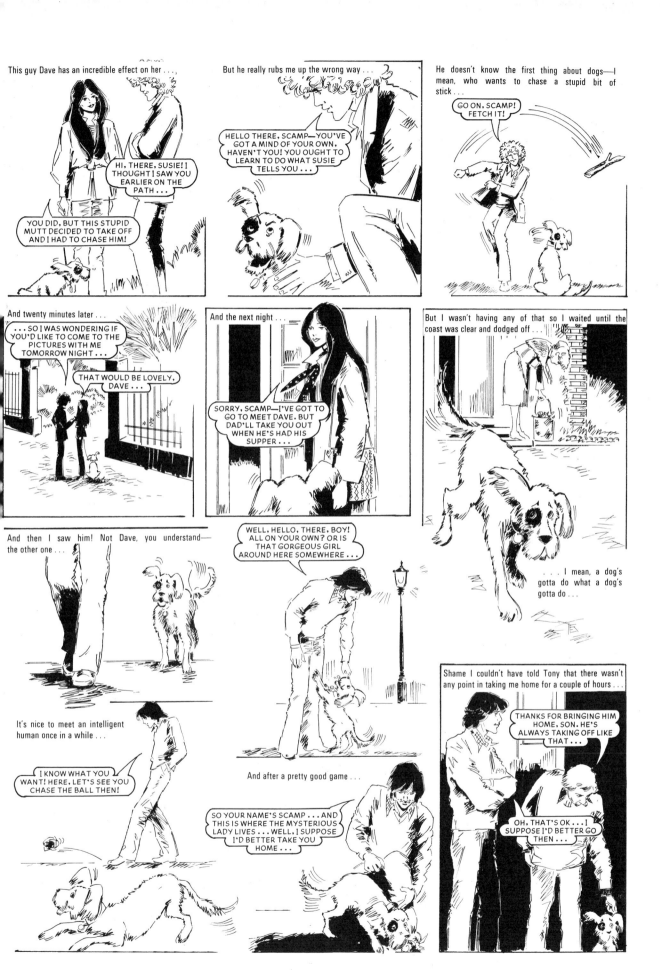

Season's Eatings!

Christmas is traditionally the season for parties and family reunions, so now's your chance to contribute to the festive table.

We've selected a few tasty but simple recipes which will make your mouth water, and we've also included some suggestions for sandwich fillings.

Get down to some simple cooking, and brighten up the table or tree!

Nut Muffins

225g/8oz. self-raising flour
Pinch of salt
50g/2oz. sugar
75g/3oz. chopped walnuts
2 beaten eggs
50g/2oz. melted butter
150 ml/5 fl. oz. milk

Sift flour and salt into a bowl. Gradually beat in all the remaining ingredients until a smooth batter is formed.

Pour into 12 well-greased patty tins, put the tins into the oven, pre-heated to 350 deg., or Gas Mark 5, and bake for about 20-25 minutes (or until a knife inserted into the centre comes out clean).

Cool in the tins for about 5 minutes and then transfer to a wire rack.

Christmas Tree Biscuits

1 lb. flour
½ lb. sugar
4 eggs

Cream eggs and sugar for 10-15 minutes. Add the flour to make a stiff dough. Roll out the dough on a floured board and cut out with small star, Christmas tree or angel-shaped cutters.

Brush with the beaten yolk of an egg and bake in a hot oven (350 deg.-400 deg.) for about 10 minutes or until golden brown.

When cool, decorate the biscuits with icing and leave to harden. Hang the biscuits on your Christmas tree with Christmas string.

Sandwich Fillings:

Smoked sardines and watercress.

Grated cheese and grated apple, mixed with mayonnaise.

Cream cheese and chopped celery.

Cream cheese and chopped cucumber.

Grated carrot and mayonnaise with sliced chicken.

Chopped, tinned pineapple and chutney.

Use brown bread if you can, or one slice of white and one of brown for an unusual looking sandwich!

Apricot Shake

Blend the contents of a large can of apricots in the mixer. Put into a glass jug, and at the last moment, add two bottles of ginger ale.

Something nice or silly or both for you to do every single month of the year!

'A Dotty Dozen'

January: January brings the sales so make sure you're fighting fit for staying out all night outside shops, or elbowing your way to the front of hordes of screaming housewives anxious for bargains, by doing lots of exercise! Don't forget to bring in the New Year in style, too – a great excuse to kiss all these boys you've had your eye on since **last** January.

February: The biggest date this month is St Valentine's Day. Write all your own verses this time, and apologise to the postman in advance for the extra mail he'll have to carry.

March: This is the month of the Mad March Hare, so it's an ideal time for doing lunatic things like wearing one leg in red tights and the other in yellow. Top it off with green shoes and you're bound to make a hit, if you're not locked up first! Remember to wear a shamrock for St Patrick's Day on the 17th and a daffodil for St David's Day on the 1st.

April: The weather is getting warmer so now is the time to burst out of your woollen cocoon and be on your guard for April Fool's Day tricks or you may end up glued to your seat or eating pepper sweets. It's St George's Day on the 23rd so wear a rose behind your ear.

May: Celebrate May Day by dancing round the May-pole – try not to get tied up in all those ribbons though. Hire a boat and go boating on the local lake – it's just the weather for it now. Start to stock up on suntan lotions so you'll be all ready for the sunbathing season!

June: Why not send the Queen a card to mark her 54th birthday, the official date is the 14th so don't forget! June 21 is the longest day of the year – get up with the sun and go to bed when it sets. Most important: don't forget Father's Day – buy a huge sloppy card and give him a big hug!

July: The sunbathing season should be well under way by now, and if you're not lapping up the sun you ought to be ashamed of yourself. Why not celebrate the 4th of July with an American-style meal, hot dogs and Coke, or turkey and cranberry sauce?

August: Now is the time to plant hyacinth bulbs for them to bloom around Christmas time. Take a trip down to the beach to watch all the beach boys showing off and splashing about in the water. Don't forget to have your summer holiday films developed.

September: Make the most of the last warm rays of the sun – go fruit-picking. Start to sweep up the leaves in your garden, your father will be really pleased. You can make jam with all that fruit you've collected – nice, sticky, sweet and fattening – Mmm . . . Try it on bread while it's still hot – lovely!

October: Now is the time to start knitting your winter woollies in preparation for the long cold months ahead. Balaclavas, leg warmers, woollen knickers, etc., should all keep frostbite at bay. Remember Hallowe'en at the end of the month, and make sure that you're doing the bewitching of the boy in your life.

November: November 30 is St Andrew's Day so thistles are the order of the day, be careful when you wear one though! It's also the month when the weather begins to get colder so stock up on your hot chocolate supplies and get ready to put on your winter woollies. November 5 is Guy Fawkes, fireworks night, so build the biggest bonfire ever. Capture at least **one** new guy!

December: Remember to stop shopping on Christmas Eve and start **enjoying** yourself . . . New Year's Day is another excuse for kissing that boy who's you've been longing to get a hold of ever since St Valentine's Day!

Your Jackie Guide To...

Kissing!

First off, it's not such a great idea to kiss a boy you're not all that interested in, even if he is great to look at. If you don't *like* him then you won't like kissing him, it's as simple as that. For any kiss to work, there's got to be some feeling behind it, so try not to kiss just any boy, especially pushy ones who try to Half-Nelson you into doing it, or you'll only end up regretting it and feeling really let down. Remember — your kisses are precious, they ought to be full of honest feeling, definitely not to be wasted on SLOBS!

OK? Now on to the fascinating subject of kissing and how to kiss . . .

YOU'VE probably imagined what it's like to kiss a boy. In your dreams, everything will be just perfect . . . In real life, though, it might not work out like that, so don't be too let down if it isn't all sweetness and light straight off. Here are a few tips to make all your first kisses that little bit special. Of course, there's no one right way to kiss but the following points to remember might help you out when it comes to the crunch, when he wants to kiss you and you think you might panic and run away from him!

Kiss your mum and tell her how much you appreciate her. Kiss you dad and tell him you think he's great. Kiss your boyfriend and *you don'* *have to tell him a thing* because here, actions speak much louder tha words!

There are kisses and kisses though, and no two kisses are alike – a friendly peck on the cheek, for instance, is a million miles from a wild passionate mouth-to-mouth clinch! So which kind of kiss should you use where and with whom, and, when you get right down to it — how shoul you kiss a boy in the first place anyway? Read our extra-special blue print on all you need to know about kissing and you'll find out!

HOW TO KISS

★ *Be prepared for the fact that he probably **will** try to kiss you after he's walked you home, although it could happen any time, any place – at the bus stop, in the disco, in the street . . . It'll help if you remember he's just as nervous as you are, so . . .*
★ *Take a few deep breaths and try to relax.*
★ *Keep your head up, don't stare at the ground.*
★ *Look at him.*
★ *When he moves towards you, don't back away.*
★ *Tilt your head.*
★ *Contact! Your lips meet.*
★ *Move your lips with his, slowly.*
★ *Depending on how things are going, you can stop kissing him now and lay your head on his shoulder. That's all there is to it!*

Once you're with a real, live boy, you ought to find everything goes really smoothly. Just make sure you *like* the boy you're kissing in the first place.

IF YOU DON'T LIKE HIM

If you've only been out with a boy once, and he's taken you home, obviously expecting a late-night snogging session, things can be a bit awkward, especially if you don't want to encourage him. So, once you get to your front door, thank him for a really nice evening, say you'll see him around, then peck him lightly on the cheek, if you like, and go indoors.

Don't allow him to put his arms around you in the first place if you don't want him to, and don't let him kiss you at all if you don't want him to — it'll only make him think you really do like him. So be honest with boys, especially the boys who are nice, not pushy, but whom you don't really fancy.

IF YOU DO LIKE HIM, AND HE LIKES YOU

Here, you'll probably expect your first kiss with him to be out of this world. If it isn't, put it down to nerves and try again. The chances are, though, that your first kiss with a boy you like *will* be wonderful, simply because it's *him* you're kissing!

IF HE WON'T TAKE NO FOR AN ANSWER

If he's too pushy, and he tries to force you to kiss him and you don't really want to, you'll have to tell him to stop. A lot of boys just don't know what's expected of them and so they go completely over the top, especially on first dates. How do you handle a boy like this? You do *not* just stand there and let him do whatever he pleases, that's for sure! You teach him to kiss naturally, the way *you* want to be kissed.

Try to make a joke out of it — say something like, "That may be OK for a female gorilla but I'm a girl." Or simply tell him what he's doing isn't welcome. Ask him to cool it. Or be honest, and tell him you don't *like* it, and will he please stop.

There's absolutely no point whatsoever in pretending to like being kissed in a certain way if you really don't, so for goodness' sake say so. Your boyfriend will probably be glad of it because then he'll stop having to live up to a big he-man image.

KISSING AND LOVEBITES

A lot of girls think lovebites are great and a lot of girls think they're pretty ugly. A lot of boys think that once they give a girl a lovebite that she's his property, while a lot of boys are really turned off by girls with lovebites.

Well, it's up to you really. Most people think kissing is a pretty private and special thing, not something you tell the whole world about. Really, though,

lovebites aren't pretty at all. And do you *really* want your boyfriend to act as if he owned you?

Too obvious lovebites can cause a lot of upsets anyway — your friends think you're a show-off, other boys think of you as being not quite nice, maybe even a bit easy, and as for your parents — it'll hurt them a lot. So is it worth it?

If you don't want lovebites, then tell your boyfriend so.

FRENCH KISSING

French kissing is when you put your tongue into your boyfriend's mouth and he puts his into yours. To a lot of people it's nice and natural. To others it's disgusting. Some people aren't disgusted by it but still don't quite like it.

If *you* don't like it, don't do it, and don't let your boyfriend force you into doing it. He may just be doing it because he thinks that's what you expect or because he thinks it's more grown up, or even a tiny bit daring.

It can be embarrassing to talk openly about your feelings when it comes to the physical side of your relationship with a boy but it's always best to air your views rather than to carry on feeling used and miserable in silence.

So speak up. If there was something he didn't like about you, wouldn't you rather he told you? At least that way, you'd understand each other a whole lot better, and feel even closer than ever.

WHICH KISS SHOULD YOU USE WHERE . . . AND WITH WHOM?

THE FRIENDLY PECK ON THE CHEEK

Use it on a boy you don't want to get serious with. If your evening out together proved a disaster, or even just OK, it's ideal — friendly without being *too* friendly.

THE ROMANTIC KISS

Use it when you're with a boy you really like — one you think you might even get to love!

THE FRENCH KISS

Kiss a boy this way and it ought to mean you've known the boy for some time. French kissing on a first date is a bit pointless and not much fun at all. A lot of boys think you must be pretty experienced if you kiss like this. Well, are you? And can you handle the kind of boy it'll encourage . . . ?

Finally, here are a few do's and dont's to remember. Follow them and you'll keep your kisses really sweet!

Don't *chatter on and on and on because you're nervous at the thought of him kissing you – he'll only think you don't want him to kiss you.*

Do *close your eyes when he kisses you. You don't want any distractions!*

Don't *get into a really heavy session with someone you don't really care about.*

Do *smile or laugh it off if everything does go drastically wrong, if you gulp really loudly, or if your false tooth falls out! Show him you've got a great sense of humour and he'll come back for more . . . and more!*

CAT

Cats are independent animals who prefer to live by themselves. They don't welcome any kind of interference. If you'd choose a cat as a pet it means you're the kind of person who likes to make up her own mind in her own time. Your ideal boyfriend will be the sort who won't push you into doing anything. At the same time you have a soft spot for special people, just like a cat, and you'll keep returning to those you like best.

BRING OUT THE BEAST IN YOU!

LION

Lions are not the most ordinary pets! If you'd like one, then it means you're pretty outgoing and adventurous. You will be the girl everybody wants to talk to at a party — always lots of fun. People sometimes don't take you as seriously as you'd like, so you could find that you don't usually have a steady boyfriend — but lots of admirers!

What's your favourite kind of pet? If you could choose the one for you (really let your imagination run riot here!) which kind would it be? A hamster, budgie, cat, dog . . . lion, lizard, elephant?? Here's just a small selection of pets *you* might like to call to heel. Choose the one you like best, then read on to find out exactly what your choice reveals about you!

BUDGIE

Girls who are quiet and nervous tend to choose budgies as pets! Unlike a budgie, though, you *don't* like to be caged in and you are very easily bored. Your boyfriend should be a quiet, dependable type who can help you calm down and get organised.

DOG

If you would prefer a dog as a pet then you are attracted to quiet, dependable people who can be relied upon to stick to you through thick and thin. You yourself would do anything for a friend and would expect them to be the same as you — kind, loyal and trustworthy!

ORANG-UTAN

If this is your ideal pet, then you're perfectly normal! Everybody in the office chose him, and we thought that Clyde the orang-utan was quite nice, too . . .

HORSE

If you're the sporty, outdoor type, then you're bound to choose a horse as your favourite pet! You tend to be as much at home in the stables with your curry combs as stomping in the disco. Your boyfriend will have to take you as you are, and put up with you coming to visit him with straw in your hair. If he doesn't, then he's *not* the boy for you!

LIZARD

Lizards are cold-blooded, just like you can be when you don't want someone around. You tend to say things without thinking and unintentionally hurt people. Your boyfriends will have to be pretty thick-skinned and take your outbursts with a pinch of salt, otherwise they won't last long!

Your Special Jackie POP-A-CROSS!

CLUES ACROSS.
1. See 7 down.
6. Band who made a discovery in 1979 — initially (1, 1, 1).
8. This group sound as though they're living in a dream world (10).
10. Led Zeppelin came "Through The Out Door" (2).
11. Christian name of punks "all-time hero." (3).
12. American town where many TV programmes are filmed — initially (1, 1).
13. The long --- of the law (3).
15. Cliff (I never grow old) Richard had a hit with a "hot" one in 1979 (4).
17. Folk group of fiddlers who like a few of these! (4).
19. Star of "M.A.S.H." sounds like a motorists club initially (1, 1).
20. "Metamatic" was the hit album for this star of the synthesizers — (surname only) (4).
21. Something that every band has in common — they're all making it (5).
24. This band was the first to bring us the "sound of ska" from the 2-Tone label (3, 8).
25. Michael Jackson's first big hit without the help of his brothers (3).
27. and 39 across. Ian Dury telling you to forget about the plumber and the joiner. Why don't *you* have a bash at it? (2, 2, 8).
29. See 22 down.
31. Middle name of DJ who has you rushing off to school each morning (3).
32. Not the sour grapes they appear to be, they're quite nice boys really (5).
33. Big hit for super group Police (7).
35. Poor BA seems a bit mixed up here — initially (1, 1).
36 across — 16 and 34 down. Darts singing about a nobleman with double honours (4, 2, 4).
38. Positive group who change their minds this time (2).
39. See 27 across.
40. American TV programme that sounds good enough to eat! (4).

CLUES DOWN.
1. Erik Estrada came to fame as a motorcycle cop in this series (5).
2. Outrageous punk band who had 11 across as their lead singer (First name, initial only) (1, 7).
3. Posh name for the Queen (1, 1).
4. "Making Plans For Nigel" was a big hit for this band (3).
5. Surname of Radio 1's late night DJ (4).
7. and 1 across. Once you've heard this girl speaking you'll know that she's not from Paradise (8, 5).
9. "Are Friends Electric" singer's got things the wrong way round (5, 4).
14. The second name of this band sounds Scottish (3).
16. See 36 across.
18. Group who sound a bit mucky. (3).
22. and 29 across. All-girl group who don't sound all that hot! (5, 7).
23. Band you might find in a pack of cards (3).
26. Supertramp have a hit with someone who's still fast asleep (7).
28. Take this band's middle name away and they sound like any old rodents (3, 4).
30. Surname of singer who's also known as "modest Bob" (6).
33. Bryan's group without the tune (4).
34. See 36 across.
37. Casey as he's better known initially (1, 1).

Solution on page 53.

43

ABC OF LIFE

APPEARANCE

This is one of the most important aspects of making the most of yourself. It's the very first thing people notice about you and the last thing they'll forget!

It's all very well avidly reading the beauty tips in magazines and wishing that you looked like a model, when you've got to be hoisted out of your armchair even to answer the phone! Don't convince yourself that it's expensive to look good — because that's just not true.

Simple, in this case, is best. When you're neat, clean and tidy, you can't help looking good, and even someone in the most fashionable clothes and make-up can sometimes look slovenly!

Take time over your appearance, because if you're feeling good then you'll radiate good looks as well!

BORROWING

It's all very well saying *never* borrow anything, but as long as you're not a consistent borrower, it often saves you buying something that you'd only use once.

But if you borrow something, make sure you return it promptly and in good condition, and if you have damaged it in any way, then tell the owner. It all depends on the situation but it's often best to buy something new if that happens. Just put yourself in their position, try imagining how *you'd* react, and you should be OK.

CRITICISM

It's easy to be critical of friends and boyfriends. Certain things about your nearest-and-dearest are bound to irritate you, but you should only criticise them rarely, and when you do, try to make your criticisms as constructive as possible.

If, for example, you think your friend treats her boyfriend really badly without knowing it, and you know that he's fed up with it, then it's obvious that a discreet word from you might work wonders. Remember, criticism is always most effective when it comes rarely and when it suggests improvements.

DATES

Dating means, simply, going out with a boy, whether once or quite regularly. The most important thing to remember about dates is that they're *not* the most important thing in the world. All they are, in fact, is just two people spending an evening together and finding out a bit more about each other. So *don't* get it out of all proportion, and you'll find that life can be really good fun.

EDUCATION

We all agree that at times, school can be very, very hard, and it can seem as though you'll *never* do anything right or understand *anything!* But another side of school is that it's the place where most of your friends are, where you can have a great laugh and join in all sorts of hobbies.

Schooldays and college days, of course, are just about the most important days of your life — and if you try your very best, then you'll never have anything to regret.

But even outside school, you're learning all the time — about relationships, about your own feelings, your strengths and weaknesses, about the way other people behave. So if you have a bad experience of any sort, just remember it'll have taught you a lot and strengthened you. It's all education for life!

FLIRTING

If you're unattached and so is he, then great! But if you're not — beware!

GOSSIP

It's hard to resist having a good old gossip, especially when there's a bit of spicy news around.

But in fact gossip never does anyone any good, and it can do real harm. So if you really want to make the most of yourself, get a reputation as the girl who *never* gossips!

HELP

Everybody, at sometime in their life, needs a little help, and it's always nice to try your best to help someone. Friends, especially, deserve some of your time when they're worried or in trouble, and even though sometimes you can't do anything, it's often just a friendly ear they need.

There's also such a thing as helping yourself, though. Whenever *you* need help, don't ever feel too proud to ask — because a problem shared isn't always just a problem halved, it can be solved as well!

INVITATIONS

Invitations are always nice to receive, proof that your company is wanted and that people like being with you.

However, don't always leave invitations to others. It's nice to have friends round now and again, and, of course that goes for boys, too. Don't always leave it to *them* to do the inviting, though, try it out for yourself.

JEALOUSY

This is one of the strongest emotions you can feel, and it never does *anything* for you. But it's also one of the most common emotions and hard to keep down. Really, jealousy isn't feeling envious of what someone else has got, it's all about what *you* haven't got — so only *you* can change that. Anyway, after reading this, you'll be well on your way — won't you!

LOVE AND YOU!

Are you really making the most of yourself, as a friend, as a girlfriend, as a daughter — as yourself, in fact? To get the best out of yourself you've got to work at it. If you sit back, and expect your life to flow happily and smoothly all the time, then you're in for quite a shock! Everybody needs to improve themselves a little, and we've got together a whole alphabet of things for you to polish up on. Go on, read it if you dare . . .!

KISSING
Many girls have a fear of kissing. They feel nervous and anxious before they've ever kissed a boy, thinking: I don't know how to do it! He'll think I'm a baby!

There's only one golden rule to kissing: kiss when you want to, and you'll find that you just *know* how to do it — it comes naturally!

LOVE
Love is wonderful, love is everything they say it is — *when* it's real, because it's so easy to fall in love with the idea of love! So just take time and don't try to convince yourself that you're in love with a boy *too* quickly — because you can get very hurt.

There are also many other kinds of love: love for your parents, your friends — love for anyone in fact whom you care for, and if you love people, then you're definitely making the most of yourself!

MONEY
Everybody would like to have money — and lots of it, but when you haven't got any it can really cause problems. Magazines often tell you to do odd jobs, etc., and if you try it you'll find that the money really does mount up. So use your imagination to get money *and* use your imagination when you haven't got any. Have some fun for free!

NAGGING
Are you a nag? If something about your friend or boyfriend irritates you, and you badly want to change it, the chances are that you mention it quite a lot.

It's always hard to get people to change their ways, and nagging certainly *isn't* the way to do it. So all we can say is, if you have the tendency to nag — button up.

ORGANISATION
There are so many groups, classes and clubs that are just crying out for members, that you've got no excuse for feeling bored. Pop along to your local library and find out all about all of the organisations in your area.

Learn new things, meet new people and thoroughly enjoy yourself into the bargain!

PARENTS
Your parents know you better than anyone else. They've cared for you through the years and have given you all they could, so it's only right that you should do the same for them.

Many girls find that when they become teenagers they don't really get on with their families as well as they used to, but you've got to realise that they *don't* want to hurt you, and they *don't* want to be nasty — they worry because they love you so much.

QUESTIONS
Questions are a vital part of life. With boyfriends especially it's always nice to show an interest in them, and it's a great way of finding out about each other and building up a relationship.

Get into the habit of asking *yourself* questions, too, about your work, feelings and ideas. That way, you're bound to keep an open mind about things.

RISKS
All we can say here is, *don't take them!* Whether it's risks with a boy, your friends or parents, it's always better to think really carefully about the worst possible outcome — and especially with boys. If they want to take risks and you don't — just tell them, and *never* do anything against your will.

SUCCESS
Success for you is what you make it. Your friend's idea of success might be being chosen to represent the school in a quiz, whereas yours might be something completely different. Success has got to be worked for, though, and being successful *proves* you've been making the most of yourself!

TRUTH
The truth sometimes hurts. And a good friend will know the right time for the whole truth, and when it's kinder to say nothing.

For instance, you might know that your friend is being two-timed. If she seems anxious and unsure, and often asks for your opinion, chances are she wants to hear the truth and it would be a relief.

But if she's immensely happy, then you run a great risk if you destroy her happiness by telling her something that will probably wreck it.

US
It's so easy to think of yourself *all* the time, that you can forget about other people's feelings. "Me, me, me" — if that's how you sound when you talk, then you're bound to appear a bit boring. Try to think of others a little bit more, and they're bound to think a little bit more of *you!*

VENOM
Hate is a terrible thing to feel for anyone. And when you're young, it's not an emotion that you should be feeling too frequently! It doesn't make you look big to cause a scene or have public arguments, it's much better to live and let live! So the next time someone does something that really annoys you, then think to yourself: Does that person really mean it the way I've taken it or am I just imagining it? It may not work *all* the time, but you never know!

WORRY
Everybody has worries, and everybody, at one time or another, can see no way out of their problem. When you're young, everybody tells you that you shouldn't worry, that you're too young to worry — but that never helps.

What you *shouldn't* do is bottle up your worries — tell someone! Even better, try not to get yourself into worrying situations!

X-TRA SPECIAL
This is what you are! Everybody on this earth is a totally unique person — and that's quite a thought!

YOURSELF
There's really not a lot we can say except — take care, and always look after yourself well.

ZEST
You should be feeling full of zest after reading this, because now you're going to start to make the most of yourself! Turn over a new leaf and try really hard to be a nice person — it may sound corny, but it'll work!

WHAT LINE IS HE HANDING YOU?

Everybody has their destiny in the palm of their hands — literally! All you have to know is how to read it. In this special feature we explain how palmistry works so that you can learn all about the secrets of a boy's true romantic nature. So read on . . . then tenderly take hold of his hand . . . and all his secrets will be revealed!

HOW TO READ HIS HANDS

The lines on his hands show his character and what's likely to happen to him, and *you* if you're with him!

The Heart line, for instance, runs across his palm above the Head line and it reveals the secrets of his romantic feelings.

He's very romantic if his Heart line is a deep strong line that cuts well into his hand. He's a boy who's never bored with love and will always be interesting to be with.

But you'll *never* receive a love letter from a boy whose Heart line runs straight across his palm without a curve. He's definitely too direct and unromantic for such sentimentality. So if it's a romantic boy you're looking for then a boy whose Heart line swoops across his palm is the one for you!

But be on your guard! If his Heart line runs *too* far across his palm, he's a boy who only imagines he's in love. He may be in love with *love* and not with *you!*

Broken marriages break the Heart line, palmists say, but a happy marriage is in store for the boy with a Heart line beginning under his index finger and running strong and unbroken across his palm.

A boy's Heart line will also show his romantic sorrows. Each small line extending down from his Heart line and each break in the Heart line is a disappointment in love.

If you want to know how much a boy's head rules his heart, compare the Head and Heart lines. Whichever line is deeper and longer rules the other. You'll have quite a time swaying the emotions of a boy with a faint Heart line and a strong Head line.

But a boy with a strong Heart line and weak Head line is bound to be over emotional and impractical in love. So, go for a boy with lines of equal strength.

Be cautious with a boy whose Heart line curves sharply upward in a right angle towards his fingers. He tends to act impulsively in love without thinking of the consequences — and you could be the one to suffer.

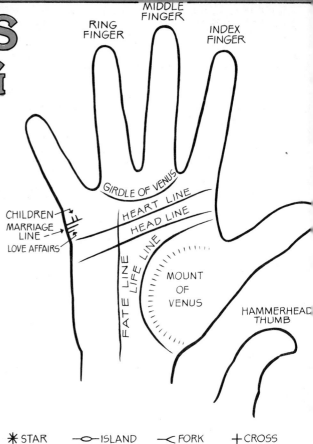

✳ STAR   ⊸ ISLAND   ⊰ FORK   ✛ CROSS

IS HE SEXY?

Yes he is, if the pad called the Mount of Venus, extending from the base of his thumb into the centre of his palm is fleshy and well developed! His sexiness is also shown by the Girdle of Venus, a semicircular line running from between the index and middle finger to a space between the ring and little finger.

When this line is strong he's a boy more interested in a girl's physical attributes than her personality! He's probably a male chauvinist, so beware! If broken in several places, he's a boy who makes many physical attachments but no long-lasting emotional ties. He'll be good fun if you don't try to tie him down.

HIS ROMANCES AND MARRIAGE

*A boy who wants to keep his past from a girl should **never** let her look at the small horizontal lines on the side of his hand under his little finger. So try to take a look before he realises what it means! Each weak line is a love affair and the deeper ones represent a marriage. You may even find **yourself** in his hand. If you're romantically involved with him you'll certainly be one of the weaker lines, at least!*

A long engagement is in store for the boy whose Marriage line begins with a fork. But if it ends in a fork this marriage will end in divorce or separation.

HIS FAULTS

The larger the thumb the stronger the ego and ambition. Girls unwilling to do just what a boy wants should avoid boys with large, long thumbs. He'll want to keep you under *his* control. A domineering boy may also have an index finger as long as his ring finger or a thumb which curves backwards like a hammerhead. Such a boy may be overbearing and childish so you'd probably do well to avoid him.

But a boy with a weak, small thumb and short index finger will let himself be nagged by a girl — he may also sweep a girl off her feet with promises he can't keep. So you won't want *him* either!

A short thumb that does not extend to the middle joint of the index finger is a sign of lack of will-power or sense of responsibility. This type of boy may let you down. If his thumb is flexible and bends easily away from his hand, he is generous and easy going and will make a great boyfriend. If his thumb lacks flexibility and does not bend easily away from his hand, he is stubborn and probably mean over money.

So now you know *his* destiny — if only he'll let you take a look at his hands!

We all know what girls are scared of . . . but what are *boys* scared of? We know boys aren't supposed to be scared of anyone or anything, but we went ahead anyway and asked a handful of boys for their honest, considered opinions about the things that frighten them — and we came up with all sorts of fascinating answers, on all sorts of fascinating subjects! Here are our results — we're sure they'll change your attitudes to the boys in *your* life . . .

THINGS THAT SCARE BOYS

...OT BEING NORMAL

Sean, 19: "You wouldn't believe the hang-...ps some blokes have about their bodies. I ...orried like mad because I didn't start shaving till ...was nearly 18. What made it even worse was ...y best mate had a moustache growing when he ...as 12! I felt like a freak. The first hair on my ...hest was a landmark for me too — I felt dead ...utch, like a man at last! It sounds stupid but ...ttle things like that can give you incredible ...ang-ups. It's even worse for small blokes, be-...ause they can get these terrible inferiority ...omplexes, especially where girls are con-...erned — I mean, it's not much fun being 5 ...eet nothing when the girl you're mad about is a ...ool 5 ft. 6 in. now, is it? It's much easier ...or girls than it is for boys, because girls ...ren't as cruel to each other, and they don't ...ave as much to live up to . . .''

...HOWING THEIR FEELINGS

Danny, 18: "I don't think boys are all *that* ...fferent to girls when it comes to feelings — ...'s just when it comes to showing their feelings ...at most blokes completely freeze up. I'm ...retty squeamish for instance, and my very first ...irlfriend dropped me because of it! It's ...nny now, but it wasn't then because I felt a ...omplete failure. Her nose started to bleed really ...adly one night — so badly that I fainted in ...ont of some of her mates just as we were going ...to a disco. Now, I suppose, I go over the top ...– go to the other extreme and act all big and ...ugh and manly. It's not me, really, but I think ...at's the image most girls go for. Boys have ...ot to hide their feelings more than girls. It's ...e same with girls though — they hide their ...elings and pretend they're what they're not ...ist as much as we do.''

MARRIAGE

Joe, 17: "I do want to get married — one day, but not now. One of my best mates who's 18 got married about six months ago — he had to because the girl was pregnant, and even I can see it's just not going to work out between them. I feel really sorry for him because he's made such a mess of his life. He hardly ever goes out with the lads anymore and when he does, his wife — *she's* only just turned 17 — kicks up a fuss. I don't want to end up like that. I'm going to get myself a really good job, play the field and meet lots of girls then settle down when I'm about 30. Why tie yourself to a wife and baby, all that responsibility, when your life's really only just beginning? I think girls are a lot to blame. All they think about is a ring and babies. They can't see in front of their noses.''

GOING TOO FAR

Sam, 15: "Sex is everywhere — on films, TV, books, magazines, and most guys do think about it a lot. I know I do. Well, it's hard not to think about it. I hate the way everything's so one-sided though — you know, guys supposed to be after *just one thing.* Well, I'm not. I know a lot of guys are but some girls just ask for it, the way they dress and behave. If they could hear the things some guys say about them behind their backs . . .! Most girls are pushovers — they go all lovey-dovey and will do anything for a guy with the right line of patter — or at least, that's what a lot of my mates say. Most of them talk a lot of hot air though, so you end up not knowing what to be-lieve. A lot of guys are really unsure when you get down to it, though. I mean, where do you draw the line? I think everything should go a lot more slowly than it does. I mean, it's not the end of the world if you don't have sex by the time you're 15. There are too many pressures on young people today. The whole thing is so mixed-up. I don't think magazines like yours help things either.'' (Well!)

GIRLS

Ian, 15: "At our school there are three kinds of girls — the snobby ones who are dead flash, — flash clothes, make-up, the works, the kind who are caught up in the ''who's going out with who and him — I wouldn't look at him twice he's not good enough for me'' syndrome; the really nice girls who aren't loud and pushy; and the yobbos — the girls who are all tough and big-mouthed. I'd really like to get to know the nice ones. The other ones I couldn't care less about and I just wouldn't want to talk to them. But it's really hard, and a bit scary too, trying to break the ice. It's still up to the boy to talk to them first, to ask them out and generally do all the running, which isn't easy to do, especially if you haven't even been out with a girl yet. Girls are like things from another planet. I just don't understand them. A guy like me finds it really hard to break the ice — I think most blokes do at first.

Finally (whew!) we think Colin deserves the last word. He's big enough to admit that lots of things scare him . . .

Colin, 16: "What am I scared of? Well, chat-ting up girls in groups for a start — I hate that. It's the same asking a girl to dance when she's with her mates. One thing I dread is when a mate and I get two girls up to dance and I get the ugly one who won't go away.

"Then there's bed-wetting, at a mate's house. Being made to look a fool by her elder brother in front of her family and knowing that I can't smash him one in the face 'cos that won't do me any good. Taking a new girl to an X film and not being able to get in. Getting beaten up. Being turned down after plucking up the courage to ask a girl out. Will that do?''

ONE morning, last winter, a Saturday, I wandered out into our garden, which was covered with deep snow. The sun was shining, and everything was a glittering world of whiteness.

At the end of the garden, there was a wall, and I happened to look over, and there, in the garden of the opposite house, was Stewart.

"Hi," I said, wanting to be friendly, but also somewhat shy, since this was the first time I'd seen him since the tragedy.

And it was a tragedy, indeed. That was the only word.

The girl he loved, Annette, had died only a week or so before.

It wasn't his fault, it wasn't anyone's fault. She had leukaemia. Something that you'd never imagine in anyone so young, but she'd died all the same.

Stewart used to visit her in hospital, more or less just watching her die, and each visit she was a little weaker, until in the end she really didn't even know him.

All this I learned from my mother, who used to talk to Stewart's mother.

I was sympathetic, naturally, but what good was sympathy, when things were as dark and gloomy as that?

So now, meeting him for the first time again that morning, in all the beauty of the sun and snow, I was shy, embarrassed, didn't know what to say, and yet wanted to say something.

"Hi, Lucy," he said back, and maybe there was a feeble trace of a grin on his lips, but it vanished again before it had time to assert itself.

I thought that if I were in his position, I'd never smile again.

"I — I'd like you to know how sorry I am, Stewart," I managed to stumble out. "About everything, I mean."

"Thanks, Lucy," he said. Just quietly, that was all.

"I wish there were something I could do . . ."

"There isn't. But thank you for suggesting it."

Well, what could there have been?

I stood there in the snow for a few moments, getting colder and colder, and somehow the radiance of the sunlight seemed to fade.

I gave an uncertain grin, and left him.

THAT afternoon, down town with Christie, we talked about Stewart. "You were interested in him, once," Christie said to me. "In fact you were very interested in him."

"Yes, I know."

"What he needs now, more than anything else, is a girl to take around," she went on. "Oh, not to fall in love with, or anything like that, but just to talk to."

"Christie!" I said, shocked. "He wouldn't even dream of taking another girl out! Maybe not *ever* again!"

"But a girl he *knows*," she insisted. "Like you, growing up side by side as you did."

"I mean, I think it might be good for *him*, but not for you, I guess."

"No, it wouldn't do at all. Anyhow, he wouldn't ask me, and I could hardly offer, could I?"

"No," she agreed, doubtfully. "Still, it seems a pity. He'll have to get over it, one day."

Still, how could *I* offer to let him cry on *my* shoulder? Did I even want to?

I think that deep down I was scared of being hurt . . . scared of giving myself a

A Jackie short story by Amanda Mandinian

To Make Him Forget

chance to fall for him all over again after taking so long to accept Annette.

"Don't you want to commit yourself?" Christie asked, reading my mind.

"Well when we were children I used to think I'd marry him when I grew up," I answered, truthfully, "and he said he'd marry me! I was ten, maybe, and he was twelve or thirteen."

"I should think I was his first real girlfriend."

Then, I remembered how I'd become used to seeing him with Annette and how I'd convinced myself that I didn't care. But I did . . .

SOMETIMES, I saw Stewart around in the days and weeks and months that followed. Spring gradually arrived, and soon summer would be here. I saw him down town, on Saturdays, always alone. He looked in a record shop window, but didn't go inside.

He walked right past the coffee bars, where in the old days he would either have been with Annette, or talking with some of the boys he knew.

I even saw him in the park, leaning against a wooden railing, staring over the lake into the distance. I suppose I could guess what he was thinking.

Memories of Annette, things they used to do together, places they went to, promises they exchanged — so unlike the childish promises that he and I had once given each other.

It seemed all very sad and romantic, at least to me.

To Stewart I supposed it must have been almost intolerably bitter.

"How's Stewart these days?" Christie asked, one afternoon a while after.

"No change."

"He *ought* to be changing!"

"Well, no-one can tell him so. That's something he'll have to discover for himself."

"You should help him discover it," she said.

"Stop, and speak. Talk. Give him a chance."

"To do what?"

"Whatever he likes," she said. "Once he knows you're not trying to move in, he'll be glad to have someone to talk to. Someone like you, I mean."

Someone like me! But I knew all the time I could never be another Annette for him, never replace Annette in his heart.

I was so mixed up. I wanted him, but I didn't want to be second best. I didn't want to be another Annette for him and I didn't want to hurt him when he was still wounded by Annette's death.

Would he remember, would he become impatient with me because I wasn't a patch on the girl, now gone and lost for ever?

All her good points, and their good times etched on his mind, forever. Could I even begin to compete with a dream?

AND yet, one warm Saturday morning, so different from that winter Saturday of long ago, I went out into the garden again, and down to the wall, and looked over, and there he was.

He even smiled.

Not much, but it was definitely a smile, even so.

"I — I'd like to talk to you, Stewart," I said, without even knowing, a second before I spoke, that I had any intention of saying something like that.

"You would?" he asked.

"Yes. About Annette."

His face clouded for a moment, and this again was something I'd never have dreamed of saying.

"There's not much we can say about her," he said, sadly.

"Yes, there is. I'd like — I mean, if you'd like to talk to me about her, I'd like to listen."

He looked at me curiously.

"Did you know her?" he asked.

"Well, not as well as you did, of course, but there was a time when we were in the same class together."

"Was she a friend of yours? In those days?"

"No," I said, truthfully, wishing I could've given a different answer. "Not exactly a friend. But we weren't enemies, either!"

"Come over," he suggested, after an awkward pause. "My family are out, come to the kitchen, and we'll have a coffee together. If you'd like."

"I would like," I said.

And so I sat in that little kitchen, with the sunlight coming through the windows, and I could remember sitting here all those years ago, when we were both children. How strange it was to look back, and how little I had thought, when I was ten or eleven, that all these years later I'd be back here again, in such different circumstances.

Slowly he began to talk. A little about Annette, a little about other things. But when he spoke of anything else, somehow the conversation seemed to drift round to Annette again.

And he seemed happier, he even seemed to like it, and I guessed that maybe his own family had never dared, or hardly ever dared, to mention her name.

It was like releasing a pent-up spring of emotion, and I was terrified in case it became a kind of torrent, but he had better control over himself than that.

"You're nice, Lucy," he said, in the end.

"I'm just me," I said.

"Yes, but — you're trying to be kind to me, aren't you?"

"No."

"Then — what?"

"We were friends once," I said. "We can still be friends again. I'm not sorry for you, or rather not just for you, but sad that something so beautiful, so right, had ever to come to an end."

"Yes," he said, slowly. "So am I sad."

When his mother came back from shopping, I left, and he walked back to the wall with me, the wall I'd climbed or jumped over so often long ago.

"Thanks, Lucy," he said.

I nearly gave some flippant answer, mostly to try to hide my own emotions, but managed not to.

"See you again, Lucy," he said, finally.

"See you, Stewart."

And I went back to my own house, thinking about the future. I knew then that I was glad I'd helped him a little, that we'd become friends again. Suddenly all my other thoughts vanished and I knew that now he just needed a friend.

AND, in fact, as the weeks went on, Stewart and I went out together. We didn't do anything sensational, just small things like walks and conversations. And slowly, we began not to talk about Annette so much, but about ourselves.

It was all very quiet, but very beautiful.

And then, one night, he kissed me goodnight. We didn't say anything, we didn't need to, but I just held on to him tightly, wishing he'd never go away.

After that, we became very close, and I knew that I was falling in love with him. But still in the back of my mind I was afraid that he didn't feel the same way, that I was just a substitute for Annette.

Then, one night at my door, something made me say, between kisses, that I knew I could never be another Annette for him.

His reply almost brought tears to my eyes, but happiness too.

"I want you Lucy . . . no-one else," he said gently. "Just you."

49

Did you know that what you write in your diary gives away an awful lot about what you're *really* like? Everyone's diary is different — as you can see from the pages we've sneaked from the diaries of five very different girls. All *you* have to do is compare their scribblings to yours, decide which is nearest your style — and find out the secrets which are lurking in the pages of your diary. (A double reason for keeping it under lock and key!)

ARE YOU A WRITE GIVE~ AWAY?

WET WENDY'S DIARY

MONDAY Felt sick, but Mum said I had to go to school, worse luck. Felt worse in Biology — no wonder, we were dissecting a horrible THING. Not sure what it was exactly, because didn't dare look at it. But Theresa threw a bit of it at me so I ran out screaming and went to the medical room to lie down.

TUESDAY Still felt very shaky after yesterday. There wasn't any hot water to wash in because the switch was off. And when I cleaned my teeth, my gums bled. I expect I've got that awful disease which makes your teeth fall out.

WEDNESDAY School dentist came so hid in the toilet. At break, John Greenfield came up, got talking and asked me out on Friday. I'm sure he was just taking the mickey so I told him I had to go to my gran's.

THURSDAY Theresa says I should have one of those new haircuts. But my hair's like old rats' tails and nothing would do any good. My hands are mottled today — I wonder if I'm going down with something?

FRIDAY Had a bit of a sore throat today. Theresa says John Greenfield really fancies me — but I don't believe her. How could he fancy me? How could anybody? Looking forward to watching TV all tomorrow.

If Your Diary's Like Wendy's . . .

We all feel like Wendy from time to time — when things go wrong. But nobody's that much of a failure. Everybody's got something going for them. When a boy asks you out, don't assume he's got to be joking. He just might be serious and attracted to you — there's no accounting for tastes!

Try increasing your self-confidence. For a start, endless fretting about your health is silly — it's usually a sign that you've got nothing whatever wrong with you.

If your life consists of watching TV, just get up and go — OUT! Anywhere: for a walk, for a bike-ride. You're far too shy — and when it comes to boys you assume you have nothing to offer, so no wonder you don't get asked out anywhere! Join a few clubs, get your free time organised so you spend it with a drama group, or a photography club, or whatever, and forget about your imaginary problems and worries!

DOROTHY DREAMER

MONDAY A strange and weird day. Dark clouds — all the birds are silent. Why? Came bottom in Geography test. Spent Needlework lesson dreaming about the French assistant M. Plaque. Miss Sullivan read us a ghost story today in English. I was so scared I had to hold on to my desk. M. Plaque still away. I wonder what's wrong.

TUESDAY M. Plaque still away. If only I could be by his bedside and nurse him back to health . . . sponge his brow and brew up his hot lemon drink. I saw a flower in a hedgerow today, picked it and made a wish.

WEDNESDAY It came true! M. Plaque came back! And that rhymes! Maybe I will write a poem about it! He looks very pale but terrifically romantic.

THURSDAY I bit my ruler in half today when M. Plaque walked past the classroom window. Splinters in the gum quite painful but for him I could bear anything.

FRIDAY M. Plaque trod on me! It was *wonderful!* He said *pardon* in his lovely French voice and looked into my eyes! I shall never wash my foot again! He *touched* me! Came bottom in History and Maths. Got run over tonight outside school, but not seriously. Was looking up at French-room windows at the time.

If Your Diary's Like Dorothy's . . .

Dreaming about things (or to be more exact boys!) is natural. But being in such a dream about them that you're out of touch with reality is another matter. And what's more, it's a very stupid state to be in. Whilst you're dreaming about Mr Right, a real flesh-and-blood boy might be trying to catch your eye . . . and failing!

It's also pretty dangerous to get yourself into such a romantic frame of mind that you believe in things like premonitions. When you think you're being psychic or feeling that something strange is going to happen you're probably only just indulging your moods.

As far as boys are concerned, you're too interested in them. It's natural to be interested. But not to think of nothing else. So give yourself a break, and get going with some pastimes that will extend you as a person. Languishing in a romantic dream-world is *not* the answer to life's problems!

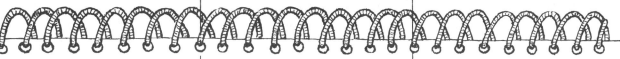

VAIN VICKY

MONDAY Woken by golden light streaming in through my curtains. The trees are covered with blossom and I have got a huge spot on my chin. A new boy got on the bus today: tall and dark, with smouldering eyes and a sulky mouth. I turned my face away so he wouldn't see my spot.

TUESDAY Washed my hair in the new **Extract of Dogrose and Cowparsley** shampoo. Smells awful — like a goat with B.O. Today my spot was worse: like a Belisha beacon. Covered it with make-up and buried my face in my scarf.

WEDNESDAY I wish Dad wouldn't wear that awful old suit. He collected me from school today because of the bus strike, and everyone could see his lapels were the wrong shape. I could've *died*.

THURSDAY A fantastic day! I shall remember this day as long as I live! The boy on the bus sat by me! I could feel his shoulder against mine! He's got the most beautiful hands — big, and brown. What's more my spot popped yesterday so I didn't have to hide my face. If only we didn't have to wear school uniform.

FRIDAY He didn't turn up. Good job, too, 'cos there was a girl on the bus who was really fantastic looking. The cow. It's not fair. Beautiful sunset today. Washed my hair in **Extract of Barley and Groundsel**. Smells foul.

If Your Diary's Like Vicky's . . .

If you think you're a bit like Vicky, well, relax a little. It's not the end of the world if you've got a spot or a blemish.

People like Vicky who are interested in beauty are usually aware of all sorts of other beauty in the world — not just their own! This is great. You probably like looking at paintings or sculpture, or just enjoying the wonders of nature. Flowers, sea-shells, feathers — you love them all, you like to collect them.

You're much too aware of your looks when it comes to meeting boys, though. You try to stun them with your beauty, whereas most boys would feel more comfortable just talking casually with a girl to break the ice.

PRACTICAL PAULA

MONDAY Got up early. Was just about to go jogging in the park when Mum asked me to go to the corner shop for some milk 'cos of the milkmen's strike. So I jogged to the shop and back. The result? A milk-shake! (Ho ho!) Mended Steve's bike puncture this evening.

TUESDAY Overslept till 7.30. In an awful rush. Forgot to feed the hamster, didn't have time to clean my shoes or iron my skirt. (Or iron the hamster, ho ho!) Hopeless day. Couldn't do hockey because of the rain.

WEDNESDAY At youth club played Steve at table tennis. Beat him hollow. He seemed fed up. It's his birthday next week. I said I'd make him a cake. That cheered him up. He *must* ask me out soon.

THURSDAY At weight-training tonight, a bloke twisted his ankle. I gave him the old first-aid treatment, and the coach was very impressed. I hope Steve noticed, but I think he was talking to that wet girl Mandy Pillick. She always comes to watch. Never lifts a finger though. (Nor a bar-bell, ho ho!)

FRIDAY I was really enjoying myself tonight making a yoghurt machine out of a few old milk-bottles and a mousetrap, when Sheila had to come round and drag me off to the disco. She said Steve would be there. He was . . . wrapped around Mandy Pillick.

If Your Diary's Like Paula's . . .

If you feel you might be a bit like Paula, well . . . congratulations! You've certainly made the most of your talents and learned a lot of skills that'll help you get on well with people. You'll always be invaluable to any group of people. You're cheery, you crack jokes, you're great in a crisis . . .

If you haven't got a boyfriend, or have trouble keeping them, you're probably putting them off by being too good at everything, too organised. *Ask* him things instead of *telling* him. There's nothing wrong with being a tomboy, but let him know you're a real girl underneath!

SUSAN SWOT

MONDAY Great day. The maths test was everything I'd been hoping for. Had a very good talk with Mark Smith at break, about the maths test. We argued about question 6. He said the answer was $ab_2 = qrt + 2.008 + zrt = 700.000006$ but I disagreed.

TUESDAY Found a terrific old book in the second-hand bookshop: called Ferrier's **Functions of the Brain**. Great stuff. Read it secretly under the desk in the needlework lesson. Pricked myself twice. Blood is interesting. I'd like to do an experiment measuring people's clotting rates.

WEDNESDAY Smashing concert on Radio 3: a new concerto for Harp, Flute and Elastic Band by Erich Twitterguts. I wonder if Mark was listening to it. I thought of him in the slow movement.

THURSDAY Asked Mark if he'd heard the concert, but he said he'd been over at the **Hope and Anchor** in Whistley, watching a band called **The Snots.** Sometimes Mark surprises me. I wonder what his clotting rate is.

FRIDAY Results of maths test! Mark was top but he did get No. 6 wrong! I was second — but I don't mind him being top sometimes. Janice says Mark might take more notice of me if I plucked my eyebrows and maybe my nostrils as well, but I know he's above such things. Read 288 pages of **War and Peace** and fell asleep to the sound of Beetroothoven's Fifth Symphony.

If Your Diary's Like Susan's . . .

If your diary extract is a bit like Susan's, it's obvious that you're highly intelligent, and very academic. Being interested in school work isn't odd — for some people it's only natural. We can't all sit goggling at *Top Of The Pops.*

When it comes to boys, you're a bit frightening to some boys because they find clever girls are a threat to them. But you *needn't* be a threat if you're just relaxed and friendly. Bright boys like bright girls to talk to.

So if you're a bit like Susan, be patient with boys. Talk to them about everyday things as well as the problems of the universe! And don't be ashamed if you want to doll yourself up now and then. Why shouldn't you be clever *and* pretty? It's a winning combination!

Every week they're there, those on-the-spots where we get you to confess to things you've never even dreamed of before! We could do *no* less for the Annual — so we went out and about and asked some of our favourite stars which Santa's knee they'd like to sit on. Read on for a few surprises!

Which Santa's Knee Would You Like To Sit On?

CELEBRITY ON-THE-SPOTS!

EDDIE KIDD
Debbie Harry of Blondie. I just think she's a very sexy girl and that'd be a great way to meet her. She wouldn't even need to give me a present, just sitting on her knee would be enough of a treat!

PETER POWELL
Wendy Wu from The Photos, I think she's absolutely delicious!

TOMMY BOYD
Lene Lovich! She's definitely a Mother Christmas as far as I'm concerned . . . I could just imagine myself sitting on her knee and asking for a present. Actually, I've always reckoned that Lene looks great in red as well — she likes unusual clothes, so she'd probably enjoy being dressed up in flowing red robes!

FRANCIS ROSSI — STATUS QUO
I'd like to sit on Prince Charles's knee if he were dressed as Santa. I think he seems like a nice chap.

D JENSEN
There's one lady, apart from my wife, ho I think is really great, and that's hrissie Hynde. I wouldn't mind sitting her knee, if she were dressed as Santa Claus, but only when my fe Gudrun wasn't looking.

EOFF DOWNES — BUGGLES
Our lovely Prime Minister, argaret Thatcher. I've never actually en her knees, but I'm sure they're ry nice and I wouldn't turn down the ance to sit on them.

ITH CHEGWIN
Farrah Fawcett. She's a very pretty ly and I think she's got nice knees. might sound weird, (it does!) but mebody once sent me a rather odd cture of her and said it looked e me! I've been a fan of hers ever ce, though I'm still not sure whether as pleased about it.
She can forget the beard, I think and had to ask her for a present it'd obably be whichever after-shave she es most. That's only fair, isn't it, if sitting on her knee . . .

SHAKIN' STEVENS
My manager. She's a very large lady called Frayer Miller and she's always really cheerful. There'd be plenty of room for me on her knee. Actually it's quite unusual to have a lady as your manager, but we're very close and really understand each other.

THEREZE BAZAAR — DOLLAR
Ian McShane would be lovely, he's my *favourite* actor at the moment. I actually met him after seeing him in the TV series "Yesterday's Hero" and had quite a chat. He's a lovely bloke, he not only looks fantastic, he's nice as well!

SOLUTIONS TO OUR SPECIAL JACKIE POP-A-CROSS!

54

And when Caroline was shown to her room . . .

OH . . . WHAT A BEAUTIFUL PAINTING! I WONDER WHO SHE IS . . . SHE'S LOVELY. BUT SHE LOOKS SAD . . . SAD AND LONELY. AS IF SHE, TOO, HAS BEEN PARTED FROM HER LOVE . . .

OH, JONATHAN . . . IF ONLY YOU WERE HERE BESIDE ME NOW. EVERY MOMENT WE'RE APART IS A TORMENT TO ME . . . IF ONLY I HAD BEEN ABLE TO TELL YOU THAT I WAS LEAVING . . .

Caroline's thoughts turned to the happiness she and Jonathan had shared in England . . . to how much she had loved him . . .

BUT FATHER DIDN'T APPROVE OF OUR LOVE. HE WAS CONVINCED JONATHAN WAS A FORTUNE-HUNTER WHO ONLY WANTED TO MARRY ME FOR MY MONEY. HE FORBADE US TO SEE EACH OTHER AGAIN . . . AND WHEN THAT DIDN'T WORK HE BROUGHT ME ON THIS TRIP TO EUROPE TO MAKE ME FORGET JONATHAN. AS IF I COULD FORGET THE ONLY MAN I'VE EVER LOVED . . .

And just then . . .

IT'S A LOVELY DAY, CAROLINE. WHY DON'T YOU BORROW A HORSE FROM THE STABLES AND GO FOR A RIDE? PERHAPS THE FRESH AIR WILL PUT SOME COLOUR BACK IN YOUR CHEEKS . . . IT'S NOT GOOD FOR YOU TO BE SO PALE!

THERE'S ONLY ONE THING WOULD MAKE MY CHEEKS FLUSH AGAIN . . . AND THAT WOULD BE TO FEEL THE TOUCH OF JONATHAN'S LIPS . . .

BUT MAMA WAS RIGHT ABOUT ONE THING. IT IS A LOVELY DAY . . . AND THE COUNTRYSIDE HERE IS SO BEAUTIFUL . . .

Then . . .

OH . . . I DIDN'T NOTICE THAT HOUSE WHEN WE PASSED THIS WAY ON THE COACH. IT LOOKS VERY OLD . . . AND A LITTLE MENACING FOR SOME REASON . . .

EXCUSE ME . . . COULD YOU TELL ME WHO LIVES IN THAT BIG HOUSE UP THERE?

NO . . . I—I KNOW NOTHING ABOUT IT . . . NOTHING!

STAY AWAY FROM THAT PLACE, MY LADY! I WARN YOU . . . STAY AWAY FROM IT!

HOW ODD! THAT MAN SEEMED TERRIFIED . . . JUST BECAUSE I ASKED HIM ABOUT THE HOUSE!

BUT WHY SHOULD I CONCERN MYSELF ABOUT AN OLD HOUSE? IT'S OF NO INTEREST TO ME . . . NOTHING IN THE WORLD INTERESTS ME NOW THAT I'VE LOST JONATHAN . . .

55

Caroline had dinner at the inn with her parents . . . but when she was alone in her room she still felt fascinated by the portrait of the beautiful girl that hung there . . .

Then . . .

JONATHAN! I—I CAN'T BELIEVE IT!

I CAN SEE THE SADNESS IN HER EYES . . . THE LONELINESS . . . JUST LIKE THE LONELINESS THAT FILLS MY OWN HEART . . .

OH . . . WHAT'S THAT NOISE? IT SOUNDS LIKE SOMEONE THROWING SOMETHING AT MY WINDOW!

NOT SO LOUD, CAROLINE—WE DON'T WANT YOUR PARENTS TO HEAR! SLIP DOWNSTAIRS QUICKLY . . . I'LL WAIT FOR YOU BEHIND THE INN.

I CAN'T BELIEVE WE'RE REALLY TOGETHER AGAIN, MY LOVE. I'VE BEEN SO LONELY WITHOUT YOU . . . SO VERY LONELY . . .

And . . .

YOU DIDN'T THINK I'D LET OUR LOVE END SO EASILY, DID YOU, CAROLINE? I'VE BEEN FOLLOWING YOU EVER SINCE YOU LEFT ENGLAND . . . AND WHEN I TRACKED YOU DOWN TO THIS INN I BRIBED ONE OF THE MAIDS TO TELL ME WHICH ROOM YOU WERE IN.

I KNOW, CAROLINE. BUT THAT'S ALL OVER NOW . . . WE'LL NEVER BE APART AGAIN, I PROMISE YOU . . .

OH, JONATHAN . . . WHEN FATHER BROUGHT ME TO EUROPE I THOUGHT I'D NEVER SEE YOU AGAIN! HOW ON EARTH DID YOU FIND ME?

OH, BUT IT'S HOPELESS, JONATHAN! ONCE PAPA FINDS OUT YOU'RE HERE HE'LL FORBID ME TO SEE YOU AGAIN. HE'LL NEVER CONSENT TO OUR MARRIAGE!

WHEN YOUR PARENTS ARE ASLEEP TONIGHT YOU MUST PACK WHATEVER YOU NEED AND SLIP AWAY FROM THE INN. I'LL BE WAITING FOR YOU AT THE EDGE OF THE WOOD OVER THERE . . . WE'LL RUN AWAY TOGETHER, AND BE MARRIED IN THE FIRST TOWN WE COME TO!

ONCE WE'RE WED YOUR FATHER WILL HAVE TO GIVE US HIS BLESSING . . . HE'D NEVER DISINHERIT HIS OWN DAUGHTER!

I KNOW THAT, CAROLINE. BUT I'VE ALREADY THOUGHT OF A PLAN . . .

I DON'T CARE IF HE DOES OR NOT . . . JUST AS LONG AS I CAN BE WITH YOU . . .

And later that night . . .

EVERYONE IN THE INN MUST BE ASLEEP BY NOW. I MUST BE CAREFUL NOT TO MAKE A SOUND OR EVERYTHING WILL BE LOST . . .

TILL TONIGHT THEN, CAROLINE. AND REMEMBER . . . NOT A WORD TO ANYONE ABOUT OUR PLAN!

I'LL BE READY, JONATHAN . . .

OF COURSE! IT'S HER... THE GIRL WHOSE PORTRAIT I SAW IN MY ROOM AT THE INN!

PLEASE... BE SEATED AND PERMIT ME TO OFFER YOU A LITTLE OF MY HOSPITALITY.

IT'S STRANGE... THE TABLE'S BEEN SET FOR THREE PEOPLE... AND YET THERE IS NO SIGN OF ANY SERVANTS IN THE HOUSE. SURELY ELVIRA DOESN'T LIVE HERE ALL ALONE...

YOU SAID YOU WERE AWAITING OUR ARRIVAL, ELVIRA... YET HOW IS THAT POSSIBLE? IT WAS ONLY THE STORM THAT DROVE US TO YOUR DOOR!

I FELT SOMEONE WOULD COME TONIGHT. IT'S BEEN SO LONELY HERE BY MYSELF... SO VERY LONELY... BUT I KNEW IF I WAITED SOMEONE WOULD COME!

I THINK YOU'RE TEASING US, ELVIRA. SOMEONE AS BEAUTIFUL AS YOURSELF COULD NEVER BE LONELY FOR COMPANY... UNLESS ALL THE YOUNG MEN IN THESE PARTS HAVE BEEN STRUCK WITH BLINDNESS!

OH... I WISH JONATHAN WOULDN'T LOOK AT HER THAT WAY! HE'S HARDLY GLANCED IN MY DIRECTION FOR THE LAST TEN MINUTES...

After they'd dined...

OH... WHAT A LOVELY PIANO. I'VE NEVER SEEN ONE SO BEAUTIFUL!

DO YOU PLAY? THEN PLEASE PLAY FOR US, CAROLINE! IT'S BEEN A LONG TIME SINCE THERE WAS THE SOUND OF MUSIC IN THIS HOUSE... A LONG TIME SINCE I DANCED TO ITS SWEET MELODIES...

As Caroline played, she watched Jonathan and Elvira dancing...

I—I FEEL SO STRANGE WATCHING THE TWO OF THEM TOGETHER... IT'S ALMOST AS IF I WERE THE OUTSIDER...

THE WAY HE'S GAZING INTO HER EYES... IT'S ALMOST AS IF HE'S BEWITCHED BY HER BEAUTY!

I'M SORRY, I—I CAN'T PLAY ANY MORE. I HAVE A SUDDEN HEADACHE...

I UNDERSTAND, CAROLINE. YOU MUST BE TIRED AFTER YOUR JOURNEY. COME AND I'LL SHOW YOU TO YOUR ROOM...

I WISH WE'D NEVER COME TO THIS PLACE. IT'S EASY TO SEE THAT JONATHAN FINDS ELVIRA FASCINATING. BUT HE LOVES ME... I KNOW HE DOES...

And...

SLEEP WELL, CAROLINE. AND DON'T BE AFRAID... IF JONATHAN REALLY LOVES YOU THEN YOU HAVE NOTHING TO FEAR FROM ME. ONLY IF HIS LOVE IS FALSE WILL THE NIGHT BRING DARKNESS!

WHAT—WHAT DOES SHE MEAN BY THAT?

Caroline's only thought was to get away from that house...

OH, DEAR LORD... WHAT'S HAPPENING TO ME? AM I LOSING MY SENSES?

Then...

THERE YOU ARE, MISS! YOUR PARENTS WERE WORRIED WHEN THEY DISCOVERED YOU WERE MISSING... THEY'RE OUT SEARCHING FOR YOU AT THIS VERY MOMENT!

OH... IT'S THE INNKEEPER...

COME... I WILL TAKE YOU BACK TO THE INN. YOUR PARENTS WILL BE RELIEVED TO KNOW YOU'RE SAFE.

NO... I CAN'T GO BACK UNTIL I FIND JONATHAN. I MUST KNOW WHAT'S BECOME OF HIM!

WE SPENT THE NIGHT AT THAT OLD HOUSE. THERE WAS A GIRL... A STRANGE GIRL CALLED ELVIRA...

YOU MUST BE MISTAKEN, MISS. NOBODY HAS LIVED IN THAT HOUSE FOR OVER FIFTY YEARS!

THE LOCAL PEOPLE SAY THAT ELVIRA'S GHOST STILL WAITS THRE... TO ENSNARE ANY YOUNG MAN WHOSE LOVE IS AS FALSE AS HER OWN LOST LOVER... AND CONDEMN HIM TO SHARE FOREVER HER LONELY VIGIL IN THE HOUSE WHERE SHE DIED....

THE OLD HOUSE HAS LAIN EMPTY SINCE THE LAST OWNER'S DEATH. IT'S SAID SHE WAS BEAUTIFUL... AS YOU MAY HAVE SEEN FROM THE PORTRAIT OF HER THAT HANGS IN MY INN...

BUT THAT'S THE SAME GIRL I MET LAST NIGHT! OH, WHAT CAN IT MEAN...

COME TO THINK OF IT, I BELIEVE HER NAME WAS ELVIRA. IT'S SAID SHE WAS BETROTHED TO A YOUNG MAN... BUT HIS LOVE WAS FALSE, AND HE FORSOOK HER FOR ANOTHER ON THEIR WEDDING DAY. ELVIRA PINED IN SADNESS FOR ALMOST A YEAR, UNTIL SHE DIED OF A BROKEN HEART. AND ON HER DEATH BED SHE CALLED DOWN A CURSE ON ALL FALSE LOVERS...

NO... IT CAN'T BE TRUE... IT CAN'T...

IT'S JUST A FOOLISH SUPERSTITION TO FRIGHTEN IGNORANT PEASANTS! AND YET... WHERE CAN JONATHAN BE? WHAT HAS BECOME OF HIM?

For Elvira had found her companion... condemned to stay by her side and share her loneliness through all eternity...

But when they returned to the inn...

THE SAINTS PRESERVE US! LOOK, MISS... LOOK AT THE PAINTING OF ELVIRA! IT... IT'S CHANGED...

OH, JONATHAN... NOW I KNOW THAT YOUR LOVE WAS FALSE. I HAVE LOST YOU FOREVER...

The End

60

SPOT THE GROT

First, check that a Grot *is* what you've got by —

HIS APPEARANCE

His appearance isn't the best guide to a Grot. Some Grots are scruffy, some are smart, some are in-between. But a too scruffy guy who obviously doesn't care what he looks like is likely not to care too much about the girls in his life, either. And that makes him a Grot.

At the other end of the scale, watch out for the *too* neat, *too* smart and *too* well-dressed guy. Ask yourself how he gets that way. All those clean shirts, the perfect creases in his trousers. You can bet he doesn't get as immaculate as that by himself. So he's already got *one* devoted slave pandering to him. Has he got you lined up as Number 2? Then he's a Grot.

THE WAY HE SPENDS HIS MONEY ON YOU

Is he generous? It's important here to separate the poor guy who's low on cash from the genuine meanie Grot. Your genuine poor-as-a-church-mouse guy will happily fork out to buy you an ice-cream. The Grot will fuss about buying you an ice-cream but he'll let you have a lick of his. Even though he could afford 100 ice-creams.

The Grot is likely to carry a purse. Men with purses are careful of the pennies. There's nothing wrong with that, but combine it with the Grot and you've got a first-class Meanie.

THE PLACES HE TAKES YOU

This is tied in with the way he spends his money on you. He's finally got round to agreeing to buy you a meal. You fancy a particular restaurant. He says "Yeah, but there's a cheaper place just round the corner." Maybe he's just being careful with his cash. Or maybe he doesn't think you rate a first-class restaurant. Some guys give girls what they think they deserve. So if you get dragged into a burger bar that's the level you're rated at in his grotty mind.

THE WAY HE ACTS TOWARDS YOU WHEN YOU'RE IN COMPANY

Is he off-hand, cool? Does he leave you standing on your own while he makes off to chat with his mates? Does he talk to people he knows without bothering to introduce you? He does? Then he's a Grot for sure. He doesn't count you as important, can't even be bothered to show you off. Face the facts, the guy is taking you for granted.

Take a long, cool look at your guy. Does he stand you up, let you down, give you the runaround and leave you stranded? Is he treating you like an old bag? If he is, then the chances are, that what you've got is — a Grot. And what's a Grot? A guy who's not so hot and doesn't care a lot, that's what! So, if you suspect that you're stuck with a Grot, read on! We tell you, first of all, how to check that you *have* got landed with a genuine Grot and if (poor fool) you find that you have, don't despair — we'll tell you what to do about it!

OK. On the evidence you find you're stuck with a Grot. The next question is — what to do.

First ask yourself if you're genuinely fond of him. Would it hurt badly if you split up? Answer *no* and all you have to do is give him the push. Simple.

Answer *yes* and you've got problems. How are you going to change a guy like that? Because that's what you've got to do, for your own sake and for his. So —

★ Start with his appearance. If he's scruffy and careless about his looks, nag him into smartening up. Or turn up looking mucky and slovenly yourself and see how *he* likes it. If he doesn't, tell him that's just how *you* feel about *him*.

The too-smart guy needs some attention, too. Ask him why he needs to be so immaculate, what's he afraid of. Guys don't like suggestions that they're afraid. It might do the trick. Or if his old mum is behind the scenes slaving away you could try getting at her instead and maybe start a rebellion so he'll have to iron his own shirts in future.

★ How are you going to knock the meanness about money out of him? Not easily, that's for sure. It might pay you to start being aggressive with him. Try lines like — "What's the matter, you don't think I'm worth spending that much on?" It might do the trick.

A gentler way is the kindly "Let me help" approach. When he's reluctant about parting with his cash, act as if you know he's really very generous and say, "Haven't you got enough? Look, why not let me make up the difference? You can pay me back later." This'll put him in a spot.

You can use the same line when he tries to drag you to the cheaper restaurant. "If you can't afford it," you can say, "let's go Dutch. I'd just love to have a real, romantic meal with you."

Even *he* will have to admit that there's not a lot of romance in a burger bar. If he has got a heart, this kind of approach should find it and, if you're lucky, he won't even take up your "going Dutch" offer.

★ When you're in company and he's doing his off-hand bit, you've got two lines of action. Stick around and ignore *him* the way *he's* ignoring *you*. He won't like you showing signs of independence. Don't hesitate to break into the group of people he's talking to if you feel like it and introducing yourself. "You may not have guessed it but I'm his girlfriend." This'll make him look like an ill-mannered yob to his friends and if he's got any sense he'll save himself future embarrassment by making sure he includes you in the action.

The second line of action is just to walk out and go home. Pretty drastic stuff, but the only way if you can't raise the nerve to do anything else. If the guy is keen on you, he's going to want to know *why* you walked out on him and you can tell him you're fed up with being ignored and treated like you're not important. (A lot of Grots don't realise just how grotty they are until it's pointed out to them.)

If he's not keen on you, then he isn't going to care why you walked out. Then you'd be better off nursing your broken heart. Don't go back to him, no matter how much it hurts not to. If you do, he's going to go on using you as a doormat.

THE important thing is to work up the nerve to be honest with the Grot. And maybe the best time, the time when least embarrassment will be caused, is when you're alone together. A heart to heart talk might do the trick. So long as the guy knows you're keen and you don't want to lose him, he's likely to listen to your list of complaints against him. Like we said, a lot of Grots don't realise how grotty they are.

But before you start, have a think about **yourself**. While you're listing **your** complaints, is he going to be matching them with complaints about **you**? So don't start on him, unless you're sure you're not also a Grot!

"Panic was rising in me, and everyone was laughing at me, laughing

I'VE always been the same. If there's a favour to be done and I'm asked to do it — I'll say yes. It doesn't matter how inconvenient it is, or how boring — I just can't say no.

" 'Course I'll set your hair," I'd say to my friend, June, when she asked — and bang would go my homework. Next day, when I got a right telling-off from the teacher, I'd vow that that was the last time — but it never was.

"Oh, Sandy, *please* come with me to this fête thing on Saturday," my friend, Wendy, would say. "The proceeds are for the old people, and I've promised to help — but I don't want to go on my own . . ."

Well, how could you say "no" to that?

"Sandra will do it" was a phrase I was often hearing — both at home and at school. And although it was sometimes inconvenient and took time when I'd rather be doing something else, it was nice to be wanted.

I think that's what made me do it, really — that, and the feeling of being liked. I just couldn't say no and risk offending people or making them dislike me.

Sometimes it caused complications, though.

"You've promised to baby-sit for the Thompsons *again?*" Mum would say. "But, Sandy, you know you promised to come with me to see Gran this Sunday . . ."

"I'll come next week," I'd promise hastily. "Without fail . . ."

NATURALLY, with all this activity, I didn't have a lot of time to spare for boys. Not that they came flocking, exactly. That was why I was so pleased when Ian came to live next door.

Ian was really nice looking. He had brownish hair, super eyes and a great smile! When he first moved in, I would rush to the window every time I heard his door close, and if I was lucky, I'd catch a glimpse of him.

It wasn't long, though, before Mum and Dad got to know Ian's parents, the Maxwells. The four of them seemed to hit it

off, and they were always going out together.

Ian was 18, I learnt, two years older than me, and didn't even have a girlfriend!

Gradually, I got in on the invitations, and soon got to the stage where I was popping casually next door. Ian was friendly and fun.

He treated me a bit as he might treat a younger sister, but he *liked* me, that was the main thing, and I got the feeling that if I stuck around, it might easily turn into something more . . .

He had his own disco equipment, it turned out, and his evenings were pretty much taken up with discos.

"Care to come with me one night?" he asked, after I'd known him a while.

Of course, I jumped at the chance. And, after that, I often went with him.

He wasn't able to pay much attention to me, of course — he was always announcing the records and operating the lights — but just to be with him was enough, and I loved the atmosphere.

"Phew, I'm exhausted!" he would say at the end of an evening. "I reckon running the show is more tiring than dancing all night! Thanks for coming with me, Sandy."

Thanks for coming with me! If only he'd kiss me, I thought, sitting in the darkness of the van beside him, gazing at him.

"Night, Sandy."

Smiling, he leaned across me to open the door.

He didn't need me at all, I reflected sadly, as I walked up the path to our door. If only he'd see me as more than a friend . . .

THEN one day, when I'd called round to drop in Mrs Maxwell's shopping — I often helped her as she had a bad back — it was Ian who answered the door, and he looked really worried.

"Oh, thanks," he said, when I handed him the shopping. "Actually, Mum's not here. She's been called away to her sister, who's been taken ill — I've got to go and pick her up later.

"I'm at my wits' end, trying to get someone to run the disco in case I can't get back in time," he went on.

"It's the rugby club tonight, down at the community hall, and I just can't get anyone to take over!"

His face creased with worry and then suddenly brightened.

"Sandy!" he shouted. "You can do it!"

"Me?" I said.

"Yes. You could do it, couldn't you? You've watched me often enough.

"There's nothing to it, really — just a matter of keeping things moving . . ."

"Well . . ." I began weakly. I shou have said that I'd never watched wha he was doing at all. I'd watched his fac and thought how good looking he wa and I'd watched the dancers, but I been only vaguely aware of his hand moving about over the switches.

"You must do it. You know how" he said eagerly. "I can explain it all you, what you'll have to do . . . please?

He fixed me with those dark eyes his, eyes that were anxious with pleadin Well, how *could* I say no . . . ?

"Of course," I said.

He was wild with delight, huggi me, thanking me, then he explained, great detail, how the disco worked.

He drew a diagram, complete wit knobs and switches, and not once d I tell him that I'd always been hopele with machinery and I hadn't understoc a word of it . . .

"You do follow?" he kept askin "Say if you don't."

And, like a fool, I'd nodded ar smiled and told him to carry on.

"I'll set it all up in the hall ready, he'd ended up happily. "And all you have to do is keep it ticking over till get there.

"It's possible I'll only be a few minut late — certainly not more than half hour. But I can't afford to keep peop waiting . . ."

I'd nodded and smiled some more ar then he'd gone off happy — and I wa left alone with my nightmare.

It'll be all right, I kept tellir myself, as that dreadful afternoon dragge on. I kept a determined picture before m of Ian's hands moving effortlessly over th switches, of his voice smooth announcing the next record.

I would manage. And it would on be for a short time.

BUT when I arrived at the hall, suddenly knew, with a sick feelir in my stomach, that I wasn't going manage at all. And what comfort was that it was only for a short time?

I looked up. There was quite a crowd the hall.

"Say, love, where's the music?" calle one of them, catching my eye.

"Is this supposed to be a disco or morgue?" called someone else.

"It's just coming!" I assured the waving an airy hand, and closing my ey and hoping for the best, I pressed a switch

A soft humming told me I'd pressed right one — at least the thing was on. scrabbled for Ian's paper, and aft frantically staring at it, pressed anoth switch. Green lights began to swing rou the room.

Stupid...

stupid girl making a fool of herself . . .''

There was a moment's surprised silence, then laughter and catcalls.

"The Martians are coming!"

"Hey, it's a new kind of disco — dancing to silent music!"

Of course! I hadn't put the record on the turntable!

Blushing at my own stupidity, I hastily snatched up a record. There were two turntables. Did it matter which . . . ?

I plonked it on the nearest one and took hold of the microphone.

Suddenly, there was a shrill, terrible whistling. People covered their ears, and I turned frantically to the nearest person — who happened to be a tall, fair-haired boy.

"I can't work it!" I blurted out desperately. "Please help me!"

He shook his head, looking blank. "Sorry, love. I don't know a thing about them."

I was almost in tears as the shrill,

dreadful whistling went on. I did the only thing I could do — I switched the machine off again.

It was then the chanting began — a loud, ragged sound, accompanied by the stamping of feet:

"Why are we waiting? Why — are — we — waiting?"

"Ian's Disco," I heard someone call out, obviously reading what was emblazoned on the kit. "For every occasion — except when you want music!"

I felt my face burn. To be talking of Ian's disco like that — the disco he was so proud of and had built up such a great reputation about. Now that reputation was being threatened because of me . . .

I was aware of the growing dissatisfaction in the hall. There was an angry buzz of voices above the persistent chanting and stamping.

"What's going on?" I heard someone say.

"Oh, some idiot can't work the disco . . ."

"I'm going to ask for my money back . . ." said another.

PEOPLE began to drift away, but still a large group stayed surrounding the disco, taunting and calling remarks. And still that dreadful stamping went on.

I just sat there, my face flaming, making no attempt now to try to see how the thing worked. It was all I could do to keep my tears back.

I was still sitting there when someone came up beside me and roughly grabbed my arm . . .

"Ian!"

"What's going on?" His face was grim. "There's a whole crowd of people outside, all asking for their money back . . ."

"I know!" I choked back my sobs.

"Oh, Ian, I'm sorry! I just couldn't do it. I couldn't see how it worked . . ."

"You stupid idiot! Why on earth couldn't you have said so this afternoon?

"I could have arranged for an announcement to be made — anything would have been better than this . . ."

He looked round at the angry crowd, then he looked back at me.

"Do you know that you've nearly ruined me tonight?" he said really nastily.

"I'll be the laughing stock of the town. Why on earth didn't you tell me that you hadn't a clue? I'll never be able to live your stupidity down!"

Tears spilling down my face, I crept away. I just couldn't bear to be there any more. People nudged each other as I passed, and I tried not to hear their giggles and remarks.

But worst of all was the memory of the look on Ian's face — that look that said I was a fool and not worth bothering with.

For *me*, who liked to please people, it was agony to see that look on anyone's face — and on Ian's of all people's! He *did* have a right to feel angry with me because I shouldn't have lied to him in the first place, and I'll never be able to look at him again.

But I know one thing now — that even though it might annoy some people — I'm just going to start saying no! Because I'll never ever get myself into a mess like that again . . .

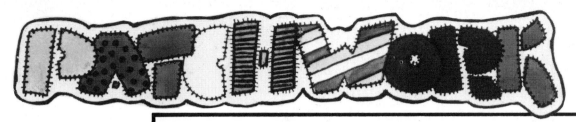

PROMISES, PROMISES . . .

A New Year should always mean a new you! Now's the time to turn over a new leaf and change yourself for the better. But this year, make a few resolutions you *know* you'll be able to keep.

Basically, most of us would like to give up a few horrid habits, and pick up some nicer ones. Here are a few examples:

GIVE UP

★ Being a pig — start eating wisely and your skin and figure will benefit.
★ Smoking — you *know* it's a stupid habit, so stop it.
★ Criticising unnecessarily — take a good long look at *yourself* before you do it!
★ Watching TV all evening — there are always better things to do, unless you want to see a specific programme.
★ Sloppiness — give your mum a hand around the house, it's only fair.

TAKE UP

★ A new hobby — there are literally thousands of things you *could* be doing in your spare time.
★ Meeting new people — don't let yourself get into a rut.
★ Saving money — a little will soon be a lot more than nothing!
★ Changing your appearance — adapt your old clothes for a 1981 look, have a haircut and experiment with make-up.
★ Being punctual — you don't like him being late, do you?
★ Exercising — it can be fun, and you'll definitely notice the difference.
★ Looking forward, instead of back, and making the most of 1981!

SWEET SURPRISE

Try making this unusual Christmas decoration for the family this year. It's a pretty candy wreath, which is simple to make, but looks really effective hanging in a decorated living-room during the festive season.

It may be wise to make more than one candy wreath, since the sweets may not last for long!

You'll need approximately 45 cm of strong, pliable wire, about 3 lb. of wrapped assorted sweets and toffees, and fine wire or cotton to wind round

and attach the sweets to the strong wire.

Make a circle from the strong wire, and fix the ends firmly. Starting from the top, wind the cotton or fine wire round the circle, attaching the wrapped sweets as you go.

The final result, as shown, will be a packed circlet of sweets. Hang the wreath from the wall with some brightly-coloured ribbon, and hang a small pair of scissors on to the circlet with another length of ribbon tied in a bow at the top.

Use the scissors to snip sweets from the wreath as required!

THE COST OF CHRISTMAS . . .

While you're preparing for, or enjoying the Christmas break, do you ever seriously consider the people for whom Christmas isn't always so much fun?

What about those people who are too sick, or poor or old, to really appreciate and enjoy Christmas? Unfortunately, there are a great many people throughout this country and the rest of the world who fall into these categories, so perhaps it's time *we* thought about them, and at the same time, thought about the real, uncommercialised meaning of Christmas, too.

The sick, lonely, old and impoverished deserve to be thought of and cared for just as much as you or me, and their plight can be relieved to a certain extent through the efforts of those who do care.

YOU can care, too, by donating money to charities (even a little can go a long way), and by raising money for various charities by staging sponsored events, such as swims, knit-ins, clean-ups and dieting, for example.

If you, or a group of friends, would like to help in this way, or would like to find out more about raising money for various causes, here are a few addresses to which you can write for more information.

There are lots of charities in need of money for aid and research — these are just a few, but you'll find many more in your local yellow pages.

Mr Christopher Robinson,
Appeals Project Officer,
The Spastics Society,
2a Conway Street,
London W1.

Save The Children Fund,
Press Office,
157 Clapham Road,
London SW9.

Oxfam,
Press Office,
274 Banbury Road,
Oxford.

Ian Stirling,
Shelter Press Office,
157 Waterloo Road,
London SE1 HUU.
(01-633-9377).

Cancer Research,
Appeals Campaign,
2 Carlton House Terrace,
London SW17 5AR.

REMEMBER TO ENCLOSE

AN S.A.E. WHEN

YOU WRITE.

IT'S A WINTER WONDERLAND!

Make the most of the wintry weather this year, and try to get involved in as many sporting activities as you can.

Skating's an obvious winter favourite, either at a local skating rink, or on a frozen pond. Wrap up well if you're going to be outside, and check that the ice is really safe to skate on.

Given a good fall of snow, sledging is the best way to spend an afternoon with a group of friends. Dig out your old sledge, scrub some of the rust off it, and get going.

If you're without a sledge, but wearing waterproof clothing (and an over-the-behind cagoule) you could try glissading instead. Simply sit down on your cagoule, tuck your legs up in front of you and you'll be speeding downhill before you know it. Make sure you try this out on a grassy, snow-covered slope — any hidden boulders, ditches or bumps could be very dangerous.

Snow fights and snowman building are the first things you think of doing when the snow falls — try a snow-castle building competition with your friends instead.

If you don't want to engage yourself in any of these exciting pursuits, the least you can do is go for long walks, breathing in the crisp, fresh winter air.

No more hogging the fire and moaning about the weather!

Get A Move On!

OK, so it's a bit more difficult to poke your nose out the door and get some exercise in wintertime. Let's face it — you don't particularly want to meet your end swimming in an ice-cold sea, and the idea of going for a leisurely stroll in a force-ten gale doesn't exactly grab you as the ideal way to spend a Saturday afternoon! So what do you do now? Well, there're plenty of *other* ways to prevent you turning into a big fat blob. Here are just a few!

DANCE AWAY

Why not better Hot Gossip and start your own dance troupe? Dance your spare tyre away and enjoy yourself doing it. Obviously, this'll take quite a lot of determination at the beginning but once you get the ball rolling it'll be worth it. Start by finding a place to practise. Your youth club or your school might set aside their hall one night if you're determined enough. Your mum's living-room is definitely out! Pool all your danceable records together and pre-record several tapes worth.

Once you've done that you're in business! Sit down together and listen to the tape a couple of times through before trying out any ideas, then swap suggestions to make a simple dance. Don't be too ambitious at first. What may seem like a simple sequence to you will turn into something horrendously difficult when six of you are trying to do it in time!

BE N-ICE!

Make up your mind now to visit your local ice rink regularly — skating is *excellent* exercise for the thighs! If you're going to make a hobby of it, it's better to buy your own skates, but until you've tried it, you're best to hire a pair the first few times. Most ice rinks have a beginners' night and it's a good idea to enrol in such a class if you can, as an area of the ice is partitioned off so you don't have to worry about experienced skaters crashing into you.

IN THE SWIM

One of the surest ways of using all your muscles is swimming. The great thing about it is that a lot of people are put off going in the water because they forget that the pool is wonderfully heated, and they shiver at the mere thought of diving into the water. So you've a good chance of having the pool all to yourself — delicious!

GLOW IN THE SNOW

Wait till the snow arrives, arm yourself with a woolly scarf, a pair of wellies, hat (did you know that most heat escapes from your head?) and gloves, and go build yourself a snowman! Or borrow your kid brother's sledge and go off in search of a nice steep slope — OK, the whizzing-down part won't do you any good, but pushing the sledge back up again will certainly make up for it! If you don't have a sledge, use an old tin tray or a

As soon as the miserable, cold weather starts to creep up on you, it's the same old story . . . you plonk yourself down in front of the telly and refuse to budge, keeping up your strength by stuffing your chops full of stodgy food. This course of action in turn results in the same old story every spring — utter *misery* as you attempt to squeeze yourself into your lighter togs. So get set for winter — and 1981 — now, with our super ideas for getting you out and about. You'll soon feel much better — and you'll look great!

large polythene bag. The most energetic way to lose weight in the snow is to organise a massive snowball fight. All that bending, stretching, ducking, throwing and running uses up more calories than you'd imagine — just try it and see!

FIGHTING FIT!

Is kung fu, judo or karate up your street? Learn the perfect art of total control over your reflexes, and get some good advice in self-defence at the same time. Again, you'll probably find classes at your local youth club, school or college.

IF you'd rather get some exercise in a slightly less energetic way, here are a few ideas. Walk up stairs rather than taking a lift, and if you're sitting watching telly, practise picking up things with your feet, or do ankle-twists — anything which will keep you moving. Lifting Mars Bars to your mouth is NOT considered good exercise!

If you want to do something constructive with all this exercise, how does the idea of an early spring clean grab you? Why not clean out all your unwanted possessions and talk your dad into letting you decorate your room? Giving walls a good lick of paint really whittles away the calories, and bending and stretching will really improve your stomach muscles. Plus that, you'll have a super fresh room all ready for spring!

Basically, if you think about it, almost *anything* you do is exercise. You've just got to remember that the main point to keep in mind is to *keep moving*. Once you get into the habit of doing absolutely nothing, you'll find it almost impossible to break out of it. We hope we've given you a few ideas on keeping fit, and more important, helped you to see that it doesn't *have* to be a drag. Here's to a healthy new you for the spring!!

How Moody Are You?

I F you want to know what sort of mood you're in and what you should and should *not* do about it, try our special quiz and we'll tell you! It's quite simple — first of all, choose your favourite colour of the moment, and just answer the questions that appear in that colour section. Your score will direct you to a certain part of the conclusions, and that'll tell you all about you and your mood of the moment!

If you find it hard to choose one colour, not to worry! You can pick two or three colours (but not more). Then, answer ALL the questions in those sections. Divide your score by two if you used two colours, or divide it by three if you used three colours.

You can do the quiz another day, if you feel in a different mood. Choose a different colour (or colours) and you'll get a different answer, to help you with your mood of that particular moment!

IF YOUR FAVOURITE COLOUR IS RED:

You start with a score of 100 in this section. Deduct the points given.

1. Would you like to have your bedroom decorated in reds?
Would you wear an all-red outfit?
Would you fancy a meal in a café decorated all in red?
 a. Yes to all 3 — deduct 1 point.
 b. Yes to 2 — deduct 2 points.
 c. Yes to 1 or none — deduct 5 points.

2. Do you ever dream of blood?
 a. Yes. Deduct 1 point.
 b. No. Deduct 5 points.

3. Choose a word from the following group: sincere, straightforward, positive, forward, action, definite.
 a. If you chose straightforward or action, deduct 1 point.
 b. If you chose forward, deduct 2 points.

c. If you chose positive or definite, deduct 3 points.
 d. If you chose sincere, deduct 5 points.

4. Would it put you off a boy if someone said he was aggressive, even if you hadn't met him?
 a. No. Deduct 1 point.
 b. It might put you off, but you'd still meet him and decide for yourself. Deduct 2 points.
 c. Definitely you wouldn't want to meet him. Deduct 5 points.

IF YOUR FAVOURITE COLOUR IS YELLOW:

You start with a score of 80 in this section. Deduct the points given.

1. Do you enjoy eating yellow food (cheese, butter, eggs, etc.)?
Would you wear yellow shoes with a yellow dress?
Would you like a bed with yellow sheets and covers?
 a. Yes to all 3 — deduct 1 point.
 b. Yes to 2 — deduct 2 points.
 c. Yes to 1 or none — deduct 5 points.

2. Do your problems seem less serious when the sun is shining?
 a. Not particularly. Deduct 5 points.
 b. Yes, usually. Deduct 1 point.

3. Choose a word from the following group: cheerful, bright, happy, fortunate, lucky, smile.
 a. If you chose smile, deduct 1 point.
 b. If you chose fortunate or lucky, deduct 2 points.
 c. If you chose any of the others, deduct 5 points.

4. If you spent the evening with your boyfriend and he was moody or unhappy the whole time for no reason, would you feel your romance was on its last legs?
 a. No. Deduct 1 point.
 b. Maybe — it would depend on your own mood. Deduct 2 points.
 c. Yes. Deduct 5 points.

IF YOUR FAVOURITE COLOUR IS GREEN:

You start with a score of 60 in this section. Deduct the points given.

1. Do you make a point of eating a lot of vegetables because you think they're good for you?
Do you think it's unlucky to bring certain green plants indoors — like lilac branches or hawthorn?
Do you like green as a colour but find it impossible to wear?
 a. No to all 3 — deduct 1 point.
 b. No to 2 — deduct 2 points.
 c. No to 1 or none — deduct 5 points.

2. Do you find that a room with pale-green walls has a calming effect on you?
  a. Yes. Deduct 1 point.
  b. No. Deduct 5 points.

3. Choose a word from the following group: belief, choice, attitude, thought, care, decide.
  a. If you chose care, deduct 1 point.
  b. If you chose belief or thought, deduct 2 points.
  c. If you chose decide, deduct 3 points.
  d. If you chose choice or attitude, deduct 5 points.

4. What do you think is the ideal length of time for an engagement?
  a. It varies according to the temperaments of the couple. Deduct 1 point.
  b. 18 months or less. Deduct 2 points.
  c. More than 18 months. Deduct 5 points.

40-2-1.5-1

IF YOUR FAVOURITE COLOUR IS BLUE:

You start with a score of 40 in this section. Deduct the points given.

1. Would you like an outfit in shades of blue?
There aren't many natural blue foods — would you fancy eating ordinary food like potatoes or bread if it were coloured blue? Would you like your bedroom to be decorated in shades of blue?
  a. Yes to all 3 — deduct 1 point.
  b. Yes to 2 — deduct 2 points.
  c. Yes to 1 or none — deduct 5 points.

2. Do you believe in the saying, "Pink makes the boys wink, blue makes the boys true"?
  a. Yes. Deduct 5 points.
  b. No. Deduct 1 point.

3. Choose a word from the following group: tension, argument, tiff, bicker, sulk.
  a. If you chose argument, deduct 1 point.
  b. If you chose bicker or tiff, deduct 2 points.
  c. If you chose any other, deduct 5 points.

4. How long do you feel it would take you to get over the break-up of a relationship with a boy you've been seeing regularly for six months, and he did the breaking-up?
  a. You'd never completely get over it. Deduct 5 points.
  b. You'd have forgotten your sorrows in six months. Deduct 1 point.
  c. It would take more than six months to forget. Deduct 2 points.

IF YOUR FAVOURITE COLOUR IS PURPLE:

You start with a score of 20 in this section. Deduct the points given.

1. Do you fancy the idea of yourself in a matching lavender nightie and negligee? When you eat coloured Smarties, do you eat the purple ones first? Do you think pansy-purple eye-shadow looks sexy?
  a. Yes to all 3 — deduct 1 point.
  b. Yes to 2 — deduct 2 points.
  c. Yes to 1 or none — deduct 5 points.

2. Do you dream in colour?
  a. Yes. Deduct 1 point.
  b. Don't usually remember dreams, so can't tell. Deduct 2 points.
  c. No. Deduct 5 points.

3. Choose a word from the following group: star-crossed, misfortune, fate, weird, jinx.
  a. If you chose misfortune or weird, deduct 1 point.
  b. If you chose fate or jinx, deduct 2 points.
  c. If you chose star-crossed, deduct 5 points.

4. Do you feel that somewhere there is a boy who is exactly right for you, and it's just a matter of luck bringing you together?
  a. Yes. Deduct 5 points.
  b. No. Deduct 1 point.
  c. You think there is more than one. Deduct 2 points.

Now count up your score (remember, if you scored for TWO COLOURS, *halve your score*, if you scored for THREE COLOURS, *divide your score by three* and turn to the conclusions.

QUIZ CONCLUSIONS

89-99 points: Steady — you could be heading for a big row or a challenge of some sort. Take a little more time to make sure that what you're doing is what you really want. Did you feel like this a week ago? Then the action you're considering could be right. If not — if you just woke up today in this dashing, crazy mood — try to put off decisions until tomorrow!

80-88 points: You're in a very positive mood at the moment, and this would be a good time to be more daring and outgoing than normal. So if you have a favour to ask, a rise to seek, or want to put your foot down, now's the time. But make sure you have all your facts right, first!

69-79 points: You're a bit too casual at the moment about everything! You have lots of confidence, but are maybe a bit too impulsive for your own good. If you're thinking of spending more than one week's money on one particular purchase, think about it for at least 24 hours.

60-68 points: You're a fairly happy-go-lucky person anyway, and today is a good day for you. Things will run very smoothly so now is the right time to tackle any chores that you've been putting off! It's also a good time to think of a change in your normal routine.

49-59 points: You're entering a more serious mood than you've been in and the next 24 hours could be important. Don't be too outspoken — remember, people aren't always as good at keeping secrets as they could be. This isn't a time to make snap judgments about important things like a job, a boyfriend, or a holiday. Take time to think about it!

40-48 points: You've got everything going for you, but you must act positively to take advantage of opportunities. What you need is some friendly help, just a friend to talk things over with. It could help you a lot to take your mind off any activities that are causing you headaches or heartaches at the moment. Get right away from the usual routine, if only for a few hours, it'll do you the world of good!

29-39 points: A bit ratty or edgy today then, are we? You're probably regretting something you said or did earlier. It's much better to kiss and make up than brood if it's a boyfriend. Try to put things right with a friendly word or two. It could be you are normally more easy going, but you're feeling tense at the moment and need to relax. Try to get more exercise, you'll find it easier to relax mentally and physically afterwards.

20-28 points: You're going through rather an unhappy phase. You definitely need a bit of cheering up so this would be a good time to indulge yourself in your favourite treat! Don't be ashamed of feeling a bit weepy, a good cry to get it out of your system will probably work wonders!

9-19 points: Could jealousy be your big problem today? Remember, if you have a problem it's much better to do something positive about solving it, rather than just brood over it. Whatever you do, don't try to solve it in some underhand or sneaky way — that'll just make things worse!

0-8 points: You're a very emotional person, and you depend a lot on luck. If you tried to be less guided by your heart and relied more on your own brains and talent, you'd be happier and probably make more of a success of your life! You have quite a lot of sex appeal even though you don't think you do, so don't under-rate yourself! Go out and make a splash!

Dresses and suits: Skirts are still slightly shorter — either on or above the knee. Soft, cuddly sweatshirts, or pretty drop-waisted dresses, look lovely with woolly tights and ankle socks, or coloured tights and low-heeled courts, for day.

The new suit is fitted, with a small box jacket and pleated mini skirt. Plaids are a strong favourite this winter, along with soft greys, pastels, and bold prints.

Have a look at some of the newest and, we think, prettiest styles for winter 1980-81. Guaranteed to warm up the most miserable winter weather!

Look Ahead!

Evening: The look for evening is definitely soft and feminine. The emphasis is on simplicity and the minimum of fuss, and fabrics are draped and silky.

Try lightly-padded print jackets, and matching tapered trousers, in pale, subtle colours. Bags are quilted too, to match the soft mood. Shell shapes in bags are complemented by chunky shell necklaces and hair decorations in muted, pearlised colours.

Separates and jumpsuits:

Plaid corduroy, and checked or tartan wool trousers are a front-runner in the separates category this season. Wear them with neat patterned twinsets, in soft, cosy colours, or boldly patterned ski sweaters, guaranteed to keep out the cold.

Jumpsuits are still with us, but with a slightly different look this time round. They're really like "Baby-gro" suits, made in soft, fleecy fabrics, and teamed with fun accessories, like the kitten-shaped hat and muff. Baby colours are definitely a strong theme for winter.

Shoes are either flat pumps, or low-heeled, comfortable courts — in pastels and bright, two-tone colours.

HAVE you ever wished that you weren't what you are? Wished, perhaps, that you were famous, rich — beautiful? Well, you're not the only one. But what about some of the famous people that *are* around, is it possible they ever wish they'd been something else — and have you ever thought that some of them *would* do better in another profession, like Anna Ford as a Sphinx? We've given a few examples below!

KERMIT THE FROG

Well, what else could we have our little friend being except a Prince Charming — not that he's not utterly charming as he is, but there's something about green skin and warts that doesn't inspire you to snuggle up to him — still, if you're a pig . . . ? Any offers for a transforming kiss?

MARIE OSMOND

What else could Marie possibly be, along with the rest of he family, but a pair of teeth advertising every new brand of toothie paste that came on the market. She must have the stronges jaw muscles in the world by now, with all that smiling.

LEWIS COLLINS

Sorry, Lewis, but there's something that's just a little shift about you — especially around the eyes — and that's why w think you'd make the ideal used-car salesman. That firm mouth those eyes — that muscled, towering body — we'll take it!!

SUPERMAN

Christopher Reeve, in the Superman role, just *has* to be a candidate for the Statue of Liberty. I mean, haven't *you* got bored with seeing that same old lady standing there with her torch every time you steam into New York Harbour(!)? Super-man could be a great help if any of the boats got into difficulty as well . . .

STAR

72

TURN!

THEREZE BAZAAR

Thereze has a face that could launch a thousand ships, or sell a few thousand pounds worth of cosmetics!

Where else have you seen someone more suited to standing behind the make-up counter in a Woolworth's store?

OK, so Thereze and David do look pretty neat together, but what would she do without *him* . . .

STING

If you've seen the Police in concert then you'll know what an energetic performer Sting is, and off-stage the athletic police-man is a keep-fit fanatic. He exercises every morning and is a past junior sports champion. So, should the Police ever get into hard times, you never know where you might find him — 1984's Olympic Games!

B. A. ROBERTSON

Perhaps you've already seen B. A. look-alikes at football grounds and outside rock venues. He's the chap who's looking rather shifty and asking for £50.00 for a ticket that would normally cost you a fiver. We're only joking, of course, but B. A. does look rather furtive here, doesn't he?

BOB GELDOF

Everyone knows what job would suit modest Bob, apart from his present profession, but would *you* vote for him if he was to stand for Parliament? Whether or not Bob would actually get elected remains a matter of some speculation — but he would certainly liven up those tedious Party Political Broadcasts.

Clothes Fo

Clothes can say a lot about you and the sort of person you are to people who don't know you. So it's important to remember that there's a time and place for everything. Who'd go hill walking in stilettos or to a garden party in denim shorts, for example? They're extreme examples, but here are some light-hearted guidelines to knowing *what* to wear, and *when!*

WHAT TO WEAR WHEN YOU'RE — MEETING HIS PARENTS

You've been going out with him for quite a while, then he suddenly announces, "Would you like to come to tea on Sunday?" And you think: Oh, no . . . ! It's not that you don't *want* to go, but the prospect of meeting his mum and dad is nerve-racking enough without the added problem of what to wear!

The mere fact that he's asked you home means that he likes you a lot and wants to show you off to his parents.

If you care about him in the same way, you'll want to create the right sort of impression with them at first, and let them see what a nice, sensible, attractive, smart and down-to-earth girl you are for their son.

What To Wear

It's a safe bet that you're choosing the right clothes if you go through your wardrobe and pick an outfit that you don't like but your mum has always raved about! The only problem with wearing the little petal-pink suit with the Peter Pan collar that your mum adores is that if you don't feel happy wearing it, it will undermine your confidence and make you feel pretty fed-up, which will show in your face.

So pick clothes you feel happy in. A skirt with a matching blouse or jumper, matching coloured tights (without ladders!), and a leather shoulder bag and matching sensible-looking shoes will appeal to his mum.

Alternatively, if you have one, wear a fairly demure, high-necked dress, which you can pretty up with a nice brooch or a scarf at the neck. Mums seem to like pretty brooches and neck scarves!

If you have long hair, pull it back or wear it up. Mothers in general don't like hair flopping round faces and fringes falling into eyes, tea, soup, etc.

Keep your make-up very simple — just a touch of eyeshadow, mascara and lip gloss. It's very difficult meeting your boy's mother for the first time — if you're too dressed up she may think you're flashy; if you're not dressed up enough she may think you couldn't care less!

The best thing is to play everything down a little to begin with, as far as clothes are concerned. Play up the happy, sweet, kind and friendly side of yourself, and that way it's a safe bet that his mum will stop looking at your clothes and begin to notice the real you.

What Not To Wear

Even if your boy sees you every day of the week in jeans and T-shirts and, more to the point, *loves* to see you in jeans and T-shirts,

the same clothes won't wash with his mum. Jeans, of any size, shape or form, are definitely *out* for that first meeting over the tea table!

In fact, even your brand-new, dead-expensive, straight-legged, £25-a-go, pink satin trousers are out, because mothers seem to prefer a girl to be an old-fashioned girl (with, don't forget, manners to match).

Don't, whatever you do, wear a T-shirt with a slogan like "See me, feel me . . . !" His dad may be impressed, but his better half will be horrified, unless she's a *very* liberated lady.

High, thin-heeled shoes are out, too. Anyway, they might leave holes in his mum's good Cushionfloor when you're drying the dishes.

Avoid anything that's shocking pink, bright yellow, passionate purple or pea-green. Don't wear anything strapless or see-through, or she'll soon see through *you*, and, even though you might be a dedicated punk, for goodness' sake leave the coal-mine eyes, rigor-mortis lips and vampire finger-nails at home.

And finally, even if you have no chest to speak of, wear a bra . . .

WHAT TO WEAR WHEN YOU'RE — ON A FIRST DATE

So he's asked you out. Whether he's se you around at school, or just around th town, he must fancy you already, and mu really like the way you look. But even s *everyone* gets into a flap about what to we for a first date, and spends hours beforeha rummaging through wardrobe and drawe finally ending up wearing what they decid they looked revolting in four hours befor

Whatever you wear, you'll think you lo awful — it's all tied up with the whole fir date scene — but remember, it's *you* he

74

All Reasons !

...terested in, and clothes aren't really all ...at important, though it helps if you feel ...at you're looking OK.

What To Wear

Unless you've met him at a party or disco, ...hen you've been dressed to kill anyway, ...ne times out of ten he'll only have seen ...ou in your school uniform or everyday ...lothes. Obviously, you want to knock him ...ut on that first date, but don't go overboard. ...ost boys find something really appealing in ...e girl who's naturally fresh and pretty, so ...o for pretty clothes, and a hint of flowery ...erfume!

Wear a self-coloured silky blouse which is ...ce to touch, and pretty it up with lace round ...e collar, or a matching piece of ribbon. ...hoose a pretty skirt in a nice fresh cotton — ...o butchy tweed or cord.

Boys like dresses, the floatier and softer ...e better, so if you have a nice peasanty or ...illy one, wear it.

Wear your flimsiest shoes or sandals to ...how off your pretty little feet. If they're big, ...ear boots, which boys find sexy, as long as ...ey're not wellies, hob-nailed or ankle-length, ...heepskin booties.

Borrow one of your mum's lacy hankies, ...e'll think it's really cute when you cry at the ...ctures (or you can use it to wipe away his ...ars when you tell him you don't want to see ...m again).

If you have long hair, wear it loose, unless ...ou can be sure it'll all tumble down at the ...rucial moment, in true Hollywood Romance ...yle.

What Not To Wear

If you were decked out at the disco like a ...ristmas tree when you met him he ...viously likes it, so it's OK to dress the ...me for the first date. But dressing up in ...rish colours, split skirts, fish-net T-shirts, ...ain belt and black stockings and ...spenders when he's only seen you in ...hool uniform is guaranteed to frighten the ...e out of him.

The punk look is too aggressive (unless he's ...punk himself). Try to avoid trousers, as all ...ale chauvinist pigs like to see the real shape ...a girl's legs (one exception here, and that's ...your nickname's Tilly Treetrunk or Claire ...icketstump).

On the other hand, if you've got a great ...gure and look amazing in jeans, slither into ...em. On the right girl, they're very sexy.

Don't wear rude brooches; he may get ...tirely the wrong idea about you. Steer clear ... military jackets, or anything vaguely ...asculine, which might frighten him.

Don't wear a woolly jumper or cardigan. ...ere's nothing very soft and sexy about ...nctional old wool.

Stay clear of stockings and suspender belts, ... your first date anyway. Again, he might get ...e wrong idea about you and suddenly ...come too hot to handle. Don't wear clumpy ...eat elephant shoes which could break his ...es when he kisses you goodnight, or tights ...ld together with nail varnish.

Don't wear anything that's not as fresh as it ...uld be — not if you want him to get closer, ...yway!

WHAT TO WEAR WHEN YOU'RE — AT THE DISCO

Now the disco's one place you can really let rip with your clothes — if you're not careful! There's absolutely no excuse for being shy and frightened about getting

dressed up for the disco. If you do feel like that, then you'd be well advised to spend your evenings in the public library instead. Discos and disco gear have never had it so good, and unless the gear's right you won't do your boogying any justice at all. You're there to let go, have a good time, and get yourself *noticed*! In all disco-goers there's a bit of the show-off, so throw caution to the wind, terrify the budgie, give your dad a seizure, and dress to kill!

What To Wear

Simply wear whatever you feel really good in, and will make you stand out from the crowd. The brighter the colour, the better — or all in white is great because it shows up well under disco lights. Silks and satins are fantastic — they glimmer in the lights and, if you've a good figure, cling to the right bits of your anatomy when you're dancing!

Choose straight-legged satin pants in any colour of the rainbow, with a skimpy little shimmery top.

The higher your heels, the better, as long as you don't keep falling over, which will ruin the image! If you're happier in a skirt, stick to the same colourful materials.

If you've a waist, nip it in with a wide, glittery or patent belt. Wear lots of jewellery, especially silver or gold to glitter under the lights.

Sprinkle matching glitter on your hair, but whatever you do, wear lashings of lip gloss which really looks good shimmering against white disco teeth!

Above all, don't be frightened to be outrageous, and remember to wear a huge smile — there's nothing worse than a miserable sea of disco faces looking as if they're only there for the beer, and even that's rotten . . .

What Not To Wear

What not to wear, basically, is anything that you wear at work or change into when you get home from school to watch the telly in. Boring everyday clothes will make you

feel boring and everyday. That means plain old jeans, deadly dull skirts and any other boring old clothes that don't turn you, or anyone else, on. Don't wear anything that you'll feel hot and uncomfortable in after half an hour.

That includes anything too tight,which might look good, but leaves you terrified that you'll get soaked with sweat which might show. Or, worst of all, split from top to bottom (literally!).

Don't wear anything blatantly braless and see-through. If you're looking for a nice guy, that's the wrong way to go about it.

In the majority of cases, boys don't really like it, unless they're only after what they can get, and that sort aren't worth knowing. And, likewise, avoid skirts slit up to your bottom, or tops slashed down to your waist.

Again, this kind of gear really will put nice boys off.

Don't wear flat shoes. They look pretty silly at a disco. Don't wear boring, flesh-coloured tights either — not when there's every colour under the sun to choose from.

And don't, *please,* wear your bag on your shoulder, or put it on the floor in front of you when you're dancing. It looks too awful for words.

WHAT TO WEAR WHEN YOU'RE — OUT FOR A MEAL

Going out for dinner does *not* mean the Wimpy Bar or the sitty-down bit of the local chipper. Dinner *does* mean a bit of luxury that doesn't happen very often because boys are usually too hard up.

But suppose your boyfriend's saved up to take you out for dinner to celebrate your anniversary, or birthday.

It's worth making a very special effort to look good for, because it's costing him a pretty penny, more likely than not, and whether it's the local Reo Stakis Steakhouse or a five-star hotel, the whole eating-out

thing in a nice atmosphere is a great experience.

What To Wear

If you're being taken out for a nice evening meal, not a luxury one, that is a Chinese, Indian or Steakhouse-type place, the best thing to go for is simply a pretty dress, provided it's not very tightly fitted because you'll never get past the first few forkfuls of rice or Steakhouse French Fries!

But if this evening meal is in a five-star hotel or expensive, romantic candlelit restaurant with soft music, finger bowls and toothpicks, do him the honour of looking gorgeous! This is the one time to wear a long dress, simple and elegant if possible, to make the best of what's underneath.

Go for halter-necks or tiny shoulder straps to show off your shoulders in the candlelight and wear one very simple silver or gold chain round your neck, with a matching chain round your wrist.

If your dress is simple and self-coloured, pin a rosebud or tiny flower on it — you can even tuck a tiny flower into your hair, which, if it's long, should be swept back or up, or softly waved.

Make sure you take a little evening purse or clutch bag — your everyday takes-everything-but-the-kitchen-sink shoulder bag will look too clumsy. Wear lashings of lovely perfume and concentrate on making your eye make-up as pretty as possible to give that big, dewy-eyed look across the table.

Wear a pretty silk or crochet shawl around your shoulders to slip off when you sit down.

What Not To Wear

No-one ever goes out for dinner in trousers — it's just *not* done! Only if you own a really fabulous silk harem suit is it acceptable, and even then some high-class hotels will frown on it. Never wear anything tight, especially if you have a midriff which will begin to expand as the meal progresses. If you're a messy eater don't wear light colours, which, horror of horrors, might show anything you spill.

Don't wear anything that's too way out. Your long shocking pink Lurex tube dress may be OK at the disco, but would look quite out of place at a ritzy restaurant.

Don't wear cheap jewellery — if that's all you have, don't wear anything at all. If you have long hair, don't wear it loose and floppy — it might fall in the soup, and anyway, it looks much more sophisticated when worn off the face.

Don't spoil the whole effect by floating into the restaurant in a plastic mac, tweed knee-length coat or cardi slung over your shoulders.

If you don't have a fur coat, silk or crochet shawl, go without. Don't wear boots under your dress and avoid floaty scarves round your neck. They'll float all right —into the soup.

WHAT TO WEAR WHEN YOU'RE — GOING TO AN INTERVIEW

Everyone, at some stage in their lives, has to face the dreaded interview. Interviews are horrible, no-one likes them, but first impressions are what interviews are all about. No prospective employer is going to be impressed with a girl who obviously hasn't made the slightest effort to look her best; that attitude will reflect on her work as far as the prospective employer is concerned, i.e. lazy, careless and untidy.

No matter whether you're trying to get a job as a dishwasher or a personal secretary, be as smart as possible, to create an image of efficiency.

What To Wear

The golden rule to remember is that everything must look clean and well cared for. Even if you can't afford a new outfit, make sure it looks neat and tidy. The best thing to wear for an interview is a smart suit, with a well-cut jacket and skirt, but, unfortunately, they don't come cheap, as most interviewers realise these days, so you just have to make do with the next best thing.

Choose a plain blouse and skirt in sober colours, for example, a cream blouse (or jumper) with an unfussy dark or matching skirt. If you feel drab like that, wear a little floral brooch or pin at the neck of the blouse, which must be fastened to a decent height.

Your skirt should be calf length, with dark or flesh-coloured tights, and smart shoes with a matching bag. If you want a touch of luxury, try a silky scarf round your neck.

Polish your shoes like mad, check tights for holes or ladders, and see that your hands and fingernails are spotless.

Wear simple make-up, and if you want to look the cool, efficient secretary type, take a notepad and pen in your bag to jot down notes, because the interviewer will expect you to ask questions.

Make sure you have a clean hankie (blowing your nose is a great diversion when you're stuck for something to say!).

What Not To Wear

Again trousers are out, even in these days of Women's Lib.and sexual equality.You have to be sensible about this. *You* may know you look great in trousers, but prospective employers will not be impressed. Even the smooth, camel, stay-press slacks should be given a miss (anyway, who'd *want* to wear them?). Dungarees aren't acceptable, either.

If you're a punk avoid anything even faintly to do with your private punk life — this includes safety-pin-style brooches, tiny silver razor-blade necklaces, even plastic banana badges. You won't get taken on for fear that you'll be more efficient at smashing filing cabinets and hurling tea urns through windows than typing.

Don't wear anything remotely slinky or sexy — you won't get the job if they think you'll spend your time climbing into the filing cabinet with the office messenger boy.

Finally, don't try to make yourself look *amazingly* good, because, if you get the job, it'll take all your pay packets to keep up the image!

WHAT TO WEAR WHEN YOU'RE — AT A FOOTBALL MATCH

It would be interesting to know what percentage of the male population are footie freaks. If you're going out with one of the minority, then you're dead lucky; if you're going out with one of the majority, then hard luck. Unless, of course, you're one of those strange females who actually *enjoys* watching fellas mindlessly chasing a ball round a field! The day will dawn when you'll have to spend the best part of a precious Saturday shivering on the sidelines, but the right gear can make the whole boring experience more bearable.

What To Wear

Well, as football is, basically, a winter sport, you'd look pretty silly in a summer dress — you'd also freeze. Yes, at last, this is where jeans come to the fore. Trousers of any shape or size are a must, but if you want to please the boy who's dragged you along, your jeans, or, even better, tracksuit bottoms, should be in the boyfriend's team colours (this is really so that the other side's fans can single you out and kick you in the bottom when you bend over to retrieve your rattle).

Wear the brightest, biggest, baggiest sweater you can find, with four other jumpers underneath, and thermal underwear underneath *them*. You may look like a Michelin man, but at least you'll be warm.

Knit yourself a bobble hat, scarf and mitts in the *right* colours, and buy one of those awful rattles — not specifically to cheer the team on, but the physical effort of swinging the thing keeps you warm.

Don't forget your dad's socks under your boots (preferably hob-nailed for defence!). Duffel coats are useful — they're warm, you can twiddle the toggles around when it gets boring, and hide under the hood when you want to fall asleep.

What Not To Wear

Don't wear a dress. That's really stupid, because it's much more draughty than trousers. Don't wear tights, you'll tear them to shreds on the wooden seats and boards, and don't wear heeled shoes. After the game you'll fall flat on your face trying to walk away — the heels will have sunk into the turf.

It's no good trying to do the model look at a football match, play up the sporty theme instead. It's simpler to avoid anything that looks pretty and feminine, because it'll get ruined with the flying mud, rain-drenched pink Andrex, flying pork-pie missiles and the liquid contents of assorted cans.

Don't wear pink lipstick, it might turn blue with the cold. Avoid red fingernails, too, they clash with blue mottled fingers.

And lastly, for very obvious reasons, don't wear the wrong colours . . .

F you haven't already heard, this is the Year of the Monkey, as dictated by the Chinese calendar. Certain boys are *really* going to come into their own this year and it's only fair, we feel, that we give you a few tips on what to look for, because there are a lot of MCM's about — Male Chauvinist Monkeys — and you *don't* want to end up monkeying around with the wrong boy, do you?

ALEC APE

STARTING with . . . Alec Ape. He's the life and soul of the party, the centre of attention, and the source of most of that annoying noise when you enter the room.

This is because he lives up to his name and is a mimic. He can ''ape'' or imitate anybody from famous comedians to yourself, and we all know how annoying bad Elvis Costello imitations have become these days. So Mr Ape's first annoying trait is that he can be a *bore*.

He'll very rarely notice if *you're* feeling bored stiff, because he's so absorbed with his own fabulously aggravating imitations of Mike Yarwood imitating somebody else. **Unless you enjoy being constantly amused, give Alec Ape a *wide* berth.**

BRIAN BABOON

BRIAN BABOON is a much more serious proposition. He's the fiercely possessive type. Baboons are notoriously fierce and will guard their ladies and their territory against anybody in the most *vicious* fashion.

At the same time they have a strong sense of humour and propriety. If you're easy-going, like people and enjoy dancing with lots of boys at parties and not being answerable for your whereabouts *24* hours a day, Brian is NOT your sort.

He'll drive you *mad* with his possessiveness; embarrass you in pubs or at parties by socking boys who so much as talk to you; and bore you silly with his regular routines and love of going to the same well-tried places.

If you feel a bit insecure and would like a permanent chap for the Year of the Monkey, then Brian Baboon will love, cherish and care for you, for ever, and ever, and . . .

CHARLIE CHIMPANZEE

CHARLIE CHIMPANZEE, on the other hand, can be *very* lovable indeed. Just think of those endearing tea-drinking chimps on telly, and you know how lovable a chimp *can* be.

Bear in mind though, as your heart begins to melt towards sweet, funny, handsome Charlie, that he can be very, very mischievous. This can take various forms.

He's quite oblivious of the fact that he's been seen two-timing you with that HORRIBLE girl from round the corner, and can't understand what all the fuss is about.

He's also the sort who thinks it's funny to miss the last bus, or get stranded without an umbrella in a rainstorm, or hide round the corner from where he's supposed to meet you and jump out and scare you silly.

If you can stand all this . . . then Charlie's your darling for sure!

GARY GIBBON

NO peace exists for anybody attracted to Gary Gibbon. Gibbons are the smallest, fastest and most agile of the monkey family and are exhausting company. Remember that Goodies song about ''Doing The Funky Gibbon'' — well it's all that and *worse*.

Gibbons can be found in squash clubs, rugger clubs, swimming pools, gymnasiums and, of *course*, every disco in the land, where they jump about and gyrate all night long, making a very elegant spectacle of themselves with hardly a bead of sweat in sight. Not fair, is it?

They also eat like pigs and stay like sticks. A trip to the cinema with one (a harrowing experience because they don't like sitting still) is accompanied by a mound of yummy chocolate which has you out in spots by Wednesday and leaves not a pimple on old Gary.

And a word of warning — they love heights, so beware of hill-walking, mountain-climbing or tree-climbing suggestions.

GRAHAM GORILLA

GRAHAM GORILLA is a misleading sort of guy. He's the boy you've been watching for a long time and silently hating, thinking he's stuck up, stand-offish, haughty and aggressive.

Then one evening at a party you see him approaching — horror of horrors! And you find he's *totally* different from how you'd imagined.

His fierce manner hides quite a strong vein of shyness and sensitivity, he's got a terrific sense of humour and is very con - siderate.

He's probably the biggest challenge of 1980 and worth the effort becuase he's full of surprises — most of them nice ones!

If you chose . . .
1. THE CASTLE

Even though you don't appear to be, you really are quite insecure. You have many hidden fears, but you manage to hide them from everybody by putting on a brave face. You're so good at it, though, that even *you* may not realise that you're as brave and bold as you try to make out!

You are scared by the outside world and try to build up your own little world around you to protect yourself. Many of the daring things that you do are only done because you feel you must. You're afraid to lose face in front of your friends, who think you're rather a daredevil.

A castle would be the best place for you to live because you could cut yourself, and your boy, off from the big, bad world. Then *you* could decide what went on around you and control everything to suit yourselves!

2. THE HOUSE-BOAT

You're a very outdoor person who's never happier than when you're doing what you want to in the open air. When you're in the city you feel as if the walls and buildings are closing in on you, and you long to be out in the country.

Do you have a secret wish to live in a castle, or an igloo, or even a tree-house? Even if you don't fancy one of these three, we're sure you already have a good idea of the kind of dream home that you'd like to live in . . .

But did you know that the type of house that you dream about is a dead giveaway to the sort of person you are and what you want from life? Well, it is!

Here are seven different homes for you to choose from. All you have to do is pick the one that you would most like for your own. Our special quiz will help you discover things about yourself that even you *didn't know!*

In the country, you feel free to come and go as you please. You can roam around to your heart's content and never meet a soul. This would suit you down to the ground, because you're sometimes ill at ease when surrounded by people.

You feel a special closeness to the sea. It's always moving and restless, just like yourself. A house-boat would be ideal for you because you'd always be near water and you could up anchor and sail away when-even, and to wherever, you wanted!

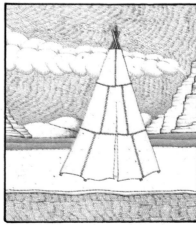

3. THE TEEPEE

Gatherings of friends and big parties scare you and if you're at one you can think of nothing better than running away to the peace and quiet of your teepee! You prefer to be alone, and find that you're happiest when you're on your own or with a special boy.

You can find it difficult to make friends sometimes, and so don't get out and about as much as you should. Not that this bothers you because you can always find something to occupy your time constructively.

You should try not to lock yourself away from people, though – they're not nearly as frightening as you think they are. Even if you do manage to become more sociable and outgoing, it's certain that you'll still want to have a lot of time to yourself.

Don't worry, the right boy and the right friends will accept you for what you are and realise that you just need more time on your own than most folk!

4. THE TREE-HOUSE

You're a bit of a romantic, aren't you? If there's a sensible way to do anything you'll avoid it, at all costs! You care nothing for common sense and *always* throw caution to the winds.

A tree-house would be ideal for you as it would raise you off the ground and you could get your head even further into the clouds! If people want a hare-brained scheme they always come to you.

Your Home?

The only problem with life as ~~yo~~u like it is that you very seldom ~~se~~e things as they *really* are. ~~Ev~~erything is wonderful as far as ~~yo~~u're concerned even though you ~~kn~~ow deep down that it isn't.

A tree-house would get you even ~~fa~~rther away from reality and ~~yo~~u'd love that. One word of ~~wa~~rning, though. Even though you ~~ha~~te to do things sensibly, try to ~~m~~ake yourself use a ladder to get ~~do~~wn from your tree-house now and ~~th~~en!

THE IGLOO

~~O~~utwardly, you're a rather cold, ~~cal~~culating person who is very ~~lo~~gical and sensible about ~~ev~~erything. The truth is that you ~~re~~ally are quite a nice, warm person ~~un~~derneath it all.

~~Y~~ou feel that you must give an air ~~of~~ efficiency to those around you ~~be~~cause that's what people like ~~of~~ you think. And you *really* do need ~~to~~ be liked, don't you? You're never ~~ha~~ppier than when you and a group ~~of~~ friends are all talking and joking. ~~Yo~~u need to be one of the crowd.

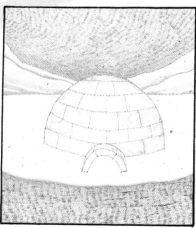

Boys, too, come in for this all-pals-together treatment as well as girls, and it tends to put some of them off. If they're used to gushy, clinging females then you come as rather a shock to them. It's not that you're any less loving (in fact, you may care more), it's just that you find it hard to let yourself go.

So, melt a little, let your inner warmth out and show everyone that you're not really an ice cube!

6. THE HOUSE ON STILTS

You're a very sensitive and creative soul and you would like nothing better than to build this house yourself. Perhaps with a little help from your boyfriend, though, because you don't really like heavy labour!

As a rule, you tend to cut yourself off from people because you're afraid of being hurt. But at the same time you need lots of friends to keep you happy and cheerful.

Your river house would probably have to be near to the bank so that people could come to visit you — but not so near that you couldn't always cut yourself off if necessary!

This attitude comes across in everything you do and say, and you're always changing your mind and your views. Although people, and boys in particular, find you very confusing, they're quite prepared to put up with you because you're so full of bright ideas!

7. THE SKY-SCRAPER

You're a sucker for every new fad and fashion that's dreamed up! You love the latest styles in *everything* — from toothbrushes to hairstyles! For this reason you're a rather difficult person to keep up with. At least, your friends probably feel a bit old-fashioned next to you.

As your hurtle along through life you tend to change friends and boyfriends very quickly. But, strangely enough, you'll probably find that your most important friends will stick by you through thick and thin. Really, you're grateful for this because without their steadying influence you'd very quickly go to pieces.

Remember that people are more important than things and that they shouldn't be changed just for the sake of change, and you'll manage just fine!

MADGE and BERYL

BOYS

In general, boys can be a bit of a pain in the neck at Christmas. A weird and unwonderful change comes over them and they really think they can take the most dastardly liberties with you. All year your brother's mate has been round at your place in the evenings, tinkering with mopeds, watching telly, drinking your mum's coffee and treating you like a sister, and you're quite glad of that because you don't fancy him all that much.

So, he comes round to see your brother on Christmas Eve, you open the door, he spots the mistletoe and suddenly he's like a thing demented, a love-starved King Kong.

Avoid this situation by (a) not answering the door to anyone over the festive season, unless it's female or you're letting the cat in, (b) asking your dad to kindly hang the mistletoe on an elastic thread, which can be hidden or pulled down at your own discretion, or (c) telling your grotty brother's grotty friends that you've got an awful cold and even worse, bad breath.

Boys take liberties at Christmas parties, too. They take the season of love and goodwill too literally and think they can just kiss and cuddle at leisure. All very well if you fancy them, but who wants the usually shy, quiet, spotty old be-spectacled office boy Bertrand to become a raving, slobbering loony at the office party and try to force you into the filing cabinet?

No, when faced with over-amorous Christmas grots, be kind but firm. Say, "Merry Christmas to you, too, but this kind of present I don't need." In other words, keep your slobbery offerings to yourself. Fanciable boys can be just the same at Christmas, but then there's no problem!

How To Cope With~ The Festive Season

stuffing, half a pound of veg., three helpings of pud and four mince pies. That's the minimum.

Then you crawl to an armchair, lie back wondering when the baby's due, put the Queen on, adjust your paper hat, and doze, waking occasionally to lift a lazy hand laden with chocolate Brazils or Christmas cake, and that, in a Brazil nutshell, is what it's all about.

Enjoy it while it lasts, because there's still the washing up to do, and tomorrow you won't get your jeans on and your face will be like a relief map of the Himalayas with too-much-of-a-good-thing spots.

FOOD

"We wish you a Merry Christmas and a Fat New Year," and that's what it all boils down to, doesn't it? People who sit down to Christmas nosh and say, "Just one tiny boiled potato, please," or "No, really, I just couldn't eat any more," after a slice of turkey breast, are so boring they make you cringe.

They're also extremely anti-social and rude. How would you like to be a Mum who'd been slav(er)ing over a hot turkey all morning just to have her more fattening goodies refused? Christmas is a time for being a pig, and the way to have a wonderful, stomach-bulging time is to have nothing but one Brazil nut and tangerine on Christmas Eve, no brekkie on Christmas Day, then tear into the turkey and pud like a demented wolf.

It's not particularly pleasant for those people sitting watching you stuff in three roast potatoes and a turkey leg at one go but you'll enjoy it, even if the turkey doesn't. To get that awful — but awfully nice — really, bloated Christmas afternoon feeling, you must have at least a pound of turkey, six potatoes, four ounces of

SHOPPING

By now, if you're one of the fantastically *organised* people, you'll have the whole thing in hand. But Britain must be a fantastically unorganised type of country when Christmas Eve sees virtually the entire red-faced, puffing population in assorted branches of Woolies, Boots and Marks & Sparks.

The thing to do is launch yourself, with a shopping list, into the seething throng, armed with steel-capped boots and a hat-pin for getting to the display stand displaying the lavender bath salts, start to sway and say loudly, "I think I've got another fit coming on."

The way ahead will open like the Red Sea and your salts will be wrapped and you'll be helped outside to the waiting ambulance to take you home. If you play the threatened fit down so no ambulance is necessary, you might get a nice cup of tea in the manager's office.

Buses are OK if you stuff a cushion up your coat or pull out your fold-away crutch to hobble on — you should get a seat no problem. Watch out for pickpockets, or pickbags in your case. They have a ball at Christmas. Tie your purse around your neck or sew it into your knickers or something — the latter sug-

gestion will provide an amusing diversion for bored shoppers when it's your turn at the till!

Wear comfy shoes, too. You'll set off with little size 4's and end up with throbbing size 7's. Above all, try to stay calm and cool. If you can't cope with seething city streets, go to your local grocer and buy them all a tin of boiled sweets. Uninspired, perhaps, but there'll be no hassles.

PRESENTS

Before you set off to buy your pressies, think hard about what people really would like to have. Would your Great Auntie Gert really like lavender bath salts when she already has six jars of the stuff in her bathroom? Perhaps she'd prefer bedsocks, a month's supply of cat food or two tubes of Steradent.

These are *practical* presents and with the cost of living these days would probably be greatly appreciated. Things like weed-killer for your dad (as long as he doesn't take it personally!), lavatory disinfectant for your mum, hair remover for your sister, laxatives for your grandad, may not be way out or pretty, but they'd be so *useful*.

PARTIES

If you're invited to a party before Christmas, and a party after Christmas, better have two suitable outfits to wear as there'll be approximately five pounds (fat, you fool . . .) difference. Christmas is a pretty, glittery time of the year, so you should be all glittery, too, to suit the occasion.

If you're thinking of throwing your own party, it needn't be expensive. You can all sing carols to dance to, play "Spot the Fairy," "Pass the Parcel" containing the mince pies your mum burnt or spare Christmas cards. For food, tell them to bring their own, and, as Christmas is all fun and fizz, give them all orange juice pepped up with bicarbonate of soda to bubble the night away.

If it's a Christmas Eve party and your dad tells you in confidence it's time they all went home, get him to walk in in a red jacket and white beard and say, "Right, scarper, you lot. Some people have to work tonight, you know . . ." and they'll all scarper all right, in terror, and it'll put all non-believers in their place . . .

Merry Christmas!

I DIDN'T TRY TO UNDERSTAND

Vicky just couldn't understand why her parents had to split up. After all, everything had been all right up until now . . .

85

Then I tried to phone him—but it was always Mary that answered the phone, and she always told me that he was out...

HOW CAN SHE DO THIS TO ME! AND WHY DOESN'T DAD STAND UP TO HER—THAT'S WHAT I WANT TO KNOW ...HE SHOULDN'T LET HER PUSH HIM AROUND ALL THE TIME...

Then the next thing I knew...

OH, VICKY...WON'T YOU TELL ME WHAT'S WRONG?

I—I...OH, MUM...

I was so upset that I just blurted out the whole story...

BUT WHY'S HE DOING IT, MUM? WHY WON'T HE EVEN TALK TO ME?

I—IT'S NOT AN EASY THING TO UNDERSTAND, VICKY...BUT I WAS SO WORRIED THAT SOMETHING LIKE THIS MIGHT HAPPEN...

YOUR DAD'S ALWAYS BEEN A BIT WEAK WHEN IT COMES TO MAKING DECISIONS. IF THERE'S SOMEONE THERE TO DO IT FOR HIM, THEN HE'S HAPPY TO SIT BACK AND LET THEM...

Y- YOU MEAN HE WAS LIKE THIS BEFORE?

THAT'S WHY I HAD TO LEAVE HIM, VICKY—EVERYTHING WAS LEFT UP TO ME...I COULDN'T TAKE IT ANY MORE. I THOUGHT WE'D BE BETTER OFF ON OUR OWN, YOU AND ME...

OH, MUM...AND I'VE BEEN SO AWFUL. IF ONLY I'D TRIED TO UNDERSTAND...

I DON'T BLAME YOU, VICKY...IT WAS ALWAYS AT THE BACK OF MY MIND THAT IT WAS MY FAULT FOR THE WAY YOUR DAD IS—THAT HE MIGHT BE DIFFERENT IF I LEFT HIM TO GET ON WITH THINGS BY HIMSELF...

IT WOULDN'T HAVE BEEN RIGHT FOR ME TO TELL YOU WHAT HE WAS LIKE—THAT WAS SOMETHING YOU HAD TO FIND OUT FOR YOURSELF...

AND I HAVE, MUM—I REALLY HAVE...PLEASE FORGIVE ME FOR THE WAY I'VE BEEN...

And we would be all right—because Mum was treating me like an adult. She was being honest with me and trusting me...

THERE'S NOTHING TO FORGIVE. IT'S UP TO BOTH OF US TO MAKE THE EFFORT NOW—WE'VE GOT LOTS TO LOOK FORWARD TO, YOU KNOW...

YOU'RE RIGHT, MUM... WE'LL BE OK...

...I WAS JUST A BABY TO DAD, SOMEONE TO HAVE AROUND WHEN HE WANTED ME. BUT IT'S DIFFERENT WITH MUM...AND I'LL MAKE IT UP TO HER IF IT'S THE LAST THING I DO...

THE END

WHERE DO THE BOYS GO IN THE WINTER?

WHERE *do* all the boys go in winter? They don't hibernate, that's for sure! But while it's easy to meet boys in summer just by hanging around the park or the pool, in winter it's different. In winter you've got to know *where* to look for them — and exactly what sort of guy you're likely to find in each place! So brush those icicles off your eyelashes and gen up on Winter Wonderboys . . .!

STEVE THE SOCCER FAN

Where to find him

Where the wind's strongest, the language ripest and the empty beer-cans are going down like ninepins. On the terraces (he'll be shouting compliments to the ref.), in the streets around the ground (he'll be welcoming the opposing team's supporters) and on the coach and car parks around motorway cafes.

What he'll look like

Steve will be wrapped in yards and yards of pink loo-paper and decorated with red and white rosettes. In fact, he'll look rather like the fairy on top of the Christmas tree.

What to say to him

If you want to make a good impression, say *"The ref. was BLIND!"* or *"We was robbed!"* (If his team lost, that is — if his team won and you said that, you'd end up in the gutter trussed up in the remains of the pink loo-paper.)

How he'll treat you

Steve wants his girlfriend to be a bit like a football match — unpredictable, exciting and a Good Match (for him, that is). But you'd better not try being fast, furious or foul or he'll send you off!

How to get rid of him

If you're stuck with soccer-stuck Steve and it's getting too boring, just say, "Isn't that Kevin Keegan?" and run like mad!

SIMON THE SKIER

Where to find him

On the slopes at St Eggflipz, cruising around the slalom course. Or in the apres-ski salon of the posh Hotel Ratz, sipping a seltzer and tucking into a Sachertortestrudel-knopfe (Ryvita and Marmite to you).

What he'll look like

He'll be tall, blond and handsome — or at least, he'll think he is, which is even *more* important. He'll be wearing a priceless sweater knitted out of yak's wool by his aunt in Argentina and a pair of trousers so sharp it's a wonder he doesn't cut himself on them.

What to say to him

Simon's basically very rich and very, *very* stupid, so don't say anything too complicated. Try, "I think you're wonderful!" for a start. No, wait — that's got a long word in it. Try, "I think you're great!" Yes, that should get him going. He'll agree with you immediately.

How he'll treat you

Simon really knows how to treat a lady. What's more, he's so thick he'll probably never realise you're not one! You'll be helped into cars, ski-lifts, ambulances, by his ever-gallant hand. And when you're back in England he'll send you at *least* a postcard telling you how unforgettable you are. The trouble is, he'll have forgotten your address.

How to get rid of him

Tie his skis together and run off into the forest.

IAN THE ICE-SKATER

Where to find him

At the skating-rink, of course — you'll recognise him immediately by the way he sweeps elegantly up and down.

What he'll look like

Ian's long-legged and chic and has his hair beautifully blow-waved. He might have a teeny earring in his teeny ear. And he's certain to be wearing Yves St Torment's **Eau Dear**.

What to say to him

Ian thrives on the adoration of his fans. And if he hasn't already got some, you can find a place in his heart by watching him for hours and "currying" favour by going up shyly to ask for his autograph. Say, " 'Scuse me — aren't you John Curry? Will you write your name on my arm?"

How he'll treat you

Ian thinks that girls are precious, exquisite things to be cherished. So don't turn up for a date in your boiler suit and feminist badge. Really, going out with him is almost as good as being with a girlfriend — you can swap earrings and perfumes

How to get rid of him

Tell him there's a Big Thaw coming.

PETE THE PARTYGOER

Where to find him

Look for Peter on a Saturday night. He'll be trudging the streets with a bottle in his hand, looking for a party to gatecrash. If he can't find a party, he'll settle for a lecture, or a meeting of the Radio Amateurs' Club, or the Hinsley Allotment Society Annual General Meeting.

What he'll look like

Pete's always dressed up to the nines (or, on special occasions, the tens). He wears the small-collar shirts, the scrubbing-brush hair and the zip-up trouser legs.

What to say to him

Pete's very vain, so tell him how great he looks for a start. Tell him he reminds you of the Boomtown Rats' bass guitarist (that is, the lowest Rat of all). You can also tell him the names of everybody there — at the party, that is.

How he'll treat you

Pete likes variety — he flits from girl to girl like a wasp on a tea-table. So you must expect him to shower you with compliments one day and pass you by without a second look when he next sees you.

How to get rid of him

Tell him the party's over!

COLIN THE CLIMBER

Where to find him

On the side of Mount Eiderdown, roped up to his stalwart buddy Joe Green, and cutting his way up the South face with an ice-axe and a look of Grim Determination on his face. Or wait for him in the mountain hut with a cup of hot Bovril and a cube or two of extra-special Captain Scott's Arctic Chocolate.

What he'll look like

It'll be a bit difficult to tell exactly what he's like, because Colin will be wrapped up in three layers of Pteradactyl underwear, six sweaters, a luminous cagoul and waterproof trousers. He'll also have a Noddy hat. And probably Big Ears, too.

What to say to him

Colin's a shy, silent type who hates fuss and bother. So the way to attract him is not to say *anything*. Just give him a nod, pass him the chocolate and sit polishing your pitons by the light of the fire. (If you haven't got any pitons, sit and pick your teeth with the ice-axe.)

How he'll treat you

Colin's the possessive type. He'll want to keep you on a string (or, more accurately, a rope). He'll also want to test your loyalty by asking you to risk your life for him in 2000 different ways, most of them freezing cold and all of them uncomfortable. And what's more, you'll have to wear horrible waterproof trousers that will make you look like a balloon.

How to get rid of him

Tell him he's come to the end of his rope, and give him the push. Right down a crevasse.

BEAUTIFUL BADDIES

Remember 1980? We decided to take a look at it and see which names and faces made it memorable. We've chosen some of our favourite goodies . . . and some of our favourite baddies. See if you agree with our choice!

OUR BEAUTIFUL BADDIES

Lemmy — Motorhead

Looks a bit wild, doesn't he? This sneering baddie is Lemmy, guitarist and vocalist with Motorhead. Maybe the sneer's for dealing with over-excited fans . . .?

James Cagney

This man is Public Enemy No 1. He's probably played more baddies than anyone else! Maybe you saw him in his latest film this year, too.

John Travolta

After failing to make a hit with "Moment By Moment," John returned to familiar ground with "Urban Cowboy" which, as you all know, was the Western version of "Saturday Night Fever." What next? "Grease" set in China?

The Professionals

If these two weren't desirable, they might be quite nasty! As it is, they're the most wanted duo — by us, that is!

Miss Piggy

Definitely a beautiful baddie! This elegant pig's karate chops are known and feared by all the cast of the Muppet Show . . . .

Joan Collins

This lady got 'Sunburn' with Farrah Fawcett which almost changed her baddy image. Keep trying, Joannie — you'll come clean soon.

Dave Vanian

No, this evil-looking character is *not* auditioning for a part in the new Dracula movie — it's just Dave Vanian of The Damned doing what he does best — looking horrible! But we reckon that this vampire can bite *our* necks, anytime!

Tony Blackburn

Beautiful? Hmmm . . . Baddie? Yes! This man is the DJ we *all* love to hate!

OUR GORGEOUS GOODIES

Humphrey Bogart

Although he may not look it, this man is always on the side of the angels! His films are often on the television and are well worth watching. Here's lookin' at you, kid . . .

Erik Estrada

Here's one speed cop that none of us would mind being stopped by! In fact, most of us would want to break the law if we knew *he'd* be on our tails!

Dr Hook

Although this bunch of unlikely looking musicians may look like baddies, you'll know from their songs that they're really goodies. Just what the Doctor ordered!

Gene Kelly

This ever-young dancer swept us off our feet in "Xanadu." It just goes to show that you're as young as you feel — and Gene obviously feels young!

Kermit

He may be the same colour as The Hulk, but that's all. This lovable little chap makes you want to give him a big hug then take him away. If only it wasn't for a certain pig, that is . . .

Luke Skywalker and Darth Vadar

Delicious Luke and diabolical Darth — the man with the sexy voice. We know already what you think about Luke but we've unmasked this baddie so that you can decide for yourself whether the face matches the voice! May the force be with you.

The Goodies

These three loonies have just *got* to be in the Gorgeous Goodies section! What more can we say?!

Captain Kirk

When he's not saving the Earth and zapping everybody with photon torpedoes, he's blasting us into warp drive. You've got to admit he's pretty dynamic, and pretty handsome with it, if you don't mind us saying so, sir.

Leonard Rossiter

Did you see him as Rigsby in "Rising Damp"? Although he plays the scheming landlord who's an out-and-out baddie, we're sure that he's not *that* bad.

The Nolans

Maybe not gorgeous, but certainly goodies — maybe even goody, goodies . . .?

nd GORGEOUS GOODIES!

YOU KNOW YOU'VE COME DOWN TO EARTH WITH A BUMP WHEN...

YOU KNOW YOU'VE COME DOWN TO EARTH WITH A BUMP WHEN . . .

. . . your country cousin comes to visit and she's more up to date than you!

. . . you dye your hair to match your kilt and nobody even notices.

. . . you've finally saved up enough cash for that flash bikini and suddenly you realise it's December.

. . . you finally pluck up courage to wear your leopardskin trousers in the High Street and someone thinks you've escaped from the zoo!

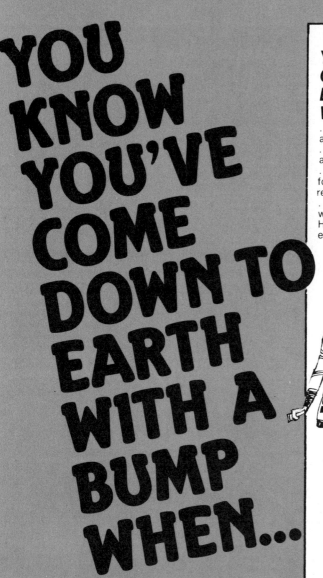

. . . you still think platform soles are fashionable.

. . . you're complimented on your new patterned tights with the intricate woven lines — and you're not wearing any.

. . . you turn up at the disco to find five other girls are wearing exactly the same dress as you.

. . . you get a free pair of oars with every pair of shoes!

. . . you give up bothering about the length of your hemline.

. . . you finally finish knitting that incredibly difficult Fair Isle twin-set — and it's four years out of date!

. . . your boyfriend thinks your new tight brown cords are jodhpurs.

. . . you wear your latest up-to-date outfit and someone tells you Hallowe'en isn't for another nine months.

. . . you walk into a room and everyone laughs.

YOU KNOW YOU'VE COME DOWN TO EARTH WITH A BUMP WHEN . . .

. . . your brother asks you to make him up as a clown for a fancy dress party, because you've had plenty of practice!

. . . your mum thinks your new foundation is a mud face-pack.

. . . you realise the make-up pencils your gran gave you two years ago are really wax crayons.

. . . you need turpentine to take off your new runproof mascara.

. . . your hairdresser asks if you've ever considered selling your hair — as Brillo pads!

. . . you tell the beauty parlour to do their best and they put a paper bag over your head.

. . . you receive seven sets of Valderma for Christmas.

. . . you stop biting your nails and they still won't grow.

. . . you use an eyelash curler and all your eyelashes fall out.

. . . the new wonder shampoo still leaves your hair looking like shredded wheat!

. . . the speak-your-weight machine shrieks, "One at a time, please!"

. . . the manicurist suggests you wear gloves.

. . . you no longer need fillings — you need dentures!

. . . the only comment that your new Eau de Cologne inspires is, "Oh de smell!"

. . . you're asked to take part in a before and after advertisement — *only* as the before.

YOU KNOW YOU'VE COME DOWN TO EARTH WITH A BUMP WHEN . . .

. . . you've only just found out that the Beatles have split up!

. . . you watch "Top Of The Pops" and you haven't heard of any of the groups.

. . . you realise that Chrissie Hynde's not going to go away.

. . . you thought Pete Briquette was some form of fire-lighter.

. . . you realise the Police are not the men in blue.

. . . you've played your new LP at the wrong speed — and didn't even notice.

. . . you've still got that record token that you got for Christmas — and it's July!

. . . you develop a liking for Nana Mouskouri.

. . . you realise David Bowie and Gary Numan are *not* one and the same person.

. . . you can't find the handle to wind your stereo up.

. . . you patriotically go to see HM and are shocked to find out that it means Heavy Metal.

. . . you're shocked to find out how much the Queen has changed her image.

. . . you go into a clothes shop and ask for a Merton Parka.

. . . someone tells you that you look like someone in Blondie — and you find out that it's Chris Stein.

YOU KNOW YOU'VE COME DOWN TO EARTH WITH A BUMP WHEN . . .

. . . the boy you've fancied for ages asks you to go out with his little brother.

. . . the dishy boy at your school says that you've got great legs — for playing rugby!

. . . you find out that the butch hulk who's moved in next door with the 1000 cc motor bike — is a girl!

. . . you're out with a gorgeous guy, having a wonderful time — and you bump into your boyfriend.

. . . you're sitting alone in a cafe, crying into your cup, and the only person who comes up to you is a Hilda Ogden-type woman who wants to discuss the price of cheese.

. . . you're at the swimming pool, looking your worst, when who walks in but the guy from last night's disco who's asked you out tonight!

. . . all the boys you start to fancy suddenly move away.

. . . you're out for a nosh-up with your boyfriend, and he's had you in stitches all night pretending to have forgotten his wallet — and he has!

. . . your rugby-playing boyfriend gives you a piggy-back and has to retire from rugby for ever.

. . . your brother makes a point of showing all your holiday snaps to his friends — including the one where you're impersonating a whale.

YOU KNOW YOU'VE COME DOWN TO EARTH WITH A BUMP WHEN . . .

. . . your legs fall off!

. . . you religiously follow a diet and put on half a stone.

. . . you start wanting to forget your birthday.

. . . you start to make a list of all the eligible boys in the neighbourhood — a week later you still haven't come up with any names!

. . . you wake up, thankful that you were only dreaming about being out in the street with your nightie, and find that you've been sleep-walking!

. . . you no longer get ten pence from the tooth fairy.

. . . your boyfriend's written "I love Julie" all over his jotter — and your name's Linda.

. . . you realise that the horrible bitch that all of your friends have been talking about — is YOU.

. . . the boy you've fancied for ages walks up, and asks your friend for a date.

. . . you've come to the end of your Jackie Annual!

LIBRA
(Sept. 22-Oct. 22)
YOUR LUCKY COLOUR

Your colour for 1981 is *emerald green* – but it's so bright that you'll need to experiment with it! You're a positive person, and with emerald green you just can't fail to stand out from the crowd. It's a great colour for helping you to solve difficult problems. You'll feel full of confidence and your plans will tend to turn out right. And when you meet an obstacle, you'll soon find a way round it. Emerald green is the colour of persistence in the face of all difficulties — and the colour of triumph, too! It's the great "Go!" colour — so don't ever wear it when you just fancy a night in front of the telly!

Smallish amounts of emerald green in your wardrobe will do wonders to get you together with other people — they'll make you full of life and good ideas. But don't wear too much of it. Emerald green is one of the strongest colours, and too much of it could make you over-confident and a bit bossy. So if you don't want to lose all your friends — go easy on the green!

YOUR ROMANTIC COLOUR

And the same goes when it comes to boys. You don't want to scare them away by being pushy, do you? So when you're off on a date this year, just a teeny bit of green for that extra sparkle — but stick mainly to your everyday colours, blue and pink. Blue is a colour for friendly dates. Pink shows you care — so save it for a very special boy!

COLOURS TO AVOID

Colours to avoid include the darker shades of red, which are much too forceful for you. And steer clear of purple, which tends to damp down your gentle feelings.

SCORPIO
(Oct. 23-Nov. 21)
YOUR LUCKY COLOUR

Beautifully, mysterious blue-green — the colour of the sea, which is your element, is your colour for 1981. Wear it to hint at the depths of your feelings — and to help you keep those feelings well in hand! Green by itself is not a safe colour for you, you're likely to let yourself get wildly enthusiastic over the most unlikely schemes — and the most unsuitable people! Blue mixed with green won't make you any less sensitive or less eager to plunge into life — but it *will* make your reactions a bit more realistic and reasoned. With blue-green as your colour, you won't be quite so impulsive. You won't change your mind (or your mood!) six times in one hour. In fact, you'll be quite consistent in your behaviour!

YOUR ROMANTIC COLOUR

When you're with a boy, stick to blue-green with a little bit of red. In fact, you can really fascinate him by wearing *both* colours together in small amounts, red *and* blue-green. Red will give him a good idea (if he doesn't know it already!) of what a rich and magnetic personality you have, and the blue-green will make him realise there's even more to you than meets the eye!

COLOURS TO AVOID

Like Aries though, you too should avoid dull, sludgy colours. They'll just make you feel dull and sludgy, too! And Scorpios should avoid wearing black. Black brings out the beast in all Scorpios and when that happens, everyone else had better watch out!

SAGITTARIUS
(Nov. 22-Dec. 21)
YOUR LUCKY COLOUR

Your colour is *blue* — true blue, not the pale or the dark shades. The middle shades of blue are the ones you should wear — strong, constant colours which will help keep you forging ahead, instead of wandering all over the place, which Sagittarians are inclined to do as soon as you pick up the trail of something new and interesting! Blue will have you going places this year and there won't be nearly so many dead ends.

Blue's a great colour for getting you on good terms with other people. You'll find it's easy to make new friends, and old friendships should run smoothly. In many ways blue is a very practical colour. But it's not at all selfish, so it won't make you go all nasty and hard-headed! It *will* make you interested in all sorts of things outside yourself. Blue isn't an easy, happy-go-lucky colour by any means — but it *can* open up a whole new world for you, if you'll let it.

blue — unless he's the brainy type! If want to start a romance going, wear turquo It will look lovely on you if you're d haired — and it's definitely a colour giving a boy the "come on!"

YOUR ROMANTIC COLOUR

Blue is a wonderful colour for making really good friends and for "going steady" with a boy you've known for ages — but if you want to catch yourself a new boy don't wear plain

COLOURS TO AVOID

Colours for you to avoid this y include camel brown (too depress and all neat, spotted or tiny f patterns (too restricting!).